# Knowledge Business and Industry

A common feature on contemporary economic policy, all over the world, is the ambition to utilise academic production of knowledge as a tool to create innovations and economic growth. However, as soon as we study this issue from a business perspective, the use of knowledge appears rather challenging.

Håkansson and Waluszewski offer a provocative and reflective treatise on the notion of knowledge and innovation in business and industry. Structuring their arguments around four cases of innovation within four entirely different contexts, the authors invite the business-minded reader to consider the costs of adopting new knowledge and innovation within a business setting. The reading is provocative to the extent that it holds in question the long-held assumption that new knowledge and innovation are universally advantageous. It follows the tremor of an innovation as new knowledge reverberates through, or is dampened by the larger economic community including the cultural structures, the industrial standards, and the foundational assumptions that rule a particular economic domain. This reading places particular focus on the interfaces where the innovative agent connects to its customers, to its suppliers, and its competitors.

This book will be of particular relevance to postgraduate students undertaking advanced courses in science and technology studies, innovation management, industrial marketing and purchasing, technological development and innovation systems.

**Håkan Håkansson** is Professor in International Management at the Norwegian School of Management BI, Oslo. **Alexandra Waluszewski** is Director at the Centre for Science and Technology Studies and Associate Professor in the Department of Business Studies, Uppsala University.

# RIOT!

## Routledge studies in innovation, organization and technology

# Knowledge and Innovation in Business and Industry

The importance of using others

**Edited by Håkan Håkansson and Alexandra Waluszewski**

Routledge
Taylor & Francis Group

LONDON AND NEW YORK

First published 2007
by Routledge
2 Park Square, Milton Park, Abingdon, Oxon OX14 4RN

Simultaneously published in the USA and Canada
by Routledge
711 Third Avenue, New York, NY 10017

*Routledge is an imprint of the Taylor & Francis Group, an informa business*

First issued in paperback 2012

Typeset in Times by Wearset Ltd, Boldon, Tyne and Wear

*British Library Cataloguing in Publication Data*
A catalogue record for this book is available from the British Library

*Library of Congress Cataloguing in Publication Data*
A catalog record for this book has been requested

ISBN13: 978-0-415-54157-2 (pbk)
ISBN13: 978-0-415-42529-2 (hbk)
ISBN13: 978-0-203-94702-9 (ebk)

# Contents

# Figures

# Tables

# Preface

This book is written for those of you who are interested in the development and use of knowledge. Our intent is to show how important others' knowledge is in these processes – especially if the user setting is in business. It is our hope that the book, if you invest in time to read it, will provide you with many good illustrations of how companies of all sizes and organisational forms, and engaged in all types of technologies, can benefit from the use of others' knowledge. There seems to be an unlimited space for improvements in this use.

This book is the result of a ten-year research programme, *Scientific Research, Technological Development and Industrial Renewal* (abbreviated VTI), involving 14 PhD projects, carried out in four research departments at two universities: Royal School of Technology, Stockholm and Uppsala University. Seven people were directly involved with the production of this book, but indirectly there were so many within and outside the VTI research program that it is impossible to give credit to all of them. It has been a journey where we experienced the same phenomena as we describe in the book – the importance of using others' knowledge.

The ambition with the book is to present "our" understanding of how knowledge is created and used in a business setting, based on the research conducted in the VTI program. However, this "our" understanding should be broadly interpreted. Along with the direct research experiences, we are building, to a large degree (as all research does), on what others have previously observed and discussed. Furthermore, we also draw upon what a large number of relatively close colleagues have noted, suggested and commented upon in a series of seminars and workshops that were part of the research project. We are grateful to all of them and hope that we are not the only ones who benefited from these discussions.

Similarly, we were extremely fortunate to have received support from the companies involved in the processes on which we have focused. The companies gave us ample opportunities to obtain the needed empirical material. Through their participation we had the opportunity to obtain rich and detailed accounts of the processes where knowledge is developed and used in a business setting, i.e. the core of our research. We are more than grateful and it is our hope that the findings might inspire new ways of approaching some of the large problems all companies face with knowledge issues. Last, but not least, we are grateful for the knowledge provided by our language improver, Linda Evans.

This programme was initiated by a research foundation that "forced" us researchers from a business setting to develop a program in cooperation with researchers engaged in the history of science, history of technology and history of architecture. The initiative helped us to create a context that we never would have been able to create ourselves, but which gave us new insights and challenging opportunities from which we have greatly benefited. Thanks to The Bank of Sweden Tercentenary Fund, which financed the program, thus significantly contributing to the creation of a research environment.

Håkan Håkansson and Alexandra Waluszewski
Uppsala, 2007

# 1 Economic use of knowledge

*Alexandra Waluszewski and Håkan Håkansson*

## Knowledge in use

Try to imagine the amount of knowledge used during a business day. Understanding all of the knowledge activated when one company sends an electronic invoice to another company is challenging enough. Behind such a simple operation there are decades of development endeavours concerning related hardware and system solutions. If one of the two parties involved in the transaction tried to develop the existing solution a bit further, the reactions from human as well as physical resources would be even more complicated to overview – at least in advance. In retrospect, however, such reactions might be seen as an illustration of all the specific knowledge that, in one way or another, was affected by the introduction of something new.

Although the amount of knowledge that is used in ordinary business and organisational life is overwhelming, it is far from all knowledge that ever becomes activated in an economic setting. Companies and organisations are as selective as final consumers are in their private consumption. Why does some knowledge become embedded into economic resources? Why do companies and organisations use some knowledge and reject other? Why does much of the radical and technological advanced knowledge, often labelled "cutting edge" science and "high tech" innovations, end up on dusty bookshelves or in museums for unsuccessful innovations? Also, why do companies and organisations often hold on to solutions built on decades or centuries-old knowledge – often produced in contexts far from any sophisticated research lab or innovation centre? Finally, does the way companies and organisations embed knowledge in a business setting affect how this knowledge is produced?

It is these issues, all related to how specific pieces of knowledge are embedded into economic resources and used, that we investigate in this book. Of course, one could ask if there is anything left to be discovered about knowledge in an economy that claims to be "knowledge-based". Centuries ago the classical economists made us aware that knowledge is a key resource in the creation of business prosperity and economic growth; Marshall's (1965, p. 115, orig. pub. 1890) message is perhaps the most well known: "Knowledge is our most powerful engine of production". Contemporary scholars engaged in studies on the "knowledge economy" express a similar understanding: "The source of productivity and growth lies in the generation of knowledge" (Castells, 1996, p. 218). However, as we will discuss in Chapter 6, this does not mean that the use of knowledge in a business setting has always been a prioritized issue in economic research. Although there seems to be a great awareness of the importance of knowledge in contemporary research, there are still many questions to ask about how knowledge is used: how is knowledge put to use in a business setting, where the prerequisite is that it has to co-exist with already activated resources?

What earlier studies touching upon this phenomenon show is that the connection between the production of knowledge and the use of knowledge in a business setting is far from simple and clear-cut. However, in the traditional economic model world this issue is not at all relevant; it is simply defined from the model. The only knowledge that is necessary to get this stylised economic world to run is the price of the resources exchanged (Wilk, 1996). On the other hand, we have all the accounts from empirical investigations carried out by scholars in the history of technology, history of science, sociology, anthropology and business studies, indicating that the relationship between the production of knowledge and the use of knowledge in a business setting is rather thorny (see Rosenberg, 1982; Hughes, 1983; Latour, 1984). What the tricky processes behind the embedding of knowledge into a business setting have in common is that they stretch over time, over space, over technologies and over organisational borders (Håkansson and Waluszewski, 2002). Thus, the creation of the use of knowledge in a business setting appears as such a delicate issue that it could be labelled as "the problems of using knowledge".

This issue is also what we will start out with in this chapter. After a closer look at the problems of using knowledge in a business setting, we will consider how this issue is related to the producers of knowledge. In the last part we will describe which research tools we have used, and in what way we have used them. In Chapters 2–5 we will present the results of four empirical studies, in Chapter 6 we will discuss what lessons we can learn from economic theory and in the final chapter we will discuss some major consequences for how to approach the use of knowledge in a business setting. But let us start with discussing the problems of activating new knowledge in the business world.

## The problems of using others' knowledge

How often do we consider that as soon as we use any produced goods, we are utilising other peoples' knowledge? Whether the items we are spending our money on are regarded as high-tech products, or whether they stem from traditional workmanship, they are the carriers of what other people know. And in most cases we do not even have to reflect upon this knowledge to use it. However, this is not always the case, especially not when the user of others' knowledge is a company. When the user of knowledge represents business activities, there are reasons both to investigate what knowledge is behind the provided solutions and to search for new knowledge – and to consider how this can be embedded into the resources the company is using. This task is complicated by the fact that the knowledge the company is already using is seldom visible, but embedded into specific physical and human resources.

Still this tricky searching for others' knowledge and figuring out how it can be combined with what is already in use is a major activity in business life. Whenever a company is engaged in exchange, it is involved in processes where it utilises and combines others' knowledge. When, for example, a company purchases components and materials, it is using both the knowledge that is embedded in these items as well as knowledge related to how to use them in combination with other resources. When buying a certain material the buyer is, in principle, buying a certain share of a production process that has given the product some specific features. If the production process is changed, then the features of the material might also change. The production process, in its turn, is dependent on the use of certain equipment and certain inputs. If these are changed, then the process will change and the features of the material might change. In this way, using a certain material implies the use of a whole set of resources combined in a specific way. If the purchasing company asks for some specific features, and if the supplying company can also benefit from changing one or several features necessary to achieve this, then it certainly is prepared to engage in a development process. Similarly, the company that activates equipment for producing or assembling things is using others' knowledge of how to develop, produce and maintain this equipment, how to combine it with other resources in the production process and what to do with the output.

These two small examples were about inputs but the same is true of the output. The company also depends on others' knowledge about the user contexts in which the output will be embedded. It must consider how its output is used, in combination with what other resources, to create what effects. And it has to consider how to relate the supplying and using sides to each other. Over time, such interaction patterns create economic resources that carry the imprint of others' knowledge. (As will be presented later on in this chapter, these interaction processes have been thoroughly studied by researchers using the IMP approach; see Johanson and Mattsson 2006; Håkansson and Waluszewski, 2002 and www.impgroup.org for an overview.)

These interactions can appear between physical resources, such as products or production facilities, systematically being adapted and related to each other. These interactions can also appear between social resources, such as business units and business relationships. Over time, such interaction patterns create systematically related business networks. What is created in such interaction processes can be characterised by its Janus-face; the result can be increased efficiency and innovativeness – which at the same time can hinder other attempts to create change (Håkansson and Waluszewski, 2002). Even if these interactions can be more or less hidden, and somewhat difficult to distinguish, every economic resource carries "traces and leavings from others" (Gudeman, 2001, p. 145), and is thus always related to other physical and social resources.

## How to acquire others' knowledge

The issue of how to acquire others' knowledge in a business setting depends on how the industrial structure works, and on how it is viewed. In general, the process of attaining knowledge has followed three different paths. One has been through buying products and facilities into which it has been assumed the knowledge is fully embedded. Another has been through integrating the parts regarded as important from a knowledge point of view. Until the middle of the twentieth century, the idea that integration could create advantages influenced the organising of many firms. For example, manufacturing firms primarily carried out production in-house. Supply of important components and materials could also be carried out by integrated units. Technologies used in-house could be handled in on-site machine shops, populated with skilled workers who could develop, produce and maintain production equipment (Gudeman, 2001; Gadde and Håkansson, 2003). Finally, the third path has been through systematic investigation, such as market research studies. The common theme among these three is that the process of getting hold of knowledge has been seen as quite structured and unproblematic. The problem has been to identify the needed knowledge and then to "buy" it.

However, over time there seems to have been a change. Through increased specialisation together with increased knowledge about different resources, which can also be seen in increased technological complexity of the exchanged goods, a number of new and more extensive ways of acquiring knowledge have developed. Business relationships have become increasingly important, but also a more recognised way of mediating knowledge (Piore and Sabel, 1984; Gudeman, 2001; Håkansson (ed.) 1982; Ford *et al.*, 2003). The contemporary company uses external specialists/suppliers not only for delivering components and insert material, but also for engagement in development issues, often involving sub-suppliers and technological experts. Complementary suppliers, or what in mainstream economic literature are simply referred to as "competitors", often work together in joint development processes. Sometimes these projects are both formal and visible, such as is often the case in the telecom industry. But often they are informal and difficult to distinguish for people outside a specific knowledge area. Another common way to utilise others' knowledge is to outsource certain activities to specialised manufacturers. However, this utilisation of others' knowledge can also be more or less hidden; an impressive network of related suppliers and producers can for example be found under a marketing company's trademark.

These different kinds of recognised or hidden interactions, where other people's knowledge is mediated through physical and social resources, is such a dominating feature in business exchange that Gudeman (2001, p. 146) labels it "the stuff of economy". The results from a study investigating the most important sources of new knowledge for 123 Swedish companies reveal that Gudeman is not exaggerating (Håkansson, 1989). A total of 496 important development relationships were identified. Of these, 172 were with suppliers, 168 with customers and 156 with "horizontal" units, such as complementary or sister companies. The structure of these relationships also illustrates that although supplier and customer interactions represent a major part of companies' knowledge development, a small number of suppliers and customers represent the major exchange processes. The ten largest customers accounted for 70 per cent of the total volume sold, and the ten largest suppliers accounted for 72 per cent of the total volume bought. The duration of these relationships averaged 13 years for customers/suppliers and eight years for horizontal units. Thus, what this study indicates is that it is within "the heavy processes", i.e. in a limited number of customer–supplier interactions, that the major part of companies' knowledge development occurs.

An important feature of these interaction processes concerning how to use others' knowledge is that as soon new knowledge is brought into use it is also reacted to – often in ways that the knowledge providers could not imagine. Who, for example, could have forecast that those machines once developed for calculations would, many decades later, be used primarily in the production and distribution of texts – and be used in the creation of "chat rooms" and "blogs" where many issues far away from mathematical calculations are dealt with? But why does new knowledge seldom retain its original shape when used in a business setting? One key aspect might be that it is always used in a very specific context, something that can be illustrated by a short look at one of the cases we will later discuss in detail.

This particular case concerns the production of newsprint. When paper is used it is clearly one of the printing houses' most important inputs, both in terms of costs and in terms of how it affects the printing process. The efficiency and reliability of the printing process is highly dependent on the paper. In the same way the finished newspaper is dependent on the paper in terms of readability and the way the paper presents illustrations or pictures. The quality of the paper is, in turn, dependent on the pulp, which in turn is dependent on the equipment used and the amount of electricity put into the process. Given this production structure there are only some types of changes, some types of new knowledge that can be incorporated. The setting has obvious limitations as to what can be used but it also gives positive effects for certain type of suggestions.

What this small example illustrates is that the role of knowledge in a business setting is far too rich a phenomenon to be reduced simply to being an input. It also appears as an active part of the output – and of the interaction patterns that characterise both the supplier and user sides. As soon as others' knowledge is used it is also reacted upon – and new knowledge is created. In this way each economic actor is involved in a number of knowledge relationships that can more or less work two ways. All together these activities form an intricate web of knowledge providers and knowledge users, where each actor can have double roles.

Scholars engaged in business studies over the last decade, particularly in the IMP setting (www.impgroup.org), have increasingly recognised the knowledge that is mediated and put into use through interaction with counterparts on the supplier and user sides. The knowledge that can be reached through interacting with skilled suppliers has been investigated by Wynstra (1998) among others, who points to the important role specialised suppliers have in a producing company's development process. Using the knowledge of advanced customers, or "lead-users" as von Hippel (1988) once labelled them, has increasingly been observed as essential for each company's development process. The knowledge that is mediated through interaction with other knowledge providers rather than direct customers and suppliers has been stressed by "knowledge management" scholars (Nonaka, 1991; Leonard-Barton, 1995).

What these authors underline is the importance of accumulating knowledge from outside the company, bringing it into the organisations where it is "stored as a part of the company's knowledge base, and utilising it by those engaged in developing new technologies and products" (Nonaka and Takeuchi, 1995, p. 6). Among these outside knowledge suppliers, academic research and R and D institutes are considered to be particularly important. However, according to the study referred to above, only about 4 per cent of the companies' most important development relationships were with scientific research units (Håkansson, 1989). Does this mean that science is not an important source of knowledge in a business setting? Let us consider "the production of knowledge" (Gibbons *et al.*, 1994) in relation to the use of knowledge in a business setting.

## The scientific production of knowledge

### The hidden use of science in business

There are probably not many users of produced goods who also consider themselves as ordinary users of scientific knowledge. Still we are – all of us. And this is true almost regardless of which economic resources we use. Make a telephone call in Moscow, chat on the net from a computer in Bombay, read a newspaper in New York or furnish a flat in Shanghai – and become the user of a mix of knowledge where science is an integrated part. There are not many businesses that are recognised as ordinary users of science either. The companies that are thought of as users of science are those that are engaged in activities where the connection to science is visible, such as pharmaceuticals or biotech. These companies are frequently labelled "science-based" firms – although in what way science constitutes a base is seldom or never declared.

Most business activities carry the imprints of science. If it is difficult to get an overview of all knowledge that is used in business and organisational life, it is even more complicated to define which part of this knowledge was mediated through science. How much science is put into use when a grocery store takes an order over the net, when a nurse vaccinates a child, when a forestry company starts to harvest, or when a car producer assembles the parts delivered by sub-suppliers? No matter what kind of company or organisation we are considering, it is probably impossible to get a fair picture of all the pieces of scientific knowledge that are embedded into technological and organisational resources. It is not even necessary to learn about all this knowledge in order to make use of it. Users of both consumer products and industrial products can most often benefit from other people's struggles with embedding science into technological and organisational solutions – about which one does not have to know every detail to activate.

Thus, the way science is used in an economic setting implies that we do not have to recognise it in order to benefit from it. First, whenever science is embedded into economic resources, it is combined with a lot of other pieces of knowledge. Science becomes, as Basalla (1988, p. 2) puts it, just "one of several interacting sources" that are combined into technological and organisational solutions. Second, to be embedded into an economic resource the scientific contributions need not be new, nor appear in a recognised form; "second and third-hand conceptions of scientific advances can and do serve technology well" (Basalla, 1988, p. 92). This means that even those who are engaged in embedding different pieces of knowledge into new economic resources are not necessarily aware of which sources these are. Thus, as soon as science is activated in a business setting, the scientific origin in general becomes both uninteresting and hidden – since it is not where a solution stems from, but what effect it creates on other resources, that is of interest.

There are also certain business contexts in which a scientific origin has a specific value. We see this, for example, when companies deliver products where a scientific origin is used as a guarantee for a certain effect or security, or when companies deliver tools and methods to science itself. In the latter case, however, it is not only the scientific origin that is of importance, but the scientific use. Certainly science can represent an important contribution in the development of a new research tool. But its role as user is of equal importance from a business perspective. Without the academic institutions' involvement in testing of new prototypes, without their use of new solutions in research, and without their producing research publications, there will never be a user side for a new scientific research tool. In these cases science has an interesting double role; it can be the source of knowledge but also the valuator of the usefulness of new knowledge (Waluszewski, 2004).

Although some industries benefit from science as a marketing channel for new scientific tools or as a guarantee for certain effects, does it in general really matter if the knowledge used by companies is mediated through what is considered as the "producers of knowledge", i.e. the academic world, or if it is mediated through problem-solving interactions with other businesses? Does knowledge labelled "cutting-edge" science or "high-tech" innovations create some special benefits when used in a business setting? Let us consider if there is something special about this kind of knowledge.

### *What is special about knowledge stemming from science?*

Not all knowledge is named science. But the knowledge that is rewarded with this epithet is generally regarded as special. Science is, as Chalmers (1999) puts it, "highly esteemed" in society:

> Apparently it is a widely held belief that there is something special about science and its methods. The naming of some claim or line of reasoning or piece of "scientific" research is done in a way that is intended to imply some kind of merit or special kind of reliability.
>
> (Chalmers, 1999, p. xiiii)

If science is held in high regard in society, the issue of what is so special with academic knowledge production has been, and still is, intensely debated – at least in social science. For some interpreters scientific knowledge is the result of a search for objective, true facts, while for others scientific knowledge is not different from any other knowledge developed in our society.[1] However, whatever camp the academic knowledge producers' hearts are in, to produce knowledge that the academic world accepts as "excellent", "cutting edge" science, they have to adapt to what is rewarded in this context.

Contemporary scientists who wish to be published in a highly ranked journal must, as it is expressed by *Nature*, present conclusions that have "immediate, far-reaching implications", and "represent a substantial advance in the understanding of an important problem".[2] Thus, a main prerequisite for science to be rewarded with publication in highly ranked journals is its uniqueness; it must contribute insight that is radically different from what is already known. The headlines that can be found in *Science* and *Nature* give a short but illustrative indication of how the editors communicate that the published knowledge really fulfils the demands of being radical challenges.[3] "Before the Bio-molecular Revolution"...[4] "Realizing the Potential of the Genome Revolution"...[5] "Are you Ready for the Revolution"... "Molecular Biology has smoothly absorbed any number of technological 'revolutions'"...[6] The most prominent research award of them all, the Nobel prize, is granted to scientists in physics, chemistry and medicine who have "conferred the greatest benefit to mankind" and who have "made the most important discovery or invention".[7]

Although most of contemporary science will never be awarded headlines on the cover of *Nature* or the Nobel Prize, because it is more about adding tiny pieces of knowledge into established knowledge fields, the basic logic is still the same. To be rewarded by the academic world, scientific contributions must be recognised as unique and at least in some aspect radically different as compared to the existing scientific knowledge base. With researchers able to produce what is considered as "excellent", "cutting-edge" science or innovations, the academic research unit that hosts them can benefit from publications in highly ranked journals. Such benefits range from being attractive for research foundations and for new researchers and/or research and business collaborations.

If uniqueness is a prerequisite for knowledge to be rewarded in the academic world, this feature has no value in itself when knowledge is embedded in the business world. If it is not the internal features of a resource that are of interest when activated in a business setting, but what effects it can create on other resources, then the uniqueness can even be a drawback. The more certainly new knowledge differs from what is embedded into already existing resources, the more difficult it is to combine it with them; i.e. the more difficult to find ways to create economic benefits. If such knowledge ever becomes embedded into economic resources, it will be through quite complex development paths. Below we will give a short illustration of the interaction that is behind the development of the creation and use of new scientific knowledge in an economic setting.

This specific search for new knowledge was triggered by a beet sugar juice contamination problem. In the early 1940s the producer, the Swedish Sugar Company, approached researchers at the Institute of Biochemistry at Uppsala University. This group of researchers provided analytical tools such as the ultra-centrifuge and electrophoresis equipment for the investigation of large proteins. The fact that beet sugar juice was contaminated by a bacterium that produced Dextran (at that time known for at least a decade) was a very interesting finding for the Swedish Sugar Company; it meant that they knew how to solve the production problem.

However, the investigation of Dextran included a very valuable finding for the Institute of Biochemistry. The fact that this type of glucose did not interfere with human antibodies certainly made sense in a research department that, like many biomedical and military research environments worldwide, was struggling with how to handle the lack of blood plasma during wartime. In 1943, the Uppsala researchers approached the Swedish pharmaceutical company Pharmacia with the possibility of developing a blood plasma substitute. In 1947 the product Dextran (later called Macrodex) was launched. For decades it was one of Pharmacia's cash cows, and today is a main product of the German-owned Fresenius Kabi.

In the early 1950s, when Institute of Biochemistry researchers were striving to improve the separation medium used in columns, the experiences from the Swedish Sugar Company's contamination problem again became valuable. Work was initiated to replace cellulose composition with cross-linked Dextran, led by a researcher at the department and a colleague who had moved to Pharmacia. These researchers were greatly impressed with the ability to use cross-linked Dextran as a separation medium. The result was presented as a new separation gel named Sephadex (an abbreviation for *se*paration, *Pha*rmacia and *dex*tran). It was presented to *Nature* in 1959 as a totally new method to separate proteins and other biomaterial by size. Despite a rather cool reaction from the academic world and some initial hesitation on the part of management, Pharmacia decided to pursue the solution and established a new business unit for biotech supply called Pharmacia Fine Chemicals. In the mid-1980s Pharmacia Fine Chemicals became Pharmacia Biotech and in the late 1990s it merged with Amersham and became Amersham Biosciences. When Amersham Biosciences was bought by GE in 2004, products based on cross-linked Dextran still represented the largest part of the sales, both for large-scale applications in industry and in analytical research instruments. While the scientific knowledge production about separation was considered as "cutting-edge" in the 1940s, 1950s and 1960s, its greatest importance in the scientific and industrial user contexts developed over the last few decades (Waluszewski, 2004).

This example can be seen as an illustration of our earlier discussion, suggesting that there are different logics behind the production of knowledge in an academic setting, and the use of knowledge in a business setting. However, it is interesting to note that when knowledge is approached from a contemporary governmental or policy perspective, this aspect is neglected. Instead, it is the uniqueness: "cutting edge" science and "high tech" innovations that are assumed to have the best potential to contribute to the renewal of businesses and economic growth. Let us consider the policy perspective on what science can contribute within business life.

### *High expectations for the ability to use science in a business setting*

Being engaged in science has always meant being exposed to expectations. However, the contemporary scientist does not only have to face expectations related to the academic world but also to its economic effects, particularly if this scientist is engaged in areas such as molecular biology, nanotechnology or biotechnology. Governments and research policy organisations worldwide are directing an increasing hope to science as a producer of innovations and economic growth. OECD, for example, ascribes science a central role as being the source of innovations and prospering businesses. "In the knowledge-based economy, science and technology and their applications in industry and communications are major sources of economic growth and well-being."[8]

The policy efforts to connect scientific knowledge with business development can be characterised by their strong focus on the supply and intermediary side. Attention is primarily concentrated on how to get science to produce innovations, and how to get an "innovation system" to deliver innovations and venture capital to entrepreneurial, high-tech oriented businesses.[9] However, a question that is less often considered, if even reflected upon at all, is how the user structure, i.e. new and established businesses and organizations, can embed this knowledge into a business world full of already activated and interdependent solutions. In order to be used, any new resources, whether social or technological, have to be embedded into technological and organizational systems, including a large number of directly and indirectly related interfaces – but this is hardly touched upon at all. So what is behind this paradox? An increased utilization of science is considered to be of utmost importance. Then why is it that the process where science is embedded into an industrial user structure is so rarely scrutinised? And why is only one side of the coin considered – how science can reach business – while the "scientisation" of industrial knowledge, as illustrated above, is absent in this discussion?

The contemporary view of science, technology and its relationship to economic growth first reflects – consciously or not – an influence from traditional ideas about how a market is constituted. In the traditional economists' idea construction about the market, supply and demand work like a communicating vessel, automatically adapting to each other. (See Chapter 6 for a thorough discussion.) New knowledge is thought to be developed outside the economic system, but, when transformed into innovations, is absorbed by the system without any technological or economic effort. Second, behind the contemporary view of the relationships between science, technology and economic growth it is also possible to trace a great trust in science as a benefactor of technological renewal and industrial development. Behind this understanding there are a variety of proponents of scientific knowledge that, for different reasons, have "exaggerated the importance of science by claiming it to be the root of virtually all major technological changes" (Basalla, 1988, p. 92).

If these ideas colour the understanding of how science is related to business prosperity and economic growth, it is rather obvious why so much effort is devoted to encourage the academic knowledge production system to increase the delivery of innovations. And it is also easy to understand why the circumstance that science often appears as being untouched by the business world is tackled as a question of "what's wrong with the existing industry". Some common explanations for this issue, commonly labelled the "knowledge paradox" (Soete, 2002) include a lack of relationships between science and business, the businesses in a region lack "absorptive capacity", or they have a "wrong production structure".[10] The academic knowledge production system, on the other hand, is thought to have a great untapped potential for economic growth. As was illustrated above, the worldwide message – from east to west, from north to south – is that science is simply not utilised enough as a benefactor of economic growth.

But, if that is true, why is it so? Are we, as representatives for private consumption or company and organisational life, not able to utilise academic knowledge production? Is it conservatism, lack of contact with science, inability to learn, or fear of new things that is behind the rejection of new scientific solutions and the keeping of traditional methods? Or are there some other solid reasons behind companies' and individual consumers' ways to select which knowledge to use? And what do these reasons imply for the understanding of how it becomes possible to create use of science in a business setting?

If all specific knowledge embedded into related technological, social and economic solutions implies that the introduction of something new into such systems is not handled by some simple and automatic mechanism, then there is a critical issue that deserves to be lifted out from the shadows: how does the new knowledge appear from the perspective of those who represent the existing technological and organisational structures where the new is supposed to be embedded?

## What is useful knowledge in a business world?

The academic disputes about what science is have been so tough that Collin and Pinch (1998) named the protagonists "science warriors". However, the issue of how to interpret the use of knowledge in a business setting has also been the object of intense discussions. On the one hand, we have the traditional economists and their model where the market is assumed to be atomistic, built by "economic atoms" (Gudeman, 2001). In such a model world, characterised by the exchange of given resources carried out by completely independent actors, any new knowledge can be smoothly absorbed by "the market" they constitute. On the other hand, we have scholars in economic history, business studies and inter-organisational theory, among others, approaching the economic world as systemic and interdependent. In such a world, all earlier investments in physical and human resources, or the "path-dependency" (David, 1985), affect what kind of knowledge contributes to value creation (David, 1985; Rosenberg, 1982; Håkansson and Waluszewski, 2002).

Thus, anyone who searches for advice about how to embed new knowledge into a business setting, whether it is the scientist who wants to commercialise a new innovation or a business company that wants to commercialise the result of a minor change in an existing product, will be faced with two rather different views. Recipes inspired by traditional economies, the policy measures included, do not see any problem with using this source of knowledge in a business setting. Instead the question is how to create a transfer from production of knowledge to a business setting.

However, if the recipe is delivered from the second camp, the use of scientific knowledge will be dealt with from a completely different perspective, which also clashes with what kind of knowledge is rewarded in the academic world. In the latter interpretation, which also colours the empirical investigations that are presented in the following chapters, the economic value of a resource is due to the effects it creates on other resources. This means that when an organisation driven by economic interests considers whether or not to go for a new solution it must deal with the issue of the results of the new solution in the context of where it will be embedded. Does the introduction of a new solution mean that the main part of earlier investments can be combined with the new? Can the new solution co-exist with established solutions with which it will interface, physical as well as social? For example, can it co-exist with interdependent solutions connecting the resources activated by several layers of suppliers and customers? Can the new solution increase the value of the resources activated in established interfaces? Or does the new solution mean that several, or even none, of the earlier investments can benefit from it? This basic logic of economically driven organisations will reward knowledge – whether stemming from scientific sources or not – that does not clash with the existing structure but can contribute to an increased value of the main part of the resources with which it will co-exist.

Thus, the different logics of the academic and business contexts, where one rewards knowledge that challenges the existing knowledge base and the other rewards knowledge that can co-exist with earlier investments, implies that there are reasons to make a clear distinction between these two fields, although they are related. This distinction refers not only to the fact that there are different kinds of knowledge that are rewarded in these two contexts, but also to the implication that if knowledge has to be related to other knowledge before it is used, then it has to be reshaped before being activated in a business setting. With this interpretation outlined, it is easy to understand why the production of scientific knowledge and the activating of it in a business context often takes place at different times, and at different places.

This understanding is also the starting point for the empirical investigations that will be presented in the following chapters. The attempt is in no way a trial to evaluate knowledge in itself, or to develop a recipe for facilitating the transfer from the production to the use of knowledge. Instead, the ambition is to see how new knowledge is activated by users in different business settings. Thus, the main focus lies in how new knowledge is created as well as how it can contribute to economic value when the users bring it into their worlds full of already activated knowledge, manifested in social, organisational and technological structures. In summary we are approaching a whole series of questions: how can we grasp the processes where knowledge is embedded into resources activated in a business setting? And how can we grasp the processes where features embedded into one resource create effects on others? Some of these created interdependencies are handled within organisations and some across the borders of organisations; they are recognised and handled in visible relationships. But many are not recognised at all, at least not until any major changes come about. How can we grasp invisible resource interaction that can still be critical for the creation of benefits?

## The research context of this project

Along with being the starting point of this book, the issues sketched above have been central themes of a larger Swedish research project called "Scientific Research – Technological Change – Industrial Renewal" (VTI)[11] financed by the Bank of Sweden Tercentenary Fund. Between 1996 and 2006, 16 PhD students and more than ten senior researchers engaged in the history of science and business studies at Uppsala University and the history of technology and history of architecture at the Royal Institute of Technology, Stockholm, carried out an extensive research collaboration concerning the relationship between science, technological development and industrial renewal.[12]

The project's main objective was to investigate alternatives to the so-called linear model, where science is supposed to lead to technological development, which, in turn, will yield commercial and economic results (Rosenberg, 1982). Special attention was directed towards the interactive effects among science, technology development and the commercial use of innovations. The idea was to give the PhD students new theoretical and methodological insights by combining the research tradition of their base institutions with the traditions represented by the other research environments/senior researchers involved. Thus, the goal was not to create an overall research consensus but to force the research students to systematically confront experiences from their own research context (which still was supposed to be the main body) with ideas and concepts from the other areas.

The projects presented in the empirical chapters, i.e. the studies on the economic use of knowledge, are the results from this idea practised by PhD students with their base in business studies. The common theoretical base for these PhD students was the IMP or industrial network approach, which is, as will be thoroughly described later, a dynamic and systemic approach to the study of economic exchange between businesses. The IMP perspective was complemented by insights provided by the STS (Science and Technology Studies) tradition, which is the common denominator for the research perspectives of the three other research institutions involved. Below we will present the main STS and IMP ideas that have inspired this project.

### *Inspiration from the STS field*

STS, or Science and Technology Studies, is a multidisciplinary research field where the focus is on the social relationship of science and technology. The field emerged in the 1970s as a reaction to the idea that science is autonomous and objective. Its main theoretical sources can be found in the history, sociology and philosophy of science and technology while its empirical-based methodology is also inspired by anthropology. Although the STS field today is represented by an abundance of research "schools", a common denominator is the interest in the production, spread and use of knowledge (Widmalm, 2004).

One of these schools is known as the LTS research field, or Large Technological Systems, with Hughes (1983, 1987, 2004) as perhaps the most representative researcher.[13] The LTS tradition made an impact on the project presented in the empirical chapters in terms of the attention to interconnections between physical resources and how they developed over time. Other important insights brought forth through the LTS tradition include the crucial aspect that any technical element in use has a systemic function and that technological systems can include elements that are less developed (reverse salient).

A second STS school that has been an important influence on the whole VTI research programme, as well as on the projects especially dealing with the economic use of knowledge, is known under the acronym SSK (Sociology of Scientific Knowledge), with the work of Shapin and Schaffer (1985) and Collin and Pinch (1998) as some of the most renowned researchers. SSK has its roots in history and sociology and is best known for the position that science must be regarded as a combination of scientific methods and social norms and values. [14]

That science is neither neutral nor independent is an insight that SSK shares with another STS school, abbreviated SCOT (Social Construction of Technology), with Bijker (1997) and Pinch (1986) as two of the key references.[15] It is evident that both of these schools have inspired the authors of this book by the attention directed to the close connection and mutual influence of social (in our terminology, organisational) and physical resources.

A fourth STS school is known by the abbreviation ANT (Actor Network Theory) with Callon (1980), Latour and Woolgar (1986), Latour (1984) and Law (1992) as some of the most renowned representatives. A central theme in this school is what happens with knowledge over time, during successive changes where some resources become stabilised but also transformed and translated between different contexts.

A commonality among all of these STS schools (which also is in line with the IMP research tradition) can be characterised as a "methodological relativism"; i.e. the understanding that the knowledge creation process is interdependent with the system where it is produced and used. Although many of the references in the empirical chapters are directed to sources commonly used in the business studies research tradition, all authors of this book owe much to the STS field – primarily because it has made us more aware of how to utilise our own research tools in a more distinct way.

### The IMP Industrial Network Approach

Like the STS tradition, the IMP Industrial Network Approach emerged in the 1970s as a reaction against a dominating research perspective – the idea that economic activities are autonomous and independent. The main theoretical impulses can be traced back to sociology, while the empirically oriented methodology carries imprints from anthropology (Johanson and Mattson, 2006; Håkansson and Waluszewski, 2002). Our ideas of how interdependent business actors behave is closely related to "bounded rationality" and other organisational restrictions that have been fuelled by inter-organisational studies, with March and Simon (1958), March (1988, 1999), Thompson (1967), Weick (1969, 1976) and Brunson (1989) as some of the most important basic sources. The understanding that companies relate to each other in a much more varied way than solely through competition has been influenced by marketing and internationalisation studies made by Alderson (1957), Levitt (1967) and Webster (1979), and by general economic studies carried out by Penrose (1959) and Richardson (1972). These authors also inspired investigations similar to those that were carried out in the LTS field, such as how an individual company's engagement is related to a larger technological and organisational structure. In total, these types of theoretical sources have coloured a large number of empirical investigations of interaction in an economic landscape, as well as the development of some theoretical models. Which research tool and how it has been used in this project's investigation of the economic use of knowledge will be presented below. But before we go deeper into this issue, we would like to present briefly some theoretical contributions that have helped us within the project to identify and focus on some specific phenomenon within the field of technological development related to businesses.

### Inspiring sources dealing with some specific aspects of technology development

There are several themes in our research of technological development in a business setting that we share with a number of other researchers. The four most important that we are aware of will be presented below. In the study of the economic use of knowledge, we have not only benefited from these researchers' published research results, but have also had the opportunity to discuss the science–technology–business interaction with some of them in common seminars.

The first theme regards the importance of the user side, which is closely connected to von Hippel (see 1976, 1978 and 1988) and his work; depicted in the early stage as the customer-active paradigm but today better known as the lead-user approach. A central theme in his studies is the interplay between users and producers to understand how technical solutions are created. This is also a key issue for our project's attention to the economic use of knowledge. Furthermore, the lead-user literature has been an important inspirational source, particularly in terms of the attention directed to the role of "sticky information" and how that forces actors who represent producer–user interfaces to interact in a much more elaborated way than assumed in market literature.[16]

The second theme is among others represented by Rosenberg (1982, 1994), and his work in the intersection between the history of technology and economic history. Rosenberg's approach as well as a number of other researchers with similar backgrounds has inspired us to focus our attention on the many indirect economic effects of technological development, due to complexities in terms of interrelationships between technologies, economic consequences and the organisation of the industry, i.e. what Rosenberg termed "opening the black box". [17]

The third theme is very much represented by van de Ven *et al.* (1999). With a background in the inter-organisational field, van de Ven and associated researchers for many years have stressed the importance of the process aspects in technological development, such as the importance of unintentional incidents, how intersections of independent courses affect development, and how parallel and coinciding events affect each other. This has certainly inspired us to try to keep a multi-process view of both developments and of the use of knowledge.

The fourth and final theme is represented by Nonaka (1991) and Nonaka and Takeuchi (1995) and the attention to the interplay between tacit and explicit knowledge in a business setting. Nonaka's view of the knowledge creating company, and the importance of deeply rooted knowledge in organisations, is very much in line with how the economic use of knowledge has been approached in this project.

## Research approach

The research issues presented earlier, in combination with our research context, mean that we have turned our attention to how economic resources are created in historical and contemporary interactions between companies. This research approach means abandoning the (more or less conscious) legacy of traditional economic theory, in which the economic value of a resource, human or material, is taken to be independent of how the resource is used and combined with other resources. Instead, it means assuming that what creates value is the very manner in which the resources are combined over organisational and technological borders.

If, as Edith Penrose (1959) suggests, it is the way a resource is activated that creates its "services", then its value is due to how it is combined with other resources within organisations, within relationships between organisations or even due to indirect interaction over the borders of visible relationships. To grasp such processes, we have used a research tool that allows us to capture the interaction between heterogeneous resources, regardless of what actors are represented. The setting of this tool, developed in Håkansson and Waluszewski (2002), is the IMP network approach and its underlying assumption that a company's technological, social and economic features are the result of its inter-action with other companies (Axelsson and Easton, 1992; Håkansson and Snehota, 1995; Håkansson and Waluszewski, 2002).[18] The interplay among companies/organisations is treated as a phenomenon that can have a wide variety of expressions – ranging from more distant relationships to close interac-tions – where both organisational and technological resources are confronted and adapted. It is an approach coloured by the understanding that developments occur when companies and organizations encounter one another (Håkansson and Waluszewski, 2002).

With these underlying assumptions embedded into a research tool that focuses on direct and indirect resource interactions, we can investigate how a company's technological and commercial solutions are developed and used. We are able to map how resources are combined, i.e. confronted and remodelled in relation to each other, within and over organizational borders. Thus, we can see how new knowledge is developed and put into use in a business setting.

This investigation tool approaches the individual company as a part of a larger network. Every company is assumed to have important business relation-ships with some specific counterpart – suppliers, customers and other companies or organisations. Each company, as well as its counterparts, is made up of some specific resources. The research model (known as the 4R model; see Figure 1.1) is based on four types of resources. Two are mainly technological: a) products (steel, paper, iron ore, mobile phones, cars, etc.) and b) facilities or equipment (railways, harbours, paper machines, buildings, warehouses, etc.). These phys-ical resources are combined with each other into different technological systems. Two types of resources are mainly organisational: c) organisational units (such as individual organisations and companies, or parts of organisations and com-panies) that bring together a certain set of physical and human resources that are useful for some specific tasks, and d) organisational relationships (quasi-organizations developed in interaction over time), systematically relating what two companies are doing. (For a detailed discussion of the theoretical back-ground, see Håkansson and Waluszewski, 2002, chapter 2.)

The four types of resources are developed over time and in relation to each other. During this process each resource is combined with other resources, i.e. specific interfaces are developed among the resources. Any user system in a business setting consists of a large number of different but related resources. In this way the resources live in an organised world, with two important character-istics. First, the existing structure is the result of a systematic combining where

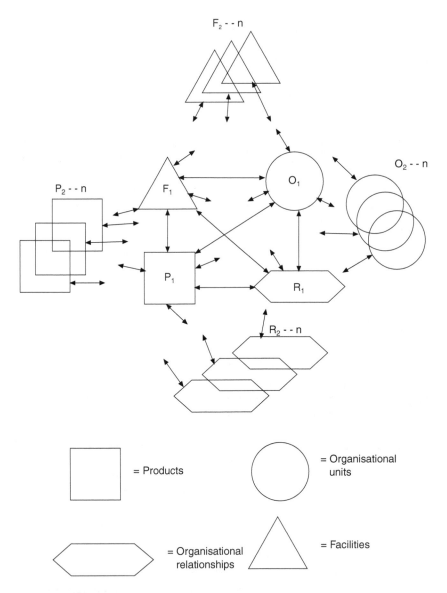

*Figure 1.1* Illustration of the 4R model.

individual resources are built together into intricate constellations. However, since most resources are used in different, sometimes contradicting combining processes, they are always exposed to tensions; to endeavours to combine them in new ways. Second, since the existing structure is the starting point for further combining, this will strongly influence the emerging changes. Thus, the use of resources in an organised world means that the replacement of one resource for another will always create reactions – not only at one, but at several related resource interfaces.

Resource interfaces can be developed and adapted to each other. Some interest may have been put into developing each interface, as well as in the combinations of a certain set of interfaces. Thus, knowledge is built into the interfaces, but will also exist in terms of knowledge about the interfaces. In this way these resource structures will exist in two forms – one as images and one as an activated structure. These two types follow different logics, where the first can easily include contradicting solutions but that is much more difficult for the other. However, both are important for how resources are used in a business setting (Håkansson and Waluszewski, 2002, p. 72f). The existence of such resource structures, where a large number of resources are systematically related to each other, makes the resource interfaces both important and complex. It also implies that important economic resource interfaces seldom are simple and highly standardised. This then implies that the introduction of something new, or change of something established, are heavy processes.

### Resource interfaces and what is behind them

This way of approaching resource interfaces has important theoretical and empirical consequences. One interesting question concerns how the existence of interfaces affects the resources. To what degree will physical resources affect each other, and how will physical resources affect organizational ones? Similarly, how will organizational resources affect each other and how will they affect the physical ones? To what degree will resources become embedded into each other? These are key questions when considering what knowledge is useful in a business setting, and they are also our focal issues, present in all of the empirical chapters.

This focus not only has important consequences for researching the use of knowledge in a business setting, but also for economic theory. The way knowledge is treated in economic theory can be regarded as a mirror of the view of resources in general. In the economic model world resources are considered as homogeneous, i.e. they are assumed to have the same value independent of other resources with which they are combined. This assumption solves some fundamental requirement for a market to function. (See Alchian and Demsetz, 1972, for a discussion on how this assumption solves the metric problem among others.) However, it also means that all resource interfaces are assumed to be completely standardised – something that explains why the only relevant knowledge in such a model world is the price.

What happens if we assume that resources are heterogeneous from an economic point of view? Then the value of the resource depends on what other resources it is combined with, and how this combination is carried out. Thus, the economic value stems not only from the internal features of a resource, but its effect on other resources. A classic example is Alchian and Demsetz' (1972) metaphor "team-effect", which illustrates how combinations of individual people into teams affect not just the value that they produce together but also the value of the individuals.

Thus, using the heterogeneity assumption, the way resource interfaces are supposed to work turns out rather differently as compared to traditional economics. Knowledge appears as essential – not in a general way, but concerning how to find better ways to combine resources. If resources are heterogeneous, it clearly has an effect on how knowledge is assumed to be created as well as used. A heterogeneity assumption suggests what is important knowledge in a business setting concerning how resources are used – and how they are combined with other resources in the using process. This puts the resource interfaces in focus. The resource interfaces will be of importance for the use of knowledge and for any production of knowledge that is assumed to be used in a business setting. Furthermore, the focal role of the resource interfaces implies that the use of knowledge in a business setting cannot easily be separated from the production of this knowledge. Knowledge that is going to be used in a business setting will be interwoven with the production of this particular knowledge – they will be parts of the same process.

In this way heterogeneity and the focus on the interfaces between resources are closely related. It is in these interfaces that development will take place. It is the role of these interfaces, from a theoretical point of view, that we will also focus on in this book.

The existence of interfaces will certainly also affect how the development processes appear. In an earlier work (Håkansson and Waluszewski, 2002) "friction" was used to characterize these processes. An attempt to change one interface will create tensions in a number of related interfaces. Thus, there will be a reacting force to any change initiative. The effects of this reaction will depend on how different interfaces are developed and how heavy each resource is. Together these are features that very much remind us of friction. However, it is important to note that this force, despite being conservative, is extremely economical. In fact, it is systematically relating the "new" investment to earlier investments and to what is invested contemporarily in related areas. The reason for this is that the tension created is related to the width and the depth of related interfaces and how they are combined including the size, i.e. the heaviness, of the resources. Given variations in these dimensions there will be more or less energy needed to change resource combinations. Furthermore, sometimes the friction can also facilitate change as when the "new" investment is positively related to earlier investments, or to contemporary, parallel changes.

In all of these development processes the interfaces will be central to the use of knowledge. However, they will also be important sources for new knowledge production. In the interfaces technical and functional features are systematically related to the economic outcome. As the process continues, these combinations are changed due to both the local knowledge production and changes in other parts of the total structure. Furthermore, as a number of these interfaces are across firm boundaries it also pinpoints the importance of relating one's own knowledge to the knowledge of others. It is a constant relating of these bodies that creates new opportunities to better use resources. It is these processes that are in focus in the empirical chapters.

## Structure of the book

The book consists of seven chapters. In this introductory chapter we have described the basic way we approach the research issue; why others' knowledge is so important and why it is necessary to consider knowledge from not only a producer but also from a user perspective. In the following four chapters we will present and discuss four larger empirical studies. Each of these studies was carried out as a PhD project within the VTI, Science, Technological Change and Industrial Renewal research programme.

The first empirical study, presented in Chapter 2, concerns the use of a resource (electricity) that is almost totally hidden from an end-user perspective. Still, this resource is important since it affects the features of several other resources related to the supply and use of the end product. Thus, although our focal resource is rather invisible, it has a strong impact on the economic value of several other related resources. We will consider how knowledge is embedded into the interfaces where the focal resource is used, and we will see how knowledge about the focal resource and the resources with which it is combined is developed in order to increase the value. However, we will also see how facets of these resources are partly unknown, implying that there are possibilities to develop the use of these resources.

In Chapter 3 we will see what happens when a new solution (wood as a framing material for tall buildings), which from a producer perspective is also regarded as an economically valuable solution, is embedded into a user setting. From the research and product development perspective, the new solution appears to be important since it can contribute to both increased quality and decreased costs. However, when embedded into an existing production structure another picture is outlined. The effects the new solution has on existing resource interfaces are not at all simple and as forecasted despite the fact that the new solution demands no new knowledge. Thus, we will see how a resource has many more facets than very experienced managers could forecast despite having a lot of earlier knowledge.

In Chapter 4 we will meet a resource that is, in contrast to the focal resource in the two first empirical chapters, very visible from an end-user perspective. However, in itself it can be regarded as neither a technically nor an economically advanced product – it is a low-priced table of wood. But when we consider all knowledge that is used in interfaces related to the creation of our focal end-product, another picture emerges. We will see how a whole network of firms are mobilized in order to develop and embed knowledge into a vast array of technological and organisational interfaces, with the common denominator that they all are adapted for the creation of our focal end-product.

Chapter 5 looks at the use of others' knowledge in a business landscape that differs radically from that presented in the three first empirical chapters. While the processes presented in these took place in business landscapes where actors both were allowed to directly interact with counterparts on the supplier–customer side and were experienced in such interaction, this is not the case for the actors appearing in this chapter. Instead, they are working in a planned economic system, where resource interfaces are governed by planning authorities. We will consider how an individual company could handle resource interfaces stretching over company borders during this era, and furthermore, what happened with the organising of interfaces when this task was left over from the planning authorities to the market.

In Chapter 6 we will leave the empirical world and instead turn to the economic literature to see what insights into these processes, i.e. the use of knowledge in a business setting, it can contribute. It is not a complete review of existing ideas concerning knowledge, but rather a highlighting of thoughts that are useful when we investigate the use of knowledge in a business setting. However, although the awareness of the importance of knowledge is high and figures extensively in economic thought, most if it does not address how it is actually used. Thus, the issue of how knowledge relates to an economic world full of already existing and related resources remains to be developed.

Chapter 7 is an attempt to contribute to such a development. While the economic literature provided us with a surplus of insights in knowledge from a production point of view, the empirical accounts pointed at the difficulties in embedding new knowledge into ongoing business processes. The empirical experiences underline that whether knowledge is going to be used or not is an issue of how it appears in the eyes of others – who are both multifaceted and already engaged in using knowledge. The chapter concludes with a discussion of what kind of theory we need in order to catch such processes, taking place in business landscapes full of earlier investments – which also are related to each other in intricate patterns. If any new venture, regardless of whether the new knowledge is presented in terms of products, processes, or services, will never be met by an open and inviting economic world or a claimless demand, then we need tools that can help us to understand the interaction between the new and existing resource patterns.

## Notes

1   At one extreme we have those for whom science really is autonomous researchers' search for objective, true facts. "Science is a structure built on facts" (Davies, 1968). Then there are the modified, but related interpretations delivered by Popper (1972) and Kuhn (1970), articulating that it is the specific methods that distinguish science from other knowledge production. At the other extreme we have those inspired by, among others, Feyerabend's (1975) argument that there is no significant difference between science and any other way of creating new knowledge through myths, traditions etc. "Knowledge is a local commodity, designed to satisfy local needs and to solve local problems..." (Feyerabend, 1987, p. 24). In this interpretation, to claim that scientific methods are a guarantee for truth and objectivity is just a way to "overrule" other ways of producing knowledge. "As science advanced and produced a steadily increased store of information, formal notions of objectivity were used not only to

create knowledge, but also to legitimize it, i.e. to show the objective validity of already existing bodies of information" (Feyerabend, 1987, p. 9). Similar arguments are brought forward by scholars engaged in social studies of science (Latour and Woolgar, 1986; Latour, 1984; Shapin and Schaffer, 1985; Collin and Pinch, 1998), who all stress that no scientific knowledge production is objective and autonomous, developed in accordance with an internal logic. "Scientific activity is not 'about nature', it is a fierce fight to construct reality. The laboratory is the workplace and the set of productive forces, which makes construction possible" (Latour and Woolgar, 1986, p. 243).

2  *Nature*, instructions to authors, www.nature.com.

3  The frequent use of the metaphor "revolutionary" is nothing new in an academic context. When this way of presenting academic results was introduced some hundred years ago, the ambition was to create an appeal that science represents a unique way of producing knowledge, which also has important and dramatic effects. Or, as Basalla (1988, p. 26) puts it: "Since the French Revolution, the work of Copernicus, Galileo, Kepler, and Newton has been described by the term 'revolution', a political metaphor that implies a violent break with the past and the establishment of a new order."

4  C. Lipinski and A. Hopkins, *Nature* 2004: 432, p. 855.

5  Marvin E. Frazier, Gary M. Johnson, David G. Thomassen, Carl E. Oliver and Aristides Patrinos, *Science* 11 April 2003, 300, pp. 290–293.

6  Dean Butler, *Nature* 15 February 2001, 409, pp. 785–760.

7  The Nobel Foundation is established under the terms of the will of the engineer Dr Alfred Bernhard Nobel, drawn up on 27 November 1895 (www.nobelprize.org).

8  oecd.org/about/0,2337.

9  A twin perspective is presented by the EU Commission. To reach the goals of the "Lisbon Strategy", i.e. "the goal of becoming the most competitive and dynamic knowledge based economy in the world", science and its ability to produce innovations is appointed a key role (europa.eu.int/comm/enterprise/entrepreneurship/action_plan). Also, in countries and regions with a "developing" economic and scientific system, such as China, science is ascribed an important role in the creation of innovations and prospering businesses. For example, on behalf of the Chinese government, the Chinese Academy of Sciences is encouraged to create a "modern science civilisation and innovation culture in China", through the "dissemination of scientific knowledge, spirit and methodology throughout society by adopting an open and networked *means*" (english.cas.ac.cn/eng2003).

10  See, for example, Edqvist (2002).

11  VTI, *Vetenskaplig forskning, Teknisk utveckling, Industriell Förnyelse.*

12  The programme has resulted in a number of publications. Along with the dissertations, four others are Håkansson and Waluszewski (2002), Widmalm (2001), Widmalm, ed. (2004) and Baraldi *et al.* (2006).

13  Two of the senior researchers active within the program have publications closely related to this field (see Lindqvist, 1984 and Kaiser and Hedin, 1995). Thomas P. Hughes has also been directly involved in seminars organised by the program.

14  In our research team we have had two senior researchers with publications with this base: Widmalm (2001) and Lundgren (2001).

15  The VTI research programme has also benefited from having Bijker as visiting researcher.

16  The VTI research programme has also benefited from guest seminars given by von Hippel.

17  The VTI research programme has also benefited from having Rosenberg as visiting researcher.

18  More recent work is available at www.impgroup.org

# References

Alchian, A.A., Demsetz, H., 1972. "Production, Information Costs and Economic Organization." *American Economic Review*, Vol. 62, No. 5, December, pp. 777–795.

Alderson, W., 1957. *Marketing Behavior and Executive Action.* Homewood, Ill.: Richard D. Irwin Inc.

Axelsson, B., Easton, G., 1992. *Industrial Networks: A New View of Reality.* London: Routledge.

Baraldi, E., Fors, H., Houltz, A., 2006. *Taking Place: The Spatial Contexts of Science, Technology and Business.* Sagamore Beach: Science History Publications.

Basalla, G. 1988. *The Evolution of Technology.* Cambridge: Cambridge University Press.

Bijker, W.E., 1997. *Of Bicycles, Bakelites and Bulbs.* Cambridge, MA: MIT Press.

Brunson, N., 1989. *The Organization of Hypocrisy: Talk, Decisions and Actions in Organizations.* Chichester: John Wiley & Sons.

Callon, M., 1980. "Struggles and Negotiations to Decide What is Problematic and What is Not: the Sociologics of Translation." In Kron, K.K., Withley, R., (eds) *The Social Process of Scientific Investigation.* Dordrecht: De Reidel Publishing Company, pp. 197–200.

Castells, M., 1996. *The Rise of the Network Society. The Information Age: Economy, Society, and Culture.* Vol. 1. Oxford: Blackwell Publishers.

Chalmers, A.F., 1999. *What is this Thing Called Science?* Buckingham: Open University Press.

Collin, H., Pinch, T., 1998. *The Golem: What You Should Know about Science.* Cambridge: Cambridge University Press.

David, P.A., 1985. "Clio and the Economics of QWERTY." *American Economic Review*, Vol. 75, No. 2, pp. 332–337.

Davies, J.J., 1968. *On the Scientific Method.* London: Longman.

Edqvist, E., 2002. *Innovationspolitik för Sverige – mål, skäl, problem och åtgärder.* Stockholm: Vinnova Forum VFI 2002:2.

Feyerabend, P., 1975. *Against Method: Outline of an Anarchistic Theory of Knowledge.* London: New Left Books.

Feyerabend, P., 1987. *Farewell to Reason.* London: Verso

Ford, D., Gadde, L-E., Håkansson, H., Snehota, S., 2003. *Managing Business Relationships.* Chichester: Wiley.

Gadde, L.-E., Håkansson, H., 2003. *Supply Network Strategies.* Chichester: Wiley.

Gibbons, M., Limoges, C., Nowotny, H., Schwartzman, S., Scott, P., Trow, M., 1994. *The New Production of Knowledge: The Dynamic of Science and Research in Contemporary Societies.* London: Sage.

Gudeman, S., 2001. *The Anthropology of Economy: Community, Market, and Culture.* Oxford: Blackwell Publishing.

Håkansson, H., ed., 1982. *Industrial Marketing and Production of Industrial Goods: A Network Approach.* New York: Wiley.

Håkansson, H., 1989. *Corporate Technological Behaviour: Co-operation and Networks.* London: Routledge.

Håkansson, H., Snehota, I., 1995. *Developing Business Relationships.* London: Routledge.

Håkansson, H., Waluszewski, A., 2002. *Managing Technological Development: IKEA, the Environment and Technology.* London: Routledge.

Hughes, T.P., 1983. *Networks of Power: Electrification in Western Society (1880–1930)*. Baltimore: Johns Hopkins University Press.

Hughes, T.P., 1987. "The Evolution of Large Technical Systems." In Bijker, W., Hughes, T.P., and Pinch, T.J. (eds) *The Social Construction of Large Technological Systems*. Cambridge, Mass.: MIT Press.

Hughes, T.P., 2004. *American Genesis: A Century of Invention and Technological Enthusiasm, 1870–1970*. Chicago: University of Chicago Press.

Johanson, J. Mattsson, L.G. 1985. "Marketing Investments and Market Investments in Industrial Networks", *International Journal of Research in Marketing*, Vol. 2, No. 3, pp. 185–195.

Johanson, J., Mattsson, L.G., 2006. "Business Networks: Background and some Basic Considerations." In Lee, J.W., Hadjikhani, A., Johanson, J. (eds) *Business Networks and International Markets*. Seoul: Brain Korea.

Kaiser, A., Hedin, M., eds, 1995. *Nordic Energy Systems: Historical Perspectives and Current Issues*. Mass.: Science History Publications.

Kuhn, T., 1970. *The Structure of Scientific Revolutions*. Chicago: University of Chicago Press.

Latour, B., 1984. *Science in Action*. Milton Keynes and Cambridge, Mass.: Open University Press and Harvard University Press.

Latour, B., Woolgar, S., 1986. *Laboratory Life: The Construction of Scientific Facts*. (2nd edn) Chichester: Princeton University Press.

Law, J., 1992. "Notes on the Theory of the Actor-Network: Ordering, Strategy and Heterogeneity." *Systems Practice*, Vol. 5, No. 4, pp. 379–393.

Leonard-Barton, D., 1995. *Wellsprings of Knowledge: Building and Sustaining the Sources of Innovation*. Boston: Harvard Business School Press.

Levitt, T., 1967. "Communication and Industrial Selling." *Journal of Marketing*, Vol. 31, No. 2, pp. 15–21.

Lindqvist, S., 1984. *Technology on Trial: The Introduction of Steam Power Technology Into Sweden, 1715–1736*. Uppsala Studies in History of Science 1. Stockholm: Almqvist & Wiksell International.

Lundgren, A., 2001. "Berzelius, Sweden, Italy, Electricity, Atoms and some Historical Reflections." In Beretta, M., Grandin, K., (eds) *A Galvanized Network: Italian–Swedish Relations from Galvani to Nobel*. Stockholm: Center for History of Science.

March, J. G., 1988. *Decisions and Organizations*. Oxford: Blackwell Publishing.

March, J.G., 1999. *The Pursuit of Organizational Intelligence*. Oxford: Blackwell Publishing.

March, J.G., Simon, H. A., 1958. *Organizations*. New York: Wiley.

Marshall, A., 1965 (1890). *Principles of Economics*. Available at www.econlib.org/library/Marshall/marP.html.

Nonaka, I., 1991, "The Knowledge-creating Company." *Harvard Business Review*, Vol. 69, No. 3, pp. 27–38.

Nonaka, I., Takeuchi, H., 1995. *The Knowledge-creating Company: How Japanese Companies Create the Dynamics of Innovation*. New York: Oxford University Press.

Penrose, E.T., 1959. *The Theory of the Growth of the Firm*. New York: Oxford University Press.

Pinch, T., 1986. *Confronting Nature*. Dordrecht: Reidel.

Piore, M.J., Sabel, C.F., 1984. *The Second Industrial Divide: Possibilities for Prosperity*. New York: Basic Books.

Popper, K.R., 1972. *The Logic of Scientific Discovery*. London: Hutchinsson.

Richardson, G.B., 1972. "The Organizing of Industry". *Economic Journal,* Vol. 82, pp. 883–896.

Rosenberg, N., 1982. *Inside the Black Box: Technology and Economics.* Cambridge: Cambridge University Press.

Rosenberg, N., 1994. *Exploring the Black Box: Technology, Economics, History.* Cambridge: Cambridge University Press.

Shapin, S., Schaffer, S., 1985. *Leviathan and the Air-Pump: Hobbes, Boyle and the Experimental Life.* Princeton University Press.

Soete, L., 2002. "The European Research Area: Perspectives and Opportunities." Paper presented for the international workshop on Research Policy: Incentives and Institutions, Rome.

Thompson, J.D., 1967. *Organizations in Action: Social Science Bases of Administrative Theory.* New York: McGraw-Hill.

van de Ven, A.H., Polley, D.E., Garud, R., Venkatarman, S., 1999. *The Innovation Journey.* New York: Oxford University Press.

von Hippel, E., 1976. "The Dominant Role of Users in the Scientific Instrument Innovation Process." *Research Policy*, Vol. 5, pp. 212–239.

von Hippel, E., 1978. "Successful Industrial Products from Customer Ideas: Presentation of a New Customer-Active Paradigm with Evidence and Implications." *Journal of Marketing*, Vol. 42, No. 1, pp. 39–49.

von Hippel, E., 1988. *The Sources of Innovation.* New York: Oxford University Press.

Waluszewski, A., 2004. "A Competing or Co-operating Cluster or Seven Decades of Combinatory Resources? What's behind a prospering biotech valley?" *Scandinavian Journal of Management*, Vol. 20, pp. 125–150.

Webster, Jr., F.E., 1979. *Industrial Marketing Strategy.* New York: John Wiley.

Weick, K.E., 1969. *The Social Psychology of Organizing.* Reading, Mass.: Addison Wesley.

Weick K.E., 1976. "Educational Organizations as Loosely Coupled Systems", *Administrative Science Quarterly*, Vol. 21, No. 1, pp. 1–11, 19.

Widmalm, S., 2001. *Det öppna laboratoriet. Uppsalafysiken och dess nätverk. Anders Ångström, Robert Thalén, Knut Ångström.* Stockholm: Atlantis.

Widmalm, S., 2004. "Uppsala STS. An interdisciplinary research centre. Final report of the project *Science and technology studies at Uppsala* and the working group's proposal." Uppsala University, Centre for Science and Technology Studies.

Widmalm, S., ed., 2004. *Artefakter.* Hedemora: Gidlunds Press.

Wilk, R.R., 1996. *Economics and Cultures: Foundation of Economic Anthropology.* Oxford: Westview.

Wynstra, J.Y.F., 1998. *Purchasing Involvement in Product Development.* (Dissertation). Eindhoven: Eindhoven Centre for Innovation Studies.

# 2 Resources in use
## Embedded electricity[1]

*Torkel Strömsten and Håkan Håkansson*

## Electricity and its interfaces

The organising process of value creation is concerned with the combination and use of both physical and organisational resources. One important consequence of this for the individual firm is the need to manage and develop the interfaces that exist between these physical and organisational resources that extend over the formal control of several firms (Wedin, 2001; Håkansson and Waluszewski, 2002; Baraldi, 2003). It can be assumed that this process continuously takes place but with a different focus and energy. Knowledge development about resource interfaces is an essential part of this process. If knowledge about resources and their interfaces is to be developed, it indicates that resources are heterogeneous (or at least can be seen as heterogeneous), and there are facets of the resources that are unknown or partly unknown to producers and users. It also specifically indicates that there are facets of the resource, through new combinations, that we want to learn more of, thus increasing the value of an economically important resource.

To illustrate this phenomenon the resource we will examine in this chapter is electricity. Electricity is traditionally seen as a very homogeneous resource that is produced and used within a physical system with clearly defined boundaries and interfaces. In fact, to function properly the flow and the quality of the electricity in the power system must be homogeneous. We will approach this resource from a somewhat different angle, and investigate and analyse the use of electricity. By focusing on the use of electricity we will also emphasise its heterogeneous aspects.

Our starting point is the use of electricity in an industrial process and, more specifically, one machine – a disc refiner producing a specific type of wood pulp, thermo mechanical pulp (TMP). The industrial process takes place in a paper mill, Hallsta Paper Mill, situated in a small city 100 kilometres outside Stockholm in Sweden. In the production of TMP, features are created that are activated by several actors in their development and their use of critical resources. We will trace how, through these features, electricity has become part of this network. The aim is to illustrate how a very homogenous and largely "hidden" or invisible resource becomes a resource with specific and heterogeneous interfaces to other resources in an industrial network as it becomes embedded both physically and organisationally over time. Thus, we will see that in this case the absence of perceived resource homogeneity is important for knowledge to be used and developed, within and between organisations.

In this chapter we investigate how the use of electricity is affected by the combination of organisational and physical resources, i.e. the interfaces between them. We examine how a single physical resource (electricity) is affected by interfaces to other physical resources and how these physical resources are embedded into organisational interfaces (such as specific business units and relationships between such units).

Moreover, in our analyses of the combination of resource interfaces we will examine the use and development of knowledge. First, there is knowledge use and creation taking place in each interface and every interface can be developed given perceived resource heterogeneity by the actors. Second, knowledge about the function and effects of one resource interface can always be related to the knowledge about some other related resource interfaces. Since all relevant resources have more than one interface there are obvious close connections through each of the involved resources between specific interfaces. In all industrial situations there are more such connections than one single organisation or single person can deal with. Thus, there must be a selection of which interfaces should be prioritised. One important issue is how interest is divided between different interfaces. Which interfaces will be in focus for knowledge development? Or which interface and what actors will benefit from a certain knowledge development?

A third aspect regarding knowledge creation in the interfaces is that there are also at least two types of knowledge creating processes. On the one hand we can identify something that can be depicted as "general interface knowledge processes" which are concerned with knowledge about how two resources behave in relation to each other in general. This type of knowledge is especially relevant for interfaces between physical resources but can also be found with organisational interfaces. The general type of interface knowledge is often "scientific" as it is often closely connected to a special scientific model including explanations for how and why the two resources influence each other (Hayek, 1945). "Specific interface knowledge processes" on the other hand deal with what happens in a resource interface in a specific context, given a certain combination of other interfaces. This type of knowledge process is often experiential in nature, where someone learns what happens when a pair of resources is combined in a specific setting, but where it might be impossible to explain why (Nonaka, 1994). Both these types of knowledge processes are important, but to varying degrees in different interfaces, and they affect and are affected by the developments within a certain interface.

In the next section of this chapter we present a framework for analysing interfaces between organisational and physical resources. Next, we give a general picture of how electricity is used in both a physical as well as an organisational environment, which consists of both direct and indirect interfaces. In the following section, we use our framework and analyse how the use of electricity is embedded in four different types of mixed resource interfaces.

Most of the empirical material was collected during 1994–2001 and was reported in Wedin (2001). A total of 103 interviews were conducted with individuals representing 40 different organisations. After that, additional interviews were conducted with managers and executives within the company. Further direct observation at Hallsta Paper Mill was conducted twice. Moreover, internal documents, company reports and industry journals were used to check and verify the information collected during interviews.

## Interfaces and the use and development of knowledge

No resource is used in isolation. Every resource has interfaces to both physical and organisational resources. Electricity is no exception. The fact that electricity has a number of physical interfaces has already been found in earlier studies, such as in Hughes (1983) where the development of the electric power systems in Berlin, Chicago, London and California are examined. Hughes analysed the development of the power system from a production perspective, where all the different components served the producers and the actors. The electricity production system has more than important physical interfaces, even though they are in the forefront in Hughes' study.

Granovetter and McGuire (1998) on the other hand identified and analysed some important organisational interfaces shaping the electricity industry in the USA. The authors found that interpersonal ties were crucial in the development of the industry and the types of technical standards that emerged. They also showed how the industry organised itself in what they called an industrial sociology, where firms interacted with suppliers, customers and other types of counterparts.

The existence and importance of different types of interfaces, where resources meet and affect each other, is the first characteristic of our analyses. In the Longman Dictionary of Contemporary English (1992) the word "interface" is defined as "a place or area where different things meet and have an effect on each other". It is further possible to "connect or be connected by means of an interface" (ibid.). The way the interfaces appear depends on historical as well as current interaction processes, between physical/technical and social/commercial resources. The interaction concerns solving problems, finding new ways to combine resource items or finding new ways to make utilisation more efficient or effective (Wedin, 2001, p. 39).

Two basic types are identified – interfaces between physical and interfaces between organisational resources. We divided each of these two types of resources into two types each – products and facilities for the physical resources and business units and business relationships for the organisational ones (see Chapter 1). In this chapter we will focus on the combination of organisational and physical resources, e.g. when a product meets a business relationship or a business unit has an interface to a production facility as in Figure 2.1.

| | | Physical resources | |
|---|---|---|---|
| | | Products | Facilities |
| Organisational resources | Organisational units | Type 1 interface | Type 2 interface |
| | Relationships | Type 3 interface | Type 4 interface |

*Figure 2.1* Four interfaces between physical and organisational resources.

There are four types of possible mixed resource interfaces according to Figure 2.1. Products and organisational units constitute the first interface. Facilities and organisational units make up the second type. Products and relationships constitute the third resource interface type, and facilities and relationships the fourth. These four different mixed resource interfaces mean special challenges, problems and opportunities for the single organisation and will now be briefly discussed.

The interface between products and organisational units implies that an organisation has identified a specific resource and is actively trying to manage it. There is a motivation to develop knowledge about the product, but what type of knowledge is not given. For example, the financial constraints an organisation faces might affect its view of the product and thereby how to maintain it, develop it, etc. However, the product also affects the organisation by its physical interfaces to other products. A product might be combined with some other products, where some features of the focal product are activated and required. This may force the organisation in a direction that was not thought about in the first place.

The second type of interface, between facilities and organisational units is also important. The knowledge in an organisation influences the way a production facility is managed, how it is used in relation to other production facilities, what type of input resources are used, etc. However, the production facility might also push the organisation in a specific direction, as facilities often involve capital investments. Then there is a clear motivation to develop knowledge so that these facilities can be used efficiently and effectively.[2] The knowledge search will then go in a direction that supports the features that increase an efficient and/or effective use of the facility.

Both type 1 and 2 interfaces are important and individual organisations are constantly trying to take care of single resources through developing these interfaces. However, there is one specific characteristic that also gives the development a certain direction and thereby important limitations. All the efforts are driven from one organisational unit's point of view. One consequence is that the knowledge of how to design the interface is limited, but also that the interest and possibility of changing the existing contextual structure is limited. If instead two or more organisations are involved, there are multiple knowledge bases, which are situated differently (have different contexts in terms of related interfaces) and thereby different interests that can drive change. If more than one firm is involved in the development effort, there are possibilities of finding new and different solutions compared to when it is just one firm.

The interface between products and relationships constitutes the third type of interface of interest for us here. A product is often a bridge between two parties, a buyer and a seller, and the product is therefore often managed by the two parties in common (even if the selling party would not necessarily agree on this). The knowledge about the product is therefore often jointly developed in the relationship, as features used and identified by the buyer (the user) are very hard for the seller (the producer) to actually have knowledge about. Knowledge that the user (buyer) develops is then often transferred and translated to the producer and the seller. Thus, the relationship as such has great impact on the product and how it is used and developed. On the other hand, products also have an impact on the direction a relationship might go. The product is used in contexts that are out of the control of both the producer as well as the user in a relationship. New types of using patterns, where new knowledge is required, might connect a producer to new users that might prove to be of more interest than old ones, and thereby lead to a terminated, or a changed relationship.

Last, the interface between facilities and relationships constitutes the fourth mixed interface that will be examined. Earlier we emphasised that there is a need for organisations to manage the physical or technical resources. The interface between a relationship and a facility implies that the evolution of how two parties link their activities, tie resources to each other and build up actor bonds, will influence how a facility is used and developed. The knowledge developed within the relationship will certainly influence the possibilities of using a facility effectively and efficiently, independent of whether the facility is on the buyer or seller side. The knowledge has to be focused not only on producing a product efficiently, but also on how the user can effectively take advantage of features created in a production facility. The knowledge that is used within a relationship will push the use of a facility in a certain direction.[3] The facility in itself will also influence the two parties in a relationship, as well as connected actors. A facility might function as an important node in a network, where the actors organise themselves in relation to this node if it is economically important enough. Thus, the knowledge that is developed in the network might therefore also be influenced by such a facility.

Even if it is possible to analyse interfaces in a stylised way, it is clear that all interfaces are embedded in other mixed interfaces. For example, the interface between a product and an organisational unit certainly has interfaces to several other products and production facilities, as well as to other organisational units or business relationships. All these interfaces will influence the focal one. Knowledge about this type of "interface embeddedness" is of importance for any organisation to anticipate patterns of behaviour or of change in the critical interfaces in the network.

## Interfaces of electricity in the TMP process

Holmen Paper (Holmen) is one of Europe's largest producers of printing paper. Holmen currently bases the absolute majority of its pulp production on thermo mechanical pulp (TMP). In the process, heated wood chips are processed between two counter rotating discs in a disc refiner. This activity is extremely electricity intensive. Holmen consumes about 2,500 kWh to produce a ton of pulp. Holmen uses a total of about 5 TWh during a year. This is more than Stockholm, the capital of Sweden, consumes during a year and constitutes about 5 per cent of the annual total production of electricity in Sweden.

Despite the intensity of its use of electricity, the TMP process is one of the most widely used industrial processes in the pulp and paper industry today. However, for a long time the dominating technology was the traditional stone wood grounding method (SGW). It is only about 30 years since the first investment in a set of disc refiners and a TMP mill was made in an integrated paper mill, where pulp production and paper making takes place within the same mill. This mill happened to be Hallsta Paper Mill, one of Holmen's major production sites. Hallsta has since 1974 invested in new TMP facilities. The latest investment was in a disc refiner from the Austrian firm Andritz (see Figure 2.2).

Disc refiners were used for several different purposes before entering the pulp and paper industry. Bauer Brothers, an American equipment manufacturer, found a refiner that was used for "breaking down cottonseeds and peanuts" and then adapted it for the pulp and paper industry (Sundholm, 1998, p. 28). A first step towards using refiners for producing mechanical pulp was taken in the 1920s when Bauer Brothers started to develop the refiner technology. In the 1950s and 1960s development of the refiner technology gained more ground. The reasons can be traced to the fact that the raw material in the north-eastern parts of the USA became more and more scarce and, therefore, more expensive. At the same time there was an excess of wood chips from the saw mill industry

*Figure 2.2* Disc refiner in Hallsta Paper Mill's TMP unit.

on the west coast. This made the development of equipment that could use wood chips as its raw material very appealing (Waluszewski, 1989).

The Swedish conditions were favourable for the introduction of the TMP technology. Wood scarcity also became an issue in Sweden in the 1970s and this made wood chips an interesting raw material. Previously wood chips were only a waste product from the saw mills' operations. Second, with a stronger pulp, chemical pulp could be excluded, which was an advantage from an environmental point of view. In addition, Sweden invested heavily in nuclear power resulting in cheap electricity. The cheap electricity made it possible for Hallsta and other paper mills to increase their costs for electricity but saving costs for other input material, due to the introduction of the TMP technology.

As indicated, even if the TMP process is a very electricity intensive process, electricity is certainly not the only resource used in this process. The most significant input cost-wise is wood. Another critical resource is also the disc refiner, which is the production equipment where the pulp is produced and where the electricity is consumed.[4] A fourth essential resource in the TMP process are the refiner segments, which are the components where the wood fibres are processed and turned into pulp. These four physical resources together make up the core of the TMP technology and are all used in Hallsta's TMP facilities.

Figure 2.3 illustrates four different physical resources that are interwoven in the TMP process and in which the electricity used at Hallsta is deeply embedded. These resources are produced and used in different industrial processes that are all connected, having interfaces to each other. First, the machines and components, the disc refiner and the segments, are developed and produced by firms that continuously try to solve problems for their customers in the paper industry. Second, the output from the TMP process, the pulp, is the input in the paper making process, which makes this process interesting if we want to understand how interfaces are designed in the TMP process. Third, the output from the paper making process is the input in the printing process. In both the paper making process and the printing process, many of the features created in the TMP process are activated, such as different strength features to keep the paper web together, thereby preventing web breaks and creating an efficient process. Fourth, the input in the TMP process, the wood, is the output from a rather complex "production process", namely foresting. The wood fibre is, in contrast to electricity, heterogeneous by its very nature. Processing the wood fibres in a way that creates the most value is certainly of great importance for the producer of pulp and paper, as wood is the largest cost component in the process.

All these resources are combined and recombined by the producers and users, and the use of each resource depends on how this matching within and between the resources works out. The use of electricity in the TMP process is dependent not only on the combination of resources with a direct physical interface (such as the wood, disc refiner and the refiner segments), but to a large degree also on the combinations of physical resource with indirect interfaces to the electricity used in the TMP process, such as the printing or the foresting processes.

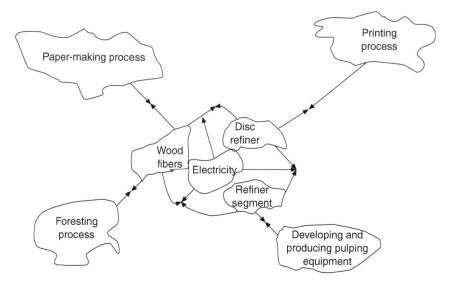

*Figure 2.3* Physical interfaces of the electricity used at Hallsta Paper Mill.

There is also an interface to the development of new pulping technologies. One such example was the development of the production of waste paper technology (Waluszewski, 1992). The waste paper process demands considerably less electrical energy in the production of pulp and this made producers of disc refiners start to develop the technology in different ways.[5] The Swedish manufacturer Sunds Defibrator, for example, developed the ThermoPulp technology, which for a while seemed promising. In this technology the wood chips were heated even more than in a traditional TMP process to make the defibration easier, and thereby save energy. However, the technology had a negative effect on the important strength features of the pulp, and the brightness of the pulp was affected by the high temperature. This lead to cost increases for the paper mill that in the end stopped the diffusion of the technology.

The organisational and interorganisational resources are important in themselves but also because they give the physical resources meaning in a social context. Certainly, there are a number of organisations that affect and are affected by how resource interfaces are designed and activated in the TMP process. An organisation that is directly involved in the defibration of wood chips and thus the use of electricity starts with the TMP unit where the pulp production takes place.

The TMP unit at Hallsta Paper Mill is responsible for the production of 500 tons of thermo mechanical pulp every day. The TMP unit supplies three paper machines (a fourth is supplied with the traditional mechanical method, SGW). There are three TMP facilities and each facility creates a production line with the paper machine it supplies. In total there are four production lines at Hallsta.

Six people run each shift in the TMP unit. Two of them run the wood yard, two of them run the debarking drum and two run the TMP unit. During one shift the operators are also responsible for not exceeding a certain load. If this happened, Hallsta and Holmen would have to pay a fee to Vattenfall, the supplier of power, since they would have used more power than they subscribed to. There is a constant trade off between producing the best possible pulp quality, at the lowest possible cost, where electricity is a large component together with wood. This is something that the operators have gradually learned to master over time.

To develop knowledge about how to produce a good pulp quality, the TMP unit interacts with several internal and external organisational units. The focal resource in this chapter, electricity, is supplied by the state-owned company Vattenfall, which has supplied the mill with power since 1915. The equipment in which the wood is processed and the electricity consumed is supplied by the Finnish firm Metso and by the Austrian firm Andritz. However, Hallsta's relationships with suppliers of disc refiners are complicated due to a consolidation phase in the equipment part of the network. In fact, over time Hallsta's relationship partners have been taken over by firms with whom Hallsta at first had chosen not to work for some specific reasons. One example is Defibrator, a close collaborator during the 1970s. When Sunds acquired Defibrator the relationship ended due to Sunds' ownership ties to SCA, a competitor to Holmen and Hallsta. Thus, in this case the organisational arrangement influenced the knowledge development, or rather the absence of knowledge development in the business relationship, as SCA, and therefore Sunds' Defibrator, was seen as an unwelcome supplier at any of Holmen's production sites.

The refiner segments (see Figure 2.4), where the wood actually directly interacts, are supplied by firms such as Metso, J&L and DuraMetall. The relationships with the suppliers of refiner segments are less sensitive as the components can be exchanged with others, while the investments in disc refiners are a long term commitment for both a buyer and a seller. Knowledge about what patterns give the best results is developed at some of the manufacturers and tried in collaboration with paper mills, the users. The interface between the wood chips and the refiner segments is seen as the key to producing a more electricity-efficient pulp. The knowledge about how the wood fibres "travel" in the refiner segments are mainly experiential, one knows what works but not necessarily why. Development becomes to a large extent trial-and-error based and as testing takes place in paper machine units, development work can be very costly if the production is affected negatively. However, these are costs that never find their way to the R&D account, but will be seen as lost revenues.

The raw material, wood, is finally supplied by an internal business unit, Holmen Forest, but behind this actor there are several independent forest owners with whom Hallsta interacts. If sorting of wood into different qualities were possible, the interface between the wood and the refiner segments would be improved in terms of electricity usage. However, there are many organisations involved with different and conflicting interests. For example, some of the wood

*Figure 2.4* Refiner segments used at Hallsta Paper Mill.

suppliers are also Holmen's competitors when it comes to selling printing paper. Therefore, Holmen and its production units sort the wood in the wood yard to make the production process more efficient.

As Figure 2.5 indicates, there is also an indirect organisational interface to the printing houses and the actors that embed this type of actor. Demands from the printing houses are important for Hallsta as they influence the choice of technology, the way that wood fibres are processed and consequently how much electricity is used in the TMP process. On the other hand, what is technically possible to achieve in the TMP process influences organisational arrangements for the printing houses and their customers, the companies that advertise in the newspapers. Knowledge of how the paper is used in the customers' printing processes is largely something that the technical marketing function within Holmen develops and brings back to the production unit (Hallsta), where different problems and possible solutions are discussed in different forums involving both marketing and production people.

As Figure 2.5 shows, just as the electricity used in the TMP process is technically embedded in a wider technological system, it is also organisationally embedded in a set of direct and indirect relationships. The TMP process has interfaces to the organisations that are concerned with printing, paper making and foresting or the production of TMP pulp, and these organisational interfaces affect the design of the TMP process and thus the use of electricity at Hallsta Paper Mill and its TMP unit. This also implies that the knowledge developed must consider different and sometimes conflicting interests in this network of actors. Balancing the different interests in the knowledge development is one of the main challenges for both the user of the TMP process and its developer and producer.

Figures 2.2 and 2.5 illustrate two distinct systems, an organisational and a

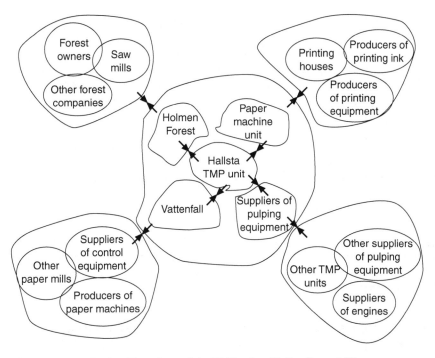

*Figure 2.5* Organisational interfaces of the TMP unit at Hallsta Paper Mill.

physical. However, these two systems interact continuously with each other and influence each other in different ways. There are organisations with different types of knowledge that manage the physical resources, but as was discussed earlier, the organisational resources are also highly influenced by the physical resources they manage. In the following we therefore investigate four mixed resource interfaces that can be found within Hallsta Paper Mill's network. All these four interfaces have great impact on the mill's use of electricity and have been chosen for that reason.

## Illustration of four mixed resource interfaces

In accordance with Figure 2.1 it is possible to identify four types of mixed interfaces: 1) interfaces between products and organisational units; 2) interfaces between products and organisational relationships; 3) interfaces between production facilities and organisational units and finally 4) interfaces between production facilities and organisational relationships.

From the empirical material presented in Wedin (2001) we selected one example for each type that directly and indirectly affects the TMP process and thus the use of electricity in this process. The type 1 interface that will be examined is the Metso-pulp interface. Second, we examine the interface between

|  |  | Physical resources | |
|  |  | Products | Facilities |
|---|---|---|---|
| Organisational resources | Organisational units | Type 1<br>Example: Metso-pulp | Type 2<br>Example: Holmen-Disc refiners |
|  | Relationships | Type 3<br>Example: Holmen/ Metso-pulp | Type 4<br>Example: Holmen/Bonnier-Printing house |

*Figure 2.6* Four interfaces between physical and organisational resources identified in the case.

Holmen's TMP unit and its disc refiners. Next, we look at the interface between the relationship between Holmen and Metso and the end product, paper. Fourth, the Holmen/Bonnier relationship and the printing house will be analysed (see Figure 2.6).

### Type 1 interface: mixed interface between an organisational unit and a product

One important mixed interface that affects the use of electricity in the TMP process is the one between Metso (the producer of disc refiners) and the pulp that is produced in the disc refiners. Metso's major task is to develop and produce equipment that produces pulp of a quality that is good for its customers' economy. The knowledge that Metso offers its customers is a high level of general knowledge that it adapts to the special conditions specific to its customers. This knowledge primarily concerns how to pick the best possible design of disc refiners and refiner segments, combine them and produce a pulp that makes it possible to produce paper of the right quality and with a good production economy. But there is also the question of using the knowledge about how to use the disc refiners.

When it comes to the issue of electricity use in the TMP process, originally this was never a problem for Metso. There was plenty of power production capacity and the price that its customers (industrial users) paid was not a big issue compared to the method's cost reductions. The TMP process made it possible to use wood chips (which was a waste product from saw mills) and to produce a stronger pulp (which made it possible to exclude expensive chemical pulp).

The role of electricity in the use of the product, the disc refiner, affects the user in several ways. It is clearly a cost item when the disc refiners are used in the TMP process. However, it can also be seen as a cost saver, as the use of TMP with the increased electricity use substituted for the use of chemical pulp,

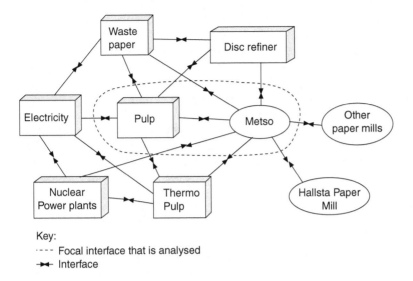

Key:
- ‐‐‐ Focal interface that is analysed
- ➤◄ Interface

*Figure 2.7* The embedded interface between Metso and pulp.

which earlier was an important cost driver for the users. Figure 2.7 illustrates how the interface between Metso and pulp depends upon several other mixed interfaces.

The interface between pulp and electricity first became of interest for Metso when electricity prices increased, and when paper producers could use a substitute product of TMP, namely waste paper, also illustrated in Figure 2.10. Metso's financial situation was hurt by the fact that it lost several potential deals due to the new technology developed for waste paper processing, and it then had clear incentives to act. For Metso disc refiners account for a large share of revenue, in both direct and indirect sales, as they get business through the sales of spare parts and maintenance.

As waste paper production facilities were developed and showed better performance[6] Metso (or rather Sunds Defibrator as the company was named in the early 1990s) lost business. Only then did the lower electricity usage in the TMP process become a real issue for Metso. One consequence was a large product development project called ThermoPulp. Metso did what it had always done – developed a general technology that they then tried to apply to specific customers' conditions. These experiences had been gained over many decades when engineers produced pulp in disc refiners. In fact one can argue that this type of knowledge was an attempt to "scientificate" practical experience.

However, these conditions proved to be too complex. As there were so many different parameters to consider, the development of the ThermoPulp method was never fully realised. Changing too many parameters produced a product that did not fit into the existing technological structure or the economic logic that dominated the investment decisions. As was mentioned earlier, the pulp's strength features were negatively affected by the ThermoPulp method and so was the brightness of the pulp. To compensate for this, customers had to use more chemical pulp to increase strength features and to add bleaching chemicals to reach the required brightness. Adopting the ThermoPulp technology meant increased costs for the paper mill and the technology could not survive in the long run, as these problems proved too hard to solve.

The development of this interface demonstrates how the importance of an interface can vary over time due to changes in related interfaces. Thus, development initiatives can often be more of a reaction than a systematic action. The interface also illustrates how knowledge development elsewhere (waste paper production) can force the development of knowledge in an interface.

### Type 2 interface: mixed interface between an organisational unit and a production facility

The second type of interface can be illustrated by how the TMP unit over the years has learned to utilise the disc refiners as production facilities. The overall goal for the unit is to produce an even and high quality pulp at a low cost. For example, the TMP unit developed a specific knowledge over the years about what type of wood quality should be used in certain disc refiners to reach a favourable cost picture. Here the use of electricity is an important parameter due to the fact that certain wood types demand more intensive refining and thus more electricity. Further, the TMP unit allows production to take place during the night shift, when capacity allows, since the electricity rates are lower at night. By doing this, they indirectly adapt to other units' consumption patterns. The TMP unit also systematically uses the disc refiner to develop the physical features in the pulp that are so critical for them in their own paper making process, and also for maintaining customer relationships to paper customers, as these features are even more crucial for them. These interfaces are illustrated in Figure 2.8. As can be seen, there are numerous different interfaces that the TMP unit has to consider in managing the disc refiners. It is not only the internal production process, but also all the other interacting interfaces illustrated in the figure.

The economy of the unit producing pulp and for the production unit Hallsta in general, relies on producing a given amount of pulp at a certain cost. However, as indicated, quality is also very important. The units producing TMP regularly meet and discuss the quality issues with the internal customers, the paper machine managers. Thus, there are attempts to make the specific developed knowledge become more general and useable elsewhere at other units. For the internal customers (paper machine unit), the quality affects the economy of their unit, and the creation of the pulp's strength feature must not be jeopardised, as the economy for the whole production unit as well as the company depends on the production in the paper machines. With a weaker pulp the economy of the paper machine and the paper mill will be in danger. Holmen

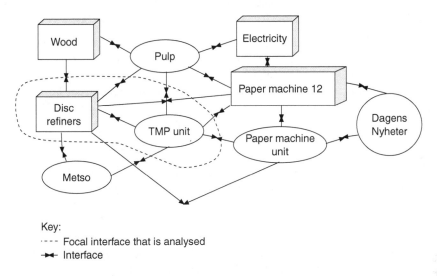

Key:
- - - - Focal interface that is analysed
→►◄ Interface

*Figure 2.8* The embedded interface of the TMP unit and disc refiners.

*Figure 2.9* PM11 at Hallsta Paper Mill.

and Hallsta's latest investment in a paper machine took place in 2002 when PM11 was built for SEK 2 billion (see Figure 2.9). Initially PM11 had productivity problems. One solution (of many) to the problem was to adapt the pulp's features better to the paper machine.

This example illustrates how a certain interface is developed over time, step by step, by a systematic relating of the interface to a number of related interfaces. This successive embedding seems to be an important ingredient in creating an economic use of a facility over time.

### *Type 3 interface: mixed interface between an organisational relationship and a product*

The third type of mixed interface is exemplified by the interface between the relationship between Holmen and Metso and the pulp produced in the TMP process. This interface is both highly complex and partly unknown. The knowledge about what creates the features of the pulp is known in terms of how it is related to the combination of wood and refiner segments, but there is less knowledge on why the pulp has these certain features. Instead the knowledge developed in this interface is largely based on practical experience and specific knowledge concerning one mill at a time, making it difficult to make quick changes. The relationship between Holmen and Metso and its influence on the pulp that is produced in the TMP unit is of great interest. As one of the key suppliers of disc refiners Metso knows much about the interface between wood fibres and disc refiners but still there are unknown areas. The existing interfaces are parts of a specific structure where the focus has mainly been on the interface between the disc refiner and the pulp. This has clearly affected the actors involved and their learning. The different interfaces are illustrated in Figure 2.10.

Which resources and which features should be in focus are highly relevant issues for the actors involved. Certainly there are diverging interests between Metso and Holmen around this; different technical and economic features are favoured by each of them. For example, initially the learning about the disc refiner's role in the TMP process was to solve problems with wood scarcity and with pulp quality. The chosen solution increased the electricity intensity of the

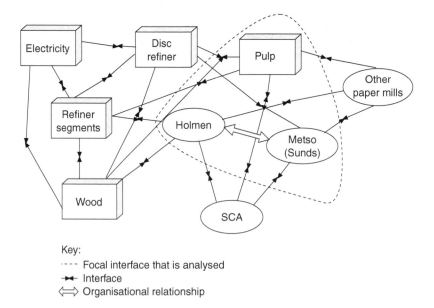

Key:
···· Focal interface that is analysed
⊶ Interface
⟺ Organisational relationship

*Figure 2.10* The embedded interface between the Holmen/Metso relationship and pulp.

process. However, since so many resources, wood, paper machines, printing presses, organisations and their routines became adapted to the features of the pulp, the knowledge and learning were directed towards these "heavy" resources. The learning is also related to the economy in the interface, represented by three types of "economies", Holmen's, Metso's and the production units producing pulp. There are both overlapping and conflicting goals in relation to economy, and of using resources efficiently. For Metso, it is important to balance the adaptations toward different customers. Every customer relationship and the solutions developed have to be some kind of compromise, as Metso supplies to customers all over the world and to different segments within the pulp and paper industry. For the production unit (the customer), an ideal situation would be to have more tailor-made facilities, to reap the possibilities from their specific prevailing conditions. This would make production even more cost efficient, but with the restriction that the disc refiners and refiner segments do not become too expensive. For Holmen as a company, the "economy" also includes how this production unit is related to all other production units within Holmen and especially the sister unit in Norrköping.

Even if certain parts or dimensions of the system are jointly defined by the actors involved, this is not always enough for cooperation. As other parts are defined differently among the actors, conflicting interests, real or perceived, might hinder the motivation to cooperate. For example, Holmen and Metso did not work together to develop the TMP process for a long time, partly due to the fact that Metso (then Sunds Defibrator) was owned by SCA, a competitor to Holmen and Hallsta. Certainly, from a technical perspective it did not make sense that an important user and one of the few producers of a technology did not cooperate. However, from an organisational point of view, this made perfect sense, at least for some of the individuals that managed the units at the time.

This example illustrates one of the key problems with connections between different interfaces. Actors involved in certain interfaces most often treat them as local problems, making them possible for the involved actors to solve. However, the local resources have interfaces to several "wholes", among them the system of which, for example, the TMP process is a part.

### *Type 4 interface: mixed interface between an organisational relationship and a production facility*

Our example for this fourth type deals with paper production and its interface to printing and how this interface affects the use of electricity. The production of paper (newsprint) is a highly automated process where the physical interfaces between pulp and the paper machine, and paper machine and paper are central, but channelled through, for example, the relationship between Holmen and Bonnier. The evolvement of the relationship can be described as a complicated problem solving process where the focus has been on finding a reasonable interface between the use of the machine and the features of the outcome – the paper. Bonnier has brought in its own production unit – DNEX (see Figure 2.11) – but indirectly also its customers, advertisers and readers into the relationship as illustrated in Figure 2.12.

The paper has a central role in the printing process and should be combined with the printing facility as well as ink. The use of colours has increased over time affecting the process (the printing process is getting wetter, leading to higher demands on paper strength) and emphasising the paper quality in terms of its appearance. These quality dimensions of the paper are directly dependent on the pulp production where they are created and thus also the use of electricity.

Knowledge about the effects of paper features in relation to specific printing presses and final newspaper is one important aspect that Bonnier brings into the relationship. This knowledge is much more developed than at smaller printing customers who do not have the same resources to collect and process this information. In the same way the organisation around the paper machine in Holmen has important knowledge regarding the interface between the pulp and the paper machine in general from its large pool of customers worldwide and its long time experience as one of the major players in the paper industry. Furthermore, this organisation unit also has close contacts with the supplier of the paper machines, who is responsible for the design of the latter both when it is designed the first time and all subsequent updating.

*Figure 2.11* DNEX printing press.

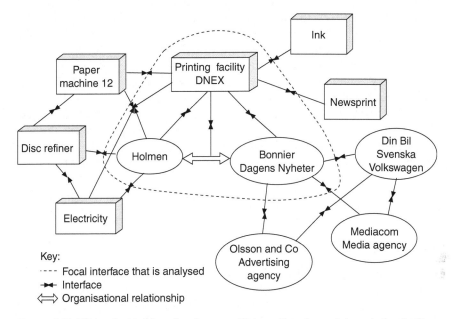

*Figure 2.12* The embedded interface between Holmen-Bonnier and the printing facility, DNEX.

Problem solving is also affected by economic considerations, which in this interface is very much related to the fact that printing presses are capital-intensive equipment that must be used efficiently and effectively. The use is dependent upon the technical design as well as how the interfaces to other resources are handled. The whole pattern around this economically heavy machine is there to "support" an efficient use in the short term. In the long term, however, there are "heavy" structures influencing this machine. These structures originate mainly from the users – the newspapers – and the suppliers – paper-producers and their suppliers. This creates an interesting paradox. On the one side there is the need to develop the use of the machine as it will be used for a very long time since it is so expensive. On the other side the capital intensity increases the need for stability. Every time a printing press stops, money is lost. Therefore using the printing press in product development, such as in testing new types of paper, is not easily carried out as it is so expensive. The user of the paper – the printing unit – wants to have a cheap paper as it uses large volumes. At the same time its economy is largely dependent upon a reliable input in the combination with the other physical and organisational resources that makes it possible to print some 300,000 copies of *Dagens Nyheter* in just a few hours every night. Losing revenue from advertisers such as Din Bil/Svenska Volkswagen can be devastating for a newspaper, and keeping them happy and making them return and increasing advertising is critical. Large advertisers often use a media agency that, from a strategic point of view, points out the right media for the advertiser. The advertising agency then handles the contact with the printing house and sees that the end result, the advertisement, is acceptable. Thus, the quality dimensions are essential and the technical dimensions of the newsprint also play an important role for the user. The appearance of the advertisement should correspond to the advertiser's so-called brand book, where all the logo-types, types of colours that should be used in the advertisement, are defined.

This illustrates how the outcome of a process – the features of a final product – is a compromise between what is technically optimal and possible and the economic priorities of the directly and indirectly involved companies. It is a compromise that in the short run must be stable but in the long run never is stable but must successively be adapted to changes in all these surrounding parameters. The relationship gives both the possibility of creating short term compromises and stability while channelling reasonable changes over time.

## Systematic combining over time

The picture we have painted through the four resource interfaces is interesting and problematic. The TMP process, and its use of electricity, consists of a set of resources being combined in a very specific way while also being closely related to a number of other industrial processes. The TMP process (and its use of electricity) is in this way embedded into a number of other processes and the resources. But the reverse is also the case. These other processes are embedded into the TMP process and its use of electricity. When the electricity is used in the TMP process all the other processes and resources are activated. Thus, these processes and resources can be seen as restrictions in the short run but as possibilities in the long run. In the short run they are fixed (given) but in the long run it is possible to change them all. Over time they will also all change and that will have effects on the use of electricity in the disc refiner (as part of the TMP process). The use of electricity in the disc-refiner is in this way directly dependent on how all these resources are related. It indicates that there are a large number of different resources that are part of the story. Furthermore, these resources are related to each other in a number of different ways. There are physical items, such as disc-refiners, pulp and newsprint, being related to each other and there are organisational resources, such as specific business units, being related to each other in unique ways. Finally, there are obvious interfaces between the organisational resources and the physical ones.

As researchers we face several huge problems. First, there are so many resource interfaces indicated in the original empirical material that we must select only a few. The question we have to ask ourselves is, how do we know which are the important ones. This issue is interesting as it is the same issue that all those actors (people as well as organisations) involved in the case have to face. They must also select and prioritise how the involved actors view the resources. Thus, the existing pattern is just one of many possible results and there is no reason to believe that it is the best one from any actor or from any resource point of view. It is a compromise at that point in time and it is only temporary. A second problem has to do with determining what type of interdependencies to look for between the interfaces. Every pair of interfaces has a common resource as the mediating mechanism – but many of the resources have a number of different dimensions that can be activated. A third problem is the identification of "patterns" including several interfaces. There are no natural borders – so these must be determined – and the pattern will also change given the reference point chosen.

None of these three problems can be decided upon before making the analysis. Instead they are closely embedded in the research process (as well as in the continuous business processes of involved companies).

In the chosen interfaces we identified a number of resources in terms of products, production facilities, organisational units and relationships that were critical for the development of the TMP process and, as a consequence, its use of electricity. These resources are successively combined with each other and the interfaces between them give restrictions and possibilities for the involved actors. Each production process creates specific interfaces among the resources used, which in turn depend on the process technology logic in combination with how the process has been organised by the business network. However, the function of each process is very much related to how they are interwoven with the other processes, which in turn depend on the existence of common resources such as a product being output from one process and input in the other. Again the physical resources are organised and related to each other through the organisational resources. In this way there are also important interfaces between the resources used in different processes and by different companies within the network. In these interfaces the features of the resources are combined and the use of each resource depends on how this matching within and between the processes works.

### Technical development as an organisational problem

We have identified a number of mixed interfaces directly and indirectly related to the use of electricity that takes place within the TMP unit. Some of the interfaces affecting the use of electricity in the disc refiner are physical ones relating products to each other or to production facilities. These interfaces create a chain. For example, given the features of the tree we get a certain type of wood. Then, depending on how the refiner segments are designed in combination with the design of the disc refiner and especially the use of electricity, a pulp is created with some specific features that affect its usefulness as input in the production of paper. This, in turn, has to be adapted to its use as an input in printing machines where newspapers are produced. Then it must be adapted to the ink used and to the fact that advertisements have to have a specific quality. Thus, electricity in combination with disc-refiners is, from a technical point of view, an interface as part of this technical chain (and some others) and the way the interface is designed is an integrated aspect of the function of the whole chain and influences all the other interfaces.

Some of the most important interfaces affecting the use of electricity in the disc-refiners are organisational interfaces, as all the involved companies have special competencies as well as economic logics affecting the handling of the physical interfaces. In this way the use of electricity is affected by how the companies organise internally as well as how they relate to others through business relationships. For example, how the forest owners organise their production and logistics, how the pulp and paper company relates to the power producer, how the pulp and paper company relates to the newsprint producers and how the latter relates to the advertisement buyers. These organising factors influence which and how much different physical interfaces become central for the others.

We have focused on the mixed interfaces, the ones where an organisational unit (a business unit or a relationship between two actors) has an interface with a physical resource (product or production facility) as we directly confront economic and technical/functional dimensions. In fact, to understand the economic use of electricity, and the possibilities of changing the use we must have a specific starting point from which we can make an "account". Any organised unit can be a starting point as they have an interest in developing and making "better" use of electricity or related resources. However, this interest can vary and so can the capability of identifying and designing changes in the interfaces.

In the above discussion we have characterised the four mixed interfaces, all with different logics. For the single firm these different characteristics are important. Taking the use and development of a resource from a single firm's perspective (an isolated view), there is not much left but to react to changes in related interfaces. Second, if looking into how a resource is used, the facilities-organisations interface helps us to understand that, when capital intensity is an issue, these interfaces are characterised by the step-by-step development efforts identified and that technical solutions are part of an embedding process in which the firm must take an active part. Third, the interface between a relationship and a product implies a more relational view, but more importantly, this view acknowledges that the actors have multiple incentives and motives to act in relation to a certain resource. Even if possibilities arise in networks that otherwise would not be possible, there is also an important issue to relate the different parts to the different wholes of which a network consists. In fact, a network is never only one network, but consists of several overlapping ones. Finally, if the interfaces between facilities and relationships are also taken into consideration, there is much more that a firm can do. However, since a firm is not the only one acting and mobilising actors, a firm will have to accept resource interfaces as characterised as compromises that are always present between what is technically possible and economically viable for the actors in the system. The degrees of freedom, what is possible to conduct, oscillate over the different interfaces, from purely reacting to the acceptance of a compromise to taking direct proactive action.

## Four interface principles

The aim of this chapter was to illustrate how what we normally perceive as a very homogeneous resource, electricity, becomes a resource with specific interfaces to other resources in an industrial network as it becomes embedded both technically and organisationally over time. Further, we saw that knowledge about these interfaces is developed within and between organisations in relation to technical or physical resources.

We identified a number of interfaces being related more or less closely to the use of electricity within an organisational unit, the TMP unit at Hallsta Paper Mill. Every time electricity is used in the disc-refiner it is done based on the assumption and knowledge that the other interfaces will have a specific set of characteristics. In the short term these interfaces are given and can be seen as restrictions. However, the degree to which they are developed determines the efficiency in, for example, the use of electricity in the disc-refiner. As a consequence, changes in all these interfaces will also influence the effects of the use of electricity in the disc-refiner. Over time all these interfaces will be developed. The development, however, does not all go in just one direction or just in relation to the use of electricity in the disc-refiner. In each interface there are a number of different forces due to interrelationships with all other resources. Thus, there is a potential in relating the interfaces to each other in a way that is optimal for the use of electricity in disc-refiners, but this is only one possibility that can be both contradictory or in accordance with other possibilities.

The first main conclusion is the importance of successive embedding of interfaces in relation to each other. The use of electricity at Holmen Paper's production unit Hallsta can only be understood if we relate it to several other interfaces as in Figures 2.3 and 2.5. The interfaces must both be related to physical interfaces such as pulp/paper, paper/printing machine, paper/ink, newspaper/advertisement. It must also be related to interfaces between Holmen/Metso, Holmen/*Dagens Nyheter* and *Dagens Nyheter*/advertisement buyer. The empirical material and the analyses that were conducted above allow us to formulate a set of principles regarding interfaces between organisational and physical resources. The first (and main) principle could be formulated as follows.

> First interface principle: *Every interface in a business network between any two resources is highly influenced by a set of other interfaces.*

One consequence of this principle is that interfaces are built on each other, which means that the function of each single interface is dependent upon all the others, and when the knowledge used and developed in these interfaces are experience-based, this makes large changes very difficult for the involved actors. Another consequence is that the value in a certain interface is created over time in a process where other interfaces affect and are affected by the focal one. This gives reason to turn to our second main conclusion.

The interfaces are related to each other in processes over time, crossing firm boundaries. In these processes it is crucial to change/adapt the focal interface to changes in the other interfaces. It is this mutual process that increases the use of electricity in the disc-refiner at the same time as this has been commercialised or "consumed" through changes in a number of the other interfaces. A number of different processes influence the interfaces. Some of them are specific and limited in time (projects) while others are more continuous (day-to-day) and constant over time. Furthermore, there are processes initiated by one actor trying to influence and integrate the interfaces from its own point of view. There are also processes that are driven by two or more actors/companies creating more joint solutions. This leads to a principle that could be formulated as follows.

> Second interface principle: *The interfaces are shaped in a number of very different processes with different origins and different time orientation.*

In these processes all interfaces do not have the same significance. First, the interest devoted to different interfaces is related to the heaviness of different resources. For example, the pulp and the paper in the case are economically heavy for the involved actors. It is a major input or output for some of the central actors and it is these reasons that are in focus in most of the relevant processes. Second, the importance of a certain interface is due to the degree to which it is "mobilised". How strong (and motivated) are the key actors within the relevant network and how aware are they of the importance of a specific interface? This leads us to our third conclusion.

The physical interfaces are in need of organisations to handle them, which is why we emphasised the mixed interfaces in this chapter. Without organisations there will be no value created out of the physical resources that are dispersed in industrial systems. The organisations take care of the physical items, combine them and design the interfaces between them. To take care of these resources, which often also represent important economic assets, there is a need to deliberately and effectively organise the interfaces between organisations. However, there are problems as there are several wholes of which any resources are a part. The different wholes indicate that there are different forces at work and a consequence is that any resource is "forced" in different and often contradictory directions. In fact, we can talk about the multiple or layered embeddedness that affects any resource. In these networks there are companies that have different interests and motives to cooperate. What is rational for one actor, or even rational for the system, will not be rational for another. This is also what creates a probable necessary tension in the network for development to take place.

In summary, the mixed interfaces have an important role as the combination of physical and organisational resources has important economic effects. These interfaces give all physical resources a certain "orientation".

> Third interface principle: *Mixed interfaces have a special role in how economy is created for physical resources.*

The knowledge that can be found within an organisational unit is not always used and this can be due to organisational structures and how information and knowledge are channelled through formal structures. For example, the TMP unit is affected by how the relationships with both the supplier of wood, Holmen Skog, and the supplier of power, Vattenfall, are managed by Holmen's central purchasing organisation. The interaction pattern with the suppliers of disc refiners and refiner segments is more direct and is managed by the individual mills. Thus, for Hallsta it can sometimes be hard to take advantage of the experiences that reside within the suppliers and customer organisations, since there always is an internal organisation in-between and the information is channelled and also filtered.

The above comment regarding the knowledge use within an organisation is only a minor consideration in relation to how important effects related to resource interfaces have for knowledge, knowledge sharing and the development of new knowledge. As soon as one interface is changed tension is created in all related interfaces, which in turn have important knowledge consequences. First, such tensions will create a need to exchange knowledge, to inform each other about the effects. Second, they have important positive effects of sharing knowledge, as changes can only be made through more or less simultaneous adaptations. Finally, all such adaptations will create some new knowledge.

Fourth interface principle: *Any change in an interface will create reactions in related interfaces that in turn might result in exchange of knowledge and/or development of new knowledge.*

In this chapter we used a "hidden" focal resource, electricity, to discuss the importance of mixed resource interfaces and the process of using and developing knowledge in these interfaces. Through the features created by the use of this resource, we were able to trace its indirect use and also the use and development of knowledge that can be associated with it.

All the processes where the interfaces are systematically related have, in this way, an important knowledge content. It might be application of new general knowledge but it will also always be creation of new experiential knowledge. Thus, in the interfaces both general as well as more specific knowledge is constantly used and developed, but not necessarily at the same time and there is not necessarily harmony between the two development processes. For the single firm, there is a need to develop knowledge that can be transferred to other relationships, thus having a more "general" content. For the user of the knowledge on the other hand, for it to be of most value, it has to be "specific" for its own conditions as the designs of the interfaces are always, to some extent, specific both physically as well as organisationally. However, even for a user demanding specific knowledge development from a supplier, there must also be an element of "economy" in the use (and thus also in the supply), as an isolated user of knowledge will never be able to reap the benefits of being connected to a wider network. What knowledge that is to be developed has to do with both the motives among the actors in the network, and about the capabilities to mobilise and thus motivate the ones that at first do not see the point of developing a certain type of resource interface (and consequently the knowledge needed).

## Notes

1  The empirical material that is used in this chapter is taken from VTI thesis "Networks and Demand. The use of of electricity in an industrial process" (Wedin, 2001). In the thesis three research questions were asked. First, how is demand for a resource formed from a focal firm's perspective? Second, how can the focal firm influence its demand for an individual resource? Third, how is knowledge about an individual resource developed and used? In this chapter, the last question regarding the use of knowledge is highlighted. Several sources of information were used in the thesis, even if interviews worked as the primary source of information. A "snowballing technique" was used and interviews with some 103 individuals were conducted and about 40 different organizations were covered in the empirical field work. This means that suppliers as well as customers, customers' customers, suppliers to customers, parallel suppliers to customers, etc., were interviewed. In the end a network pattern of the demand for electricity was formed from the interviews.

2  When market conditions change (or rather network conditions) or when the organisation faces a financial downturn (often these conditions co-vary) the production facilities of an organisation are often handled in two different ways. They might be used more tightly, where every inch or hour of capacity is used to cover variable costs and contribute to the organisation's economy. Or, the facilities might be shut down or sold to outside (partners) suppliers in an outsourcing agreement.

3  In addition, the way the relationship is embedded will also influence the way a facility is utilised. For example, this will influence a producer when the buyer is embedded in a network of relationships where growth first is on the agenda and then a downturn takes over. Suddenly the relationship will have probably created an over capacity in the facility due to the embeddedness in the volatile network.

4  Disc refiners are run by electric motors and they can have loads up to 20 MW. Disc refiners are simply large pieces of equipment, about $2 \times 5$ metres long. The electric motor is even significantly larger.

5  But since a large share of the electricity consumed in the disc refiners can be recovered and re-used in the paper machine's drying sections, the overall energy consumption is actually equivalent if drawing the boundary around the whole production line and not only around the pulping equipment. The reason is that oil is needed to create the steam used to dry the paper in the drying section of the paper machine.

6  Waste paper was and still is cheaper as a raw material, and less electricity is used in the production of pulp based upon waste paper.

## References

Baraldi, E. (2003) *When Information Technology Faces Resource Interaction: Using IT Tools to Handle Products at IKEA and Edsbyn*, PhD Thesis, Department of Business Studies, Uppsala University.

Granovetter, M. and McGuire, P. (1998) The Making of an Industry: Electricity in the United States. In Michel Callon, editor, *The Laws of the Markets*. Oxford: Blackwell, pp. 147–173.

Håkansson H. and Waluszewski A. (2002) *Managing Technological Development. IKEA, the Environment and Technology*. London: Routledge.

Hayek, F.A. (1945) "The Use of Knowledge in Society", *American Economic Review*, Vol. 35, pp. 519–530.

Hughes, T.P. (1983) *Networks of Power. Electrification in Western Society, 1880–1930*. Baltimore: Johns Hopkins University Press.

Longman Dictionary of Contemporary English (1992) Burnt Mill, Harlow: Longman.

Nonaka, I. (1994) "A Dynamic Theory of Organisational Knowledge Creation", *Organisation Science*, Vol. 5, No. 1, pp. 14–37.

Sundholm, J. (1998) *Papermaking Science and Technology. Mechanical Pulping.* Helsinki: Fapet Oy.

Waluszewski, A. (1989*) Framväxten av en ny mekanisk massateknik. En utvecklingshistoria*. Avhandling. Företagsekonomiska institutionen, Uppsala universitet.

Waluszewski, A. (1992) *Vedfiber eller returpapper?* Ingenjörsvetenskaps-akademien, Uppsala universitet.

Wedin, T. (2001) *Networks and Demand. The Use of Electricity in an Industrial Process.* PhD Thesis, Department of Business Studies, Uppsala University.

# 3 Introducing "old" knowledge in an established user context

## How to use wood in the construction industry[1]

*Anna Bengtson and Håkan Håkansson*

### Reintroducing an "old" solution in a user context

What happens when old knowledge, which from a producer perspective, however, is regarded as an economic valuable solution, is reintroduced into a user setting? In this chapter we will follow the attempts to replace an established technology with an alternative solution that was used 100 years ago. From the producer point of view, the new/old solution appears beneficial, since it can contribute to both increased production quality and decreased costs. Thus, it appears to belong to the few innovations that actually can also contribute to generation of income when embedded in a user setting. However, when the "old" solution is starting to get used, another picture is outlined. The effects the "old" solution has on existing resource interfaces intervene in the process in a way that was quite surprising from the producer perspective.

The resource in focus is far from what is traditionally considered as a high tech innovation. On the contrary, it concerns a (re)introduction of a low tech technology into a structure where it had not been used for a long time due to legal restrictions. The situation was one of an easy technology transfer rather than of a new breakthrough in science. The amount of learning needed to start using the technology for business purposes in this structure was therefore limited; the technology was simple, well known and had been used for decades in other locations. The production structure on the supply side was also well established and there was excellent access to a vast amount of research that for decades had already been spent on the materials and components. Still, it proved to be very difficult for this solution to contribute to a positive bottom line. This raises the question of what is required in order for innovations that are considered as beneficial from a producer perspective to contribute to economic benefits also in a user setting.

### *Legal change opens up for new possibilities*

The technological change situation that we focus on was found in the Swedish construction industry in the mid and late 1990s. An amazingly large amount of time and resources were spent by Swedish construction companies on something as basic as timber construction. Aspects that were discussed in seminars and in articles concerned not only this basic material, but also its most fundamental functions such as fire insulation, acoustics and stability (Andreasson, 1999; Andreasson and Thelandersson, 1998; Eriksson, 1995; Norén, 1996; Östman, 1997a, 1997b, 1998; Persson, 1998). This sudden fling between the construction industry and the well known material timber in the old timber nation of Sweden had, however, its natural reasons. A large city fire in Sundsvall in 1888, the last in a long line of city fires in the nineteenth century, had put an end to the construction of timber framed residential buildings of more than two storeys for a little more than 100 years. In the early 1990s, however, new research findings showed that the legislators had most likely confused timber frames and timber facades at the time of the prohibition and thus forbidden both. New fire tests proved that timber frames provided rather good fire insulation compared to other materials used such as steel. In 1993/1994 the building regulations in the Swedish building code BBR94 were changed in favour of functional requirements. The prohibition against burnable materials such as timber was replaced by requirements that stated how long a building must hold in the event of a fire (Interview Östman; Miller and Stone, 1995).

To explain the interest shown by the construction industry, one also needs to know that this legal change came at a time when the Swedish construction industry was looking for ways to lower production costs, which according to several statistics had been rising steadily for some years (Engebeck and Wigren, 1997; SCB, Bostads- och byggnadsstatistisk årsbok, 2002). Swedish industry representatives looked at the USA at the time and were able to show that the American construction industry, which had not been burdened with the same timber prohibition as the Swedish industry, used timber frames in more than 90 per cent of its multi dwellings. The technique had been popular for decades and comparisons to Swedish production costs revealed that it resulted in much lower costs than those in Sweden. This was so even when considering differences in taxes, climate, quality demands, etc. (Miller and Stone, 1995). The interest in timber construction shown by the Swedish construction industry in the mid-1990s was based on the fact that they were given an opportunity to lower their production costs by perhaps as much as 40 to 50 per cent simply by switching to another framing material. The material, timber, was well known and widely used for many other industry-wide applications.

The prevailing situation in the Swedish construction industry in the mid-1990s gives us, as researchers of technological change, an interesting opportunity to study how the existence of a specific limitation influenced the development of the total structure of physical and organisational interfaces within a specific network. This analysis would, we assumed, help to better understand the importance of knowledge for technological change and economic reconstruction in knowledge-rich change situations. In the US subnetwork, use of one material for a specific function (timber for framing) has been allowed while it has been forbidden in the Swedish (Scandinavian) one. However the material in itself is also used in the latter subnetwork in a large number of other applications. We can therefore assume that the total knowledge of the material is at the same level (it could even be higher in Sweden as Sweden is more dependent on the forest industry than the USA). Any difference in the two subnetworks must then be related to the blocking of one specific interface, i.e. the one between the material and the function. The situation remains of a designed classical experimental situation with one group where, at a certain time, there was a change and a control group with no change and where, 100 years later, it is possible to measure the long-term effects as there is a change back to the old solution.

In this chapter we will look further into these networks and the physical and organisational resource interfaces that are related to the design and the production of a building using timber and the concrete technologies. By starting with the legal change concerning the use of timber in Sweden described above, we will be able to show that, from a knowledge point of view, the construction of the economy is far from a neutral process. Through time, resources and resource interfaces were directed into certain "paths" or "use areas" from which new use potentials emerged, making the resources even less neutral. We will study how the Swedish construction network, with its experimental "change" starting situation, evolved from one technological situation to a somewhat different one in an attempt to reconstruct the economy. This change is affected by both technological and organisational interfaces as well as by the industrial parties' knowledge and/or ignorance of these interfaces.

In the next section we will give a short introduction to the resource structure behind a building. Thereafter we will begin the analysis by looking closer, from a technical point of view, at the relationship between the focal interface and other types of interfaces in the construction industry. Next, important organisational interfaces in housing construction are related to the focal interface. The chapter ends with an analysis of the technological change that we studied from a knowledge point of view. The question raised is: Does the technological simplicity of this change (well established supply structure that gave the producers the knowledge input they needed, good access to a vast amount of research on the subject, as well as more or less free access to the knowledge in the network that already uses the technology) imply an absence of the knowledge obstacle in the creation of wealth through this innovation?

## Physical and organisational resource interfaces in a building

For anyone interested in how resources become combined into larger valuable and functional "wholes" or products, the construction of a building is an ideal object of study. The functionality aspects related to the product are quite complex since there are several functions that any building must have, and that must be considered during the design process. The most fundamental function of a residential building is to provide shelter for its residents. Providing shelter can, however, be further broken down into more specific functions such as safety (for example resistance to wind, moisture and fire), and comfort (such as ventilation and sound insulation). Some of these functions are described in laws and regulations, either on a national basis or in a larger setting. Other functions are still perceived as given, i.e. over processes in time they have become part of our very definition of a building. Designing a building – aesthetically and technically – is thus a question of considering all these functions.

These functions, whichever they are, also raise certain demands on the individual materials and components used to construct the building, on how these materials and components are combined in the construction, i.e. on various physical resource interfaces, and on the larger technical resource structure needed for the construction of the building. All functional and aesthetic requirements for a certain product – in this case a specific building – are also affected by the production processes hidden behind the construction of the various components and materials of which the building is fabricated. Producing all of these components and materials that fulfil these functions requires an extensive and highly complicated production structure. The various production processes in the production structure are then affected by the requirements on the building, but also primarily by demands on economical and organisational aspects, such as efficiency and the long-term production planning of each specific component in each specific production unit. The production side of the resource structure is composed of a number of suppliers and sub-suppliers each having specialised production equipment as well as design and production knowledge/experience.

We have distinguished between the product and its requirements, and the production structure behind it and its other requirements. It can thus be stated that the logic behind the design of a building and the logic behind the production of the same building may differ. We also concluded that there are clear dependencies between these two processes, which could lead to a dynamic and interactive process of design and production as a whole. However, as we will see in the descriptions of the reconstruction process, the design and production of buildings are generally treated as separate processes bridged by a market and its price mechanism rather than by interaction and co-development. In the following analysis of resource interfaces related to design and to production we will make a distinction between physical interfaces, which relate to the products and production equipments needed, and the organisational interfaces, which are made up of competences, skills and economic reasoning made by the involved companies and organisations.

## Important physical interfaces: starting out from the frame

When Sweden prohibited the use of timber in tall residential buildings in the early nineteenth century, its use for house construction had just started to become more industrialised. For example, an expansion of the saw mill industry in the 1870s made light timber construction more common, and an industry branch with housing catalogues and prefabrication was expanding. After the prohibition, however, there were other materials that took over. Non-burnable materials such as stone and brick had already become more commonly used as the cities were expanding due to the urbanisation at the turn of the century. It was these materials that one now reached for in the absence of the possibility of using timber for construction of more than two storeys. Soon, however, concrete became more common, and more recently has dominated the application, even though steel and steel/concrete combinations are alternatives that might be considered. The shift from timber to concrete for framing clearly meant a lot for those producing concrete, but also for others who produced materials or components that in some way were related to the frame. Let us look a little closer at this by starting out from the role of the frame.

### The frame and the building

The frame is an important part of the building as it is directly related to several of the key functions (stability, fire protection, sound insulation, design, etc.). The choice of framing material impacts both the design phase and the production phase as well as the final use of the building. The standard choice for framing of Swedish multi-storey residential buildings is concrete, which is a robust and thermally efficient material. As the material grew popular for house building in the 1960s one learned, however, that concrete contains a large amount of moisture before it dries, making certain interfaces, such as surface materials and the glue used for the surface material on floors, vulnerable if not used properly. Cast in situ concrete also has some disadvantages in the construction phase in a cold climate country like Sweden, since the construction becomes vulnerable to changes in temperature, rain, snow etc. Prefabricated framing elements have therefore become an often used alternative. Because the country is so large, high transportation costs for the heavy and ungainly concrete elements became a major obstacle. Another obstacle is the need for heavy equipment such as load-bearing cranes. Due to the large span width that can be accomplished, recent decades have seen a rise in the popularity of steel for the construction of large buildings that demand open-plan space, such as garages or open offices.

When we consider timber frames, the standard choice for residential buildings in the American construction network, we find that it is generally not possible to determine the material from which it is made from the appearance of the building. Some of the buildings that were built with timber frames after the legal change in Sweden were originally planned as regular concrete buildings. When the development started, its aim was to reach the same result in all functional dimensions independent of the framing material that was used. Later in the development, however, the timber material was sometimes used as a sales argument, as explained by a builder from the building company Skanska, engaged in the development. "People tend to like timber, which has positive associations, in comparison to concrete that one may have somewhat of a dislike for." Fulfilling the same functional requirements independent of the framing material used, demands, however, different efforts related to the two materials. For example, concrete is non-flammable, whereas timber is flammable and requires coverage with a material such as plasterboard to fulfil the same fire-safety requirements.

The fact that timber is a lightweight material, while concrete is heavy, puts different demands on the design of the construction in relation to stability. Acoustic conditions also vary between a timber and a concrete framed building.

### The production process of frames

As indicated in the previous section, the production of concrete frames can take place either on the construction site or in a factory. A site-made concrete frame is constructed in several steps. After the ground has been prepared, the shuttering for the first storey frame is built and concrete is poured into it. The concrete then must dry for some time before the same procedure can follow for the second storey and so on. A prefabricated frame is constructed on large moulding tables from which it is lifted after a short drying time. When enough elements have dried they are transported to the site and lifted onto the building one by one. Properly made sections are vital to reach good strength and bearing capacity for a prefabricated frame of this type. Whereas both methods have their pros and cons, the choice of either method is normally decided on in the planning phase of the building project, based on such considerations as time schedule, time of the year, availability of construction workers, etc.

A great deal of knowledge on how to produce concrete frames has emerged through the little more than 100 years that the material has dominated the application. The technology had a good chance to mature during the production peak caused by the so-called "million programme". The programme was based on a resolution in 1965 that was passed by the Swedish Parliament on a production goal of one million new apartments to be produced in ten years. The million programme declaration made it worthwhile for large contractors to invest in factories and heavy machinery to make their production more efficient. Much knowledge regarding productivity factors was gained through these rather extreme conditions. A great effort, for example, was made to make the interface between the frame and the production process more efficient, and to ease the interface between design or architecture and production. The houses built during that era were often claimed to use "crane architecture" since the design was made to ease both scale production and the production process at each construction site. As already indicated, much was learned during the million programme era, but many mistakes and shortcomings in different features became apparent several years after completion of the buildings. One of the large obstacles in technological development related to housing is the long lifespan of the product, which means that learning from mistakes shown in the use phase can take place many years after the time of production.

Subsequent production volumes of residential buildings have never been as high as they were during the million programme era. This means not only that the incentives of scale production have been much lower, but also that there has been time to consider and reconsider the methods and routines used then. For example, had today's construction workers had more experience with the material, less emphasis would be put on (often quickly revised) assembly instructions.

A more long-term structure of heavy equipment rental firms has also been created, meaning that the construction firms rent the machinery (and often even the personnel handling the machinery) by the hour for the time that it is needed on the construction site.

If we temporarily move away from the concrete frame and instead consider the interface between a timber frame and its production process we find, by looking at the US network, that it is somewhat different. Since the timber frame is a light construction much less construction equipment and machinery is needed (no cranes, for example), and there is less waiting time involved. The lightness of the construction also means simplified foundation laying and access roads during construction in comparison to concrete. The technology of site-made timber construction is most common in the USA. A great deal of man-power (nailing power) is needed for this type of frame construction. The whole frame can, however, be raised in a few days. Whereas much of the construction is completed as soon as the frame has been constructed on a concrete building, many "layers" – insulation, gypsum board, etc. – are still needed in a timber framed building. As is further described in the next section, this makes time tables and organisational procedures based on the technology for one framing material difficult to translate and use for the other.

### The frame and the production process of a building

The frame is also important for the production process of the whole building, and must be considered for the entire project to be efficient. Experience with concrete as a framing material has created knowledge about routines to min-imise the time loss in production caused by such things as drying without decreasing quality. A modern Swedish building project is organised around careful time schedules showing when deliveries are due, when each production activity must take place, etc. Typical features of concrete production have thus been built into other production processes at the construction sites, as well as into the activity structure of the project as a whole. The activity structure of the building project is thus arranged according to the frame assembling on the different storeys, so that surface materials and other finishes might be made on the first storey, while installations are made on the second storey and frame assem-bling or moulding on the third. The specialisation of the work done by the work-force can thus be rather high in large buildings, as the buildings are constructed in stages related to a cycle with a certain circulation period. The workers move from one storey to the next and continue with the same type of activity there.

Returning to American site-made timber construction, we find a different activity pattern from the one found on a regular Swedish construction site. The American construction workers are carpenters specialised in the different pro-duction phases. There are, for example, some carpenters (often young, strong and willing to travel) who nail the frame whereas there are others who do more of the finishing parts. A timber construction also enables the workers to work on all storeys at once since the whole frame is assembled in just a few days. All installations in the building are, for example, usually made at once, instead of divided by storeys as they are in a concrete construction. Another cost advantage with timber in the USA is the ability to use the same materials in interiors as in the frame thereby reducing overheads.

### The frame and the design and production of other components

The components or building materials needed for the construction of a building can be sorted into five "branch groups": 1) frame materials, 2) supplementary materials, 3) interior materials, 4) installation materials and 5) expendable supplies. A large portion of these components and materials are currently produced in process industry characterised by capital intensive production facilities, indicating that there are scale effects to consider. The scale economies of components together with a reliance on a tendering system have led to "batch production" and use of standards. Standard components are thus bought for the specific building projects and must be adapted on the sites to fit the design and requirements of the specific building. Hence, even if the production of a building normally is in a project form and thus "unique" to a certain extent, the production of its different components are made with "standardised interfaces". The term standardised can be misleading if one believes that the components are designed to fit equally in all situations. On the contrary, the standards are based on the general conditions faced in a specific use situation.

In the Swedish case, the general use situation consists, at least it did until 1994, of building projects in which a concrete frame is used. Over time, the standardised interfaces became adapted to these conditions, since the requirements put on such things as pipes, board or insulation material differ depending on the framing material that was used. (This phenomenon has been termed by some researchers "collective adaptation", see for example Dubois and Gadde, 2002.) The use of standards to reach scale economies often makes it difficult to engage suppliers in development efforts. For example, the contractor for the early Swedish building projects using timber framing tried to engage both plasterboard producers and insulation suppliers in their development trials. These parties were, however, sceptical of making any large efforts before any substantial change of framing technology had occurred in the Swedish construction network. Through the change efforts it became clear that the Swedish long-term attempts to reach a general construction standard with standardised interfaces as part of this effort led to a specific structure optimised towards the included resources, and that changes in one resource interface in this structure led to difficulties in several other interfaces.

### Economy in physical interfaces

We will end our analysis of technological interfaces by more thoroughly discussing the economical aspects. Before any investment was made in timber framing of tall buildings in Sweden in the 1990s, developers from the Swedish construction firm Skanska, together with others interested in the reintroduction, wanted to learn more about the economy behind the framing technique. A comparison was made between production costs for tall residential buildings in the USA and in Sweden. (For broader comparisons of the framing technologies in the two countries, see also Eriksson, 1993a; 1993b).The comparison confirmed a) that Swedish production costs were much higher, and b) that this difference was most likely due to the use of different framing technologies in the two countries. A change from concrete to timber framing was due to these findings perceived as and described by Swedish enthusiasts as a rather "quick fix" that could be of great value in lowering production costs. Table 3.1 is a comparison between construction costs in the two countries that was made by the investigators in the early 1990s and published in a book on the matter in 1995.

The second column (concrete Swedish) lists all costs in the production of a typical Swedish housing project at the time of the investigation, i.e. a residential building with a concrete frame. The third column (Concrete Swedish in USA) is an estimate of what the costs of the same project would have been if it had been produced in the USA. The fourth column (Concrete American) gives the costs of an American project using concrete frames, and the last column shows the costs of a building in the USA with a timber frame. Looking at the index in the last

*Table 3.1* Construction costs: comparison between Sweden and the USA (US$000)

| Materials and labour | Concrete Swedish | Concrete Swedish in USA | Concrete American | Wood American |
|---|---|---|---|---|
| Concrete | 271 | 320 | 145 | 17 |
| Brickwork | – | – | 29 | 40 |
| Steel | 44 | 58 | 18 | 1 |
| Lumber | 25 | 30 | 21 | 164 |
| Thermal insulation | 13 | 18 | 9 | 10 |
| Roofing | 15 | 23 | 7 | 1 |
| Doors, windows | 66 | 70 | 31 | 20 |
| Drywall, ceilings | 32 | 12 | 56 | 38 |
| Stone, tiling etc. | 23 | 26 | 7 | – |
| Carpeting | 11 | 9 | 17 | 23 |
| Parquet flooring | 8 | 14 | – | – |
| Paintwork | 27 | 11 | 11 | 8 |
| Acoustic boards, etc. | 1 | 2 | – | 3 |
| Bathroom equipment, etc. | 10 | 12 | 5 | 12 |
| Kitchen cabinets, closets | 15 | 27 | 16 | 13 |
| Appliances, kitchen, laundry | 23 | 24 | 27 | 24 |
| Elevator | 32 | 41 | 40 | – |
| Plumbing, ventilation, control equipment | 72 | 75 | 73 | 65 |
| Electrical installation | 26 | 48 | 60 | 29 |
| Total | 717 | 820 | 578 | 469 |
| Index | 100 | 114 | 81 | 65 |

Source: Miller and Stone, 1995, p. 60.

row we find the results that made the investigators so excited: the Swedish concrete framed building was 50 per cent more expensive to produce than the American timber frame building. Looking at the other figures, we also see that the American concrete building was less expensive to produce than the building built in Sweden. It is stated, however, that "American builders are unanimous in claiming that, all things considered, wood frame buildings are 20–30 per cent cheaper than concrete ones" (in the USA) (Miller and Stone, 1995, p. 64).

Something that surprised the investigators was the estimated cost for producing the Swedish building in the USA. The figures show that the production cost would be 14 per cent higher if the building had been produced in the USA. We believe that part of these costs has to do with a lack of both technological and organisational interfaces to Swedish concrete frames, and that had the building actually been produced, the real costs could have been even higher. The difficulties involved with early attempts to introduce timber framing in Sweden support this statement. Each material and component as well as the production unit in which it is produced were designed to function in accordance with other materials and components in the larger technological resource structure from an economic point of view. In component production, the resource structure on an aggregate level became used to and adapted to a certain scale of production, and adjustments in similar but originally non-identical components were made to reach even larger scale advantages. Over time, interfaces were also built up between these components and the production of the buildings on the production sites. It is therefore not surprising to find that a) there was a lack of certain components and materials in Sweden that were suitable for timber framing, and b) the costs for adjustments and trials related to the use of unknown components were high. But there is an even more important conclusion to make. The design of the physical interfaces was affected by economic considerations. There are not just physical interdependencies between the different interfaces but also a large number of economic interdependencies. Over the years the physical interfaces were adapted to find economically efficient solutions in both production and use. Thousands of people – technicians and others – over the years developed better solutions from an economic point of view.

The conclusion of the description and analysis made so far is that production of the frame material developed over the last 100 years, and that this is the case in both our "test group", the Swedish network, and in the group with "non-restricted" conditions, the US network. The production of the frame developed both in terms of the production structure of the frame itself as well as in terms of how the production of the frame is handled at the site. We have argued that other components used in building houses have been adapted to the use of a specific material in the frame. This also affected – at least in certain cases – the way these components are produced. Hence, what has been shown is that the specific framing material, through adaptations in the interfaces with all the other technical attributes, has become embedded into both the use of the specific features of these others as well as into a number of production processes both before and on the site. And all of these adaptations were made under economic considerations. Table 3.2 gives a

*Table 3.2* Comparison of concrete and timber technology in Sweden

| Concrete technology | Timber technology |
| --- | --- |
| A heavy construction<br>• analysis of ground conditions important<br>• need for heavy equipment on the site | A light construction<br>• more difficult to stabilise |
| Non-flammable | Flammable<br>• frame covering and testing |
| Known acoustical characteristics | Unknown acoustical characteristics |
| Choice between prefab or in situ | No pre-existing prefab alternatives |
| Frame assembling determines the production structure on the site | The frame assembled in a few days – different activity structure needed |
| A workforce composed of concreters and carpenters needed on site | Many carpenters with different skills needed on site |
| Components and materials adjusted for the specific use area | No pre-adaptations of components and materials for this use area |

summary of some of the differences found in using concrete framing technology and timber framing in Sweden in an analysis of physical interfaces.

## Important organisational interfaces: starting out from the frame

The choice of a certain material does not just influence physical interfaces but also involves organisational actors. In this section we will present some of the most important actors in regard to design of the frame and production of the components and the building. We will discuss both how they developed in terms of internal resources (including competence and experience) and how these resources were influenced and moulded together through the interaction between the actors. We will also discuss the economic logic behind the action of various actors, i.e. how they interact in certain modes because it is rational from an economic point of view given their resource possessions.

### The frame and the construction firm

Until the turn of the twentieth century, construction work was a handicraft in which all components and materials needed, such as windows and paint, were produced on the construction site. Today construction firms can best be described as central nodes, bringing together products, materials and skills from a large set of specialised companies. Several of today's large construction firms (such as Sweden's largest construction firm, Skanska) became interested in the construction of residential homes in the 1950s and 1960s, after the first "industrialisation" of the construction work when it started to become more rationalised and specialised. These companies had their background in construction of the state-owned railroad system, which started around the mid nineteenth century, and in the building of roads, bridges and other infrastructure projects (dams, etc). With their resource base and their knowledge from heavy road construction they made important contributions to the continued efforts to mechanise construction work. Their efforts were also further supported by a special fund for machine loans that was started in 1952, and in the passing of unitary building regulations in the early 1950s. This background was relatively perfect for the use of concrete as a basic building material.

The current Swedish construction sector consists of one group of small construction firms and one group of large firms. There are about 10,000 small firms that have less than 50 employees and nine large companies with more than 1,000 employees each. The two groups are rather equal in both total number of employees (45 and 40 per cent respectively) and in total turnover (41 and 42 per cent). If we concentrate on the large construction firms we find that they operate in the entire country through regional offices that are spread geographically for national coverage. Most of them are still devoted to both house building and heavy construction work such as road and railway construction. At times it is argued that this mix of operations gives the large firms the opportunity to move resources from one area to the other, or from one region to the other, in relation to changes in demand (Nordstrand, 1993, p. 138). Furthermore, they can continue to build on their earlier background for the use of "heavy" construction methods (such as using concrete for frames) in both application areas.

Construction firms' costs for components, materials and sub-contractors are estimated to average around 70 per cent of total production costs. Hence, as indicated above, the competence needed by the construction firms consists mostly of "combining skills", both regarding materials and components and in regard to different sub-contractors and suppliers. Many sub-contractors and suppliers are (or at least have been) smaller local companies located in different regions. This is one of the reasons why the construction firms have a decentralised organisational structure, and perhaps especially so on the purchasing side. The construction companies have learned to work decentralised – on a large number of different locations within the large company. This structure indicates that most of the skills must be spread out in the organisation so each building project works efficiently. All these features enhance the use of one dominating production design. This is further strengthened by the fact that most of the purchasing activities are done within single projects despite attempts to centralise some of the purchases to reach better long-term supplier deals. The relationships to suppliers are often tight within building projects since many technical and economic considerations must be discussed and handled throughout the production phase. Between projects, however, most relationships are handled at arms length because of the strong reliance on tendering procedures for each project.

Looking at the American situation at the time we see a rather different organisational interface. Whereas multi-family houses in Sweden were built by general contractors operating in the whole country, the large American contractors concentrated on projects of a particular kind, such as offices or large-scale industrial facilities, and seldom in housing production. Thus the construction companies active in the housing sector differed between the two countries with a dominance of large construction firms in Sweden and small firms in the USA. The small American firms have been noted to "display a big capacity for survival, by virtue of their flexibility, good local knowledge and small over-heads" (Miller and Stone, 1995, p. 20). There were also other differences that could be noted. Whereas Swedish general contractors had a large number of construction workers on their payrolls, American companies largely relied on sub-contractors. Another difference concerned unionisation, which was almost 100 per cent in Sweden, but low in the American housing construction sector. (There were at the time of the investigation of the American conditions 24 nationwide construction unions in the USA. The unions, among other things, define which tasks each trade is allowed to carry out.)

### The frame and the architect

Architects have a rather independent position in the Swedish construction network. The architect's work effort in giving the building its aesthetic appearance is usually made first and thus sets the boundaries for the work that needs to be conducted by other parties in the building project. For example, it is common for commissioners to arrange architectural competitions to which certain architects are invited. The prize for "best" design is, of course, the assignment. Compared to the interaction between the construction firm and sub-contractors, such as the consulting engineer, the relationship between the architect and the construction firm is more distant within projects, with the majority of the architects' efforts preceding the intense production phase in which most interaction takes place.

When the first building projects using the timber framing technology in Sweden were conducted, it became apparent that the "independent" architects were also adapted to the fact that their main customers – the large construction firms – were heavily directed towards concrete frames. When comparing Swedish multi dwellings with American ones one finds that the Swedish buildings are, generally speaking, narrower so that each apartment has windows in several directions whereas the American buildings are larger – often covering a whole street block. The fact that these design preferences were created in different resource sub-networks, and thus based on different interfaces to the frame, was not anything that most had considered. However, as the Swedes constructed their first timber houses using Swedish design criteria, resulting in tall and narrow buildings, problems arose related to stability for unexpected horizontal wind forces, which had not come about with a more American design. Being used to concrete, the architects were not aware of the resulting effects on such aspects as stability and spread of sound in light construction, and could therefore not make a thought-through evaluation of design in relation to function based on timber conditions.

## The frame and the technical consultant

A consulting engineer in charge of making all technical calculations for the building is always assigned to a building project. The technical calculations are required so the construction firm will know how to construct the building to function in accordance with all technical requirements (load bearing capacity, stability, moisture resistance, acoustics, etc.). Since a concrete building is a heavy construction, a sound analysis of the ground conditions and their demands on the construction is needed. Where the ground conditions of the area in which the building is made are known to be difficult, a certain engineer is chosen for his or her previous experience in the area, or who is known for his or her skills on the topic. Another task of the consulting engineer is to find a suitable frame alternative, choosing between prefabrication and in situ, between concrete and steel or a combination of the two materials. After the frame system has been determined, the calculations for load bearing capacity are made. For most multi dwellings, another consideration is the elevator shaft and the staircases that contribute to the building's load bearing capacity. Besides load bearing capacity, the consulting engineer also makes sure that the building will function according to stability and acoustical requirements, which are given in an acoustic standard. The consulting engineer also ensures that the system conforms to the fire safety requirements, which in Sweden can be found in the building code BBR 94 that refers to the standard time-temperature curve.

After the legal change, when the technical consultants assigned to the first Swedish timber building projects were making calculations for the maiden buildings, it became apparent to them that the interface between concrete frames and their competence area had resulted in several adjustments that made their task more difficult when working with timber. Along with the difficulties in stabilising the tall and narrowly designed buildings, which was described above, they ran into some interesting difficulties in sound testing. From a legal perspective there were no problems in reaching an acceptable acoustic environment in the buildings. However, the scale used for measuring sound was based on concrete noises and the frequency in which timber noises occur was lower and thus not taken into consideration in the standard. Until a new standard could be accepted the consulting engineers had to test and decide on their own what spread of sound could be considered acceptable, knowing that an uncomfortable acoustic environment could be too negative a hallmark for the technology to survive.

A third area that made the consulting engineers' work on the maiden projects difficult concerned fire testing. Timber is a flammable material, and the investigators who made comparisons between the American production technology using timber and the Swedish concrete-based technology gave this fact special consideration and checked costs for fire insulation in the USA. The fire safety requirements stated in BBR94 in Sweden were almost identical to the American requirements, but despite this, the fire tests that were conducted showed that almost double the amount of gypsum would be needed. A first conclusion drawn by the engineers was that "it burns better in Sweden than in the U.S." Later, however, because the consequences of this difference were rather devastating from a cost perspective, a more thorough investigation of the real reasons for the difference was conducted. It showed that the American testing had been made a long time ago, and that changes in components had been made since then. The American construction would thus be unlikely to pass their own test if they were retested. The investigators also found differences in testing procedures. The American fire tests were, for example, made with elements loaded from one side, whereas the Swedish test elements were loaded double-sided and therefore more vulnerable to fire. Taken together, one finds small and rather coincidental differences in testing procedures, etc., that resulted in negative economic effects in the Swedish network.

### The frame and the supplier of framing materials

The choice of concrete supplier for site-made concrete frames is usually based either on distance from the project site, since the cost of transportation time of the pump truck is the highest, or on price if there are several suppliers available. Suppliers of prefabricated elements are often larger in size and less local, even though transportation costs are taken into consideration in the tendering procedure. To give a specific example: for the construction of the frame of a hospital building in Uppsala the construction firm engaged several suppliers. One supplier constructed prefabricated load bearing wall elements and transported them to the site. Another supplier delivered prefabricated elevator shafts and stairwells. A third party, a sub-contractor, who was well known to the consulting engineer, was engaged for the system of joists. The system was semi-prefabricated and consisted of steel components produced by three different steel firms. All calculations and logistics were, however, handled by the sub-contractor. At the building site the system of joists was assembled according to instructions, and fresh concrete was poured into form, leaving the concrete to dry one-sided. A top storey containing the fan system was added to the building. It was made of steel to add as little extra weight to the building as possible. The deliveries were made by a local supplier, who also delivered steel components for the entrance roofing, the staircases, etc. Thus, in summary, the supply of framing materials in a concrete project is made within a highly specialised structure based on concrete technology.

The first two timber frame building projects, conducted after the legal change in Sweden in 1994, were made in Linköping and Växjö and bear witness to much more trial and error, of trying to find ways to organise a functional supply structure. Despite the fact that the same construction firm, Skanska, was responsible for the construction of both buildings, and the fact that they were parallel in time, different technologies were tested and minor experiences were shared between them. The project in Linköping was an attempt to copy as much as possible of the American site-made construction technology (Figures 3.1 and 3.2 show construction of the timber framing in progress at Linköping), whereas

*Figure 3.1* Constructing the timber framing at Linköping (1).

*Figure 3.2* Constructing the timber framing at Linköping (2).

the Växjö project was linked to technical research efforts on the timber material and tried out a technology for prefabrication of timber elements.

The supply of lumber for the frame was not considered an important aspect in the Linköping project. They were inspired by the Americans, who use standard lumber of one type ($2 \times 4$ inches), varying the amount of lumber put next to each other and the width of span between girders. The lumber for the project was delivered from a local manufacturer. Some of the other components and materials needed for the project were viewed as central to the quality reached. For example, they had problems finding a good board for the floors, a crucial aspect for both handling moisture during production and achieving well functioning working conditions in the building. An American board, developed and used for this very purpose, was therefore imported, together with the glue that the Americans used for attaching the boards to the joists.

In the other project in Växjö, the production management had a vision of continuing the efforts with more prefabrication even though the new framing material was tested. This project had been initiated by one of Sweden's large forest owners' societies, Södra Skogsägarna, and was located next to their head office by the lake Växjösjön. Neither they nor Skanska, however, had the necessary resources, such as factories for production of timber elements. Therefore a solution with a field factory made of reused building material was tested. The elements (inner walls, outer walls and floor components) were produced in the factory and then assembled pretty much in accordance with the procedures for a concrete building. The lumber needed to make the elements was delivered from Södra's own saw mills. There were some special demands on the lumber that was delivered but most efforts were made in relation to logistics. The saw mills were not used to delivering such small quantities (deliveries were made by apartment) of a specific quality and in exact dimensions, rather than their standard delivery: a bulk product for foreign markets sold in large quantities on an international spot market.

### The frame and the supplier of components

Earlier we stated that the physical interfaces between the concrete frame and the design and production of other components used in the production of a building are based on standardised interfaces. The organisational side of the coin helps explain this since the interface between the same concrete frame and the suppliers is also largely based on standards. The earlier described ambition of construction firms to be independent and able to always look for the lowest price available at that moment, combined with their decentralised organisational structure, influences the interfaces between them and their suppliers. It is risky from the suppliers' perspective to invest in long-term adaptations towards a certain construction firm. The next time they do business with the construction firm, they will most likely be dealing with another purchaser without the experience of their former joint accomplishments. They might also be bidding for a standard product knowing that they have a higher priced but better adapted solution to the tender. The decentralisation of construction firms thus leads to difficulties in the transfer of knowledge not only within the construction companies, but also between them and various suppliers. Much of the experience gained and the knowledge needed in the industry has become institutionalised into building regulations, standardised products and production processes as described earlier. It has also been built into standardised organisational interfaces or standardised "role descriptions", leaving little room for specific counterpart changes in the interaction patterns between a contractor and a certain type of supplier or subcontractor. Hence, the expectations put on each party are to a great extent given.

For a long time the suppliers to the large construction firms in Sweden lived in an environment that demanded efficient components in a setting in which concrete technology was by far the dominant regime. Consequently, over time their products became better and better adapted to this technology, i.e. to fit as well as possible into most use situations at the building sites. This is also the reason why gypsum board producers, insulation suppliers, etc. were rather unwilling to "de-invest" in all these experiences and "re-devote" themselves to timber technology efforts. These producers and suppliers had already invested a great amount of effort into the interfaces combining user knowledge and experiences of construction firms with their own experiences and knowledge of component production. If a supplier's R and D expenditures for decades were devoted to making the interface between concrete frames and their product, e.g. insulation, more efficient it is rather obvious that a request to invest resources into the development of a new interface is met with some scepticism.

### *The frame and the supplier of "systems"*

Along with component and material suppliers, some system suppliers are involved in the creation of a building. Usually these systems involve two types of interrelated actors in each building project. There are consultants that design water systems, electrical systems, etc., needed in the building. The architectural drawings form a base for their work, which is closely coordinated with calculations made by the consulting engineer responsible for technical calculations on stability, fire resistance, moisture, etc. After their efforts have been completed and added to the drawings the production phase of the project begins and a system supplier responsible for the installation of the system is hired. These suppliers have usually worked with the construction company in the region before, which can be a good starting point since their activities on the construction site need to be closely coordinated. Even if a detailed timetable for the different activities is designed before the project begins, different production setbacks and delays will always prevail, making flexibility and coordination with the construction company and with other system suppliers and sub-contractors a necessity throughout the project.

Looking at the organisational interfaces between the construction companies and the other parties involved in the production on the construction site, such as the system suppliers, one finds two different interaction patterns if comparing the Swedish and the American networks. American construction firms together with subcontractors and installation firms make up what can be referred to as informal networks, which are rather stable over time. As explained by Miller and Stone (1995, p. 21), "Most often the general contractors operate with a chosen group of subcontractors. On average 20 percent of projects are put out on bids, and then only to check price levels." The more distant relationship between the parties among projects that can be found in Sweden was probably a draw-back for economical results in the early Swedish timber framing projects due to lack of communication and sharing of risks and outcomes. The investigators of American timber technology from the Swedish construction companies had found that costs for system installations could be reduced using timber framing due to simplified installation procedures and a more flexible production struc-ture. What they discovered in the production phase for the first timber projects, however, was that the Swedish system suppliers had raised their prices instead of lowering them, due to perceived risk and to their insecurity with the new technology. Later it turned out that it was also difficult to achieve cost reduc-tions on a more long-term basis due to differences in working routines and safety requirements, which had been developed in the Swedish setting with its concrete framed buildings.

### Economy of the actors

The organisational interfaces that have been described are vital for the economy of each actor with an interface to the frame. Our description has shown that far more actors have an interface to the frame than one might believe at first glance. One important clue for working with the reintroduction and its economic effects is to identify these relevant actors. Let us give one example. It is not very surprising that the frame material being used is economically important to the construction company. In fact, this was the very reason why Skanska started the effort to reintroduce timber framing in tall Swedish buildings. To make the reintroduced framing technology permanent in the Swedish setting, it was vital that there were also economic benefits in the development for other involved parties, such as the previously described system supplier. The fact that the framing material is economically important to an actor such as the plumbing supplier might be more difficult to grasp. Looking at the American network, however, it is obvious that this actor group was one towards whom the investigators of the American technology had believed that cost saving could be made. Beside what were described as simpler working drawings, one also described the production situation for system sup-pliers on the site as much simpler:

> A wood frame simplifies the installation of plumbing and wiring. Concrete casting is complicated by the need to provide openings and recesses for plumbing and wiring. Complicated sealing is required for penetration of acoustical insulation and fire cells. In concrete frame buildings, electrical

installations are complicated as conduits must penetrate concrete walls and floors. Mistakes are costly.

(Miller and Stone, 1995, p. 64)

This is also clearly reflected on the cost side, where the costs for electrical contracting and plumbing for the timber framed building was half the cost for the same installations in the American concrete building as shown in Table 3.1. What the investigators did not know when considering the cost differences was all the time and effort required of the different parties (contractors, installation firms and authorities among others) to build up the interface that made it possible to provide the low cost structure present in the American network. The timber frame installations were not that much cheaper per se, but had become so through testing, documentation, product development, creation of skills and of routines on behalf of the involved actors. Another angle to the same example is whether any cost savings that could be reached in the Swedish network using the American procedures would benefit the system supplier, the construction firm or both. Skanska was the actor investing most in the new framing technique and the one taking most risks in the reintroduction. However, by agreeing to share any cost savings that could be reached they might have had a better bargaining position to get other parties, such as the system suppliers, involved in and dedicated to the development.

The economy for the actors in the US "wood" network as well as in the Swedish "concrete" network was in this way a "construction" that was based on an intensive interaction over many years where the choice of frame had been one important ingredient. It was perhaps not the most important component in the building but central enough to have influenced a large number of physical and organizational interfaces. It was not easy suddenly to now try to take away the "concrete" as well as to introduce the "wood"!

Every construction project consists of a rather tight network of companies that needs to be coordinated and interrelated in an efficient way. Each party must know what the others are able to do and how to do it in an economical way. The role descriptions given to each party are therefore rather inflexible and based on institutionalised and economised roles that are fixed within a certain context but that may vary between contexts. This fact becomes apparent in the difficulties construction companies experience when attempting to internationalise business, except for specific construction such as large bridges or other large constructions. There are many changes in the involved parties between individual Swedish building projects but few in how the parties work together. Still, there are clear long-term relationships in the construction network in terms of working together over time, in finding patterns and routines of how to work together, of how to solve problems, etc. The strong wish to maintain their "independence", however, creates a need to standardise all physical interfaces. All components have been standardised, not randomly, but to be efficient relative to the use of some specific frame technology. A standard is always built on some given other interfaces.

The organisational interfaces in relation to frames that have been described in this section are summarised in Table 3.3. The table is based on a distinction between the interfaces found using concrete framing and the ones between timber framing and the different parties involved, both based on the situation found in the context of the Swedish construction network at the time of the reintroduction.

## Embedding as a specific process

In this chapter we looked more closely at a technological change situation to discuss what is needed to make money on an innovation and what role knowledge plays in this matter. It has been argued in earlier research on the subject that lack of knowledge about a new technology and thus the need to learn about it is one clear obstacle in technological change processes. The matter has been

*Table 3.3* Organisational interfaces and framing technology in Sweden

|  | *Concrete framing technology* | *Timber framing technology* |
|---|---|---|
| Construction firm | A decentralised structure enhances the use of one dominating design – a concrete design with which the firms have many years of experience. | The responsible builder, Skanska's experiences were limited to small projects constructing single family houses, etc. made by another unit within the company. |
| Architect | Design preferences and "style" based on historical experiences with the technology. | Earlier experiences of material were, for the architects at Wälludden, Mattsson and Wik Arkitektkontor, limited to "high profile" projects with large design budgets. |
| Technical consultant | Much experience. Tables and programs to fall back on. | The consultant in charge of both timber projects – Skanska Teknik – had no former experience – much testing and documentation was needed. |
| Supplier of framing materials | A highly specialised structure based on the technology. | Trial and error. No clear structure available, great need for co-ordination. Södra Timber made all timber deliveries to Wälludden |
| Supplier of components | Scale production of standardised components. | Need for adaptations and difficulties in finding all necessary components. |
| Supplier of "systems" | Much experience – knows what setbacks might prevail. Earns money on efficient workflow – if costs are lower than the pre-set payment rate. | No experience – difficulties in knowing the real costs. |

analysed extensively, as early as 1835 in Charles Babbage's book *On the Economy of Machinery and Manufactures*. (A thorough discussion on the contributions of Babbage can be found in Rosenberg, 1994.) In his book Babbage offered what has been described as the first systematic analysis of the economies associated with increased returns on scale, and identifies what later generations would refer to as a "learning curve". Following in Babbage's footsteps, failures in the commercialisation of scientific breakthroughs have been analysed by several scholars, and statements have been made such as "scientific breakthroughs are, at best, only the first step in a very long sequence of knowledge accumulation, if we think in terms of an economic perspective". Taking the reasoning made by earlier researchers on knowledge and innovation one step further, the aim of this chapter has been to analyse a situation where knowledge should not be of a major concern. Therefore, at the beginning of the chapter the question was raised whether technological simplicity of a change implies an absence of relating to obstacles; knowledge thus facilitating the creation of economic surplus.

The choice of study focus affected the study design. To be able to discuss the matter we looked closer at a technological change in which the amount of knowledge and technological difficulties were perceived as low by those involved. The timber framing change offered such an opportunity since the technology that was reintroduced had been abandoned for juridical reasons rather than for pure technical or economical ones. The technology was also well known and widely used in other locations such as in the USA. The firms operating in the context to which the technology of timber framing would be reintroduced were also well acquainted with the material and strong interfaces to other functional areas were built up throughout the years. In the study we were able to compare two networks: the American in which the technology was used and the Swedish one in which the interface between the material timber and its use for construction purposes of tall buildings had been blocked for a little more than 100 years. Starting from this situation we were able to follow the reintroduction and its effects on the Swedish network in which efforts were made to create an interface between timber and the construction of residential homes, comparing it to the situation in the other, American, network.

The reintroduction of timber into the Swedish construction network and its use situation turned out, despite the believed ease of the task from a knowledge point of view, to be quite a difficult and time consuming task. Neither of the two early timber framing projects, located in the cities of Växjö and Linköping, was an economic success. Several shortcomings of both a technical and an economic nature had to be dealt with in the projects and in the continued timber framing efforts. (For more detailed information on the Wälludden project see also Hansson, 1997 and Persson, 1998). This can be explained using a resource network perspective. The change effort in the Swedish context was confronted with an already established network of resources and resource interfaces that had constructed a specific economy with certain logics and interaction patterns on behalf of the involved parties. Establishing the timber framing technology would, hence, imply a reconstruction of this economy that had evolved during the last 100 years. Such a reconstruction will demand great effort and take time. This is primarily so because it involves a large degree of deconstruction – of moving away from a well functioning and well developed economic structure towards something else that might, or might not, generate larger revenues for some of the involved actors. Some parties in the construction network control resources, which made it interesting for them to move towards the change. Timber suppliers were, for example, presented with an opportunity to sell a more adapted product on their national market. Other parties, such as several component suppliers, had invested much in the already established interfaces and saw the efforts towards timbering as a "disturbance" of this development and thus more as a threat.

Coming back to our question then: is it lack of knowledge that is hindering economic success in this technologically quite simple change situation? Interestingly, there were certainly some knowledge gaps identified in the case. These are especially related to the "new" context in terms of other designs of the buildings in the Swedish network as compared the US network. Thus, there is always a context related part of the knowledge that will be new even if the technology itself is well known. However, that is probably not the most important obstacle. The timber framing change was a simple change from the perspective of demands for *new* technological knowledge. However, the framing application in the already established construction network is, as has been described in the case, a much embedded function with dependencies on a wide set of resources in housing design and in housing production. Changing thick and multi-levelled interfaces is demanding, especially since there is a gap between design and production as in this case. No new knowledge was missing in the change effort that we have studied. There was a well-established supply structure for timber and components made of timber that was willing to support the builders, they had access to research on the matter, and were able to study the use of timber in the networks that already use timber. However, the difficulties that prevailed tell us that there was a lack of something else. The lack was based on the fact that in all use situations, such as the one in the Swedish construction network, there is not one given economic potential for a certain technology or a certain resource. Rather, the technological option and, especially, its economic potential are created through an interaction process by the parties in the network. The success of this interaction process depends on the use of already existing resources and resource interfaces.

What then becomes interesting to discuss is network functioning, which concerns the way the already established resources and resource interfaces are working, and the ability to forecast economic effects of changes and reconstruction based on the knowledge embedded into this network. An interesting aspect of this knowledge is the fact that the knowledge possessor (*who* knows) and the knowledge frame of each knowledge possessor (who knows *what*) is of vital importance to understand a certain change process. Another interesting aspect is the clear process driven character of network knowledge. A certain use situation is the result, or mirror, of earlier learning about use potentials of certain resources and technologies. However, this mirror just reflects the results, it by no means gives anyone the full story or complete knowledge of its construction. Changing one small piece – in this case the framing material – in the use structure shows that this mirror reflection is far from enough. The knowledge that has been built into the structure (into the various resources and resource interfaces), which lies underneath the reflection, will be, and needs to be, activated, understood, questioned and tested based on the new piece. A functioning economy based on a certain technology is thus earned through interactive and stepwise efforts rather than given at a certain moment. Hence, economy is constructed through time based on actions that result from various pieces of network knowledge.

The empirical study of the reintroduction of wood framing for higher buildings in Sweden tells us that knowledge gaps always seem to exist even in low tech situations related to the use of a product in a new context. There is always context specific knowledge that must be acquired when moving a product from one to another technical and economic setting. More importantly, however, seems to be that knowledge in itself is not such a key issue. Instead it is the fact that all technical artefacts and the way they are related are based on a certain used knowledge. In this way, knowledge has become embedded and manifested in a physical structure as well as in a number of using processes not just within single users but also across actor boundaries. The network consists of artefacts and processes built on an economic logic that in turn is built on the used knowledge. As a consequence, knowing is not enough in an economic setting. The knowledge must also be built into technical artefacts and organizational processes stretching over a number of firm boundaries.

## Note

1  The material discussed in this chapter constitutes the empirical basis of a VTI thesis "Framing technological development in a concrete context – the use of wood in the Swedish construction industry" (Bengtson 2003). The material for the thesis was collected through both primary and secondary sources. First a referential study of a traditional building project using the concrete technology was conducted through interviews with involved parties such as the construction firm, architect, constructing engineer and several suppliers and sub-contractors. Thereafter information and data concerning the technological change attempts in Sweden was gathered through interviews with persons involved in the first two projects using the timber technology. Material was also collected through media and through research reports and technical articles on the subject as well as through participation in project groups working on the technical aspects of the change. Finally, a Scandinavian comparison of the change attempts concerning timber framing was made in cooperation with researchers from Norway, Denmark and Finland. More than 50 interviews were completed. For further information on the methodological aspects of the study, see Bengtson (2003), chapter 3.

# References

Andreasson, S. (1999) *Three Dimensional Interaction in Stabilising of Multi-storey Timber Frame Buildings*. Report TVBK-7061. Lund Institute of Technology, Division of Structural Engineering.

Andreasson, S. and Thelandersson, S. (1998) *System Aspects of Force Transfer in Multistorey Timber Framed Buildings*. Lund University, Department of Structural Engineering.

Bengtson, A. (2003) *Framing Technological Development in a Concrete Context: the Use of Wood in the Swedish Construction Industry*. Uppsala: Department of Business Studies.

Dubois, A. and Gadde, L.-E. (2002) "The Construction Industry as a Loosely Coupled System: implications for productivity and innovation." *Construction Management and Economics*, 20, pp. 621–631.

Engebeck, L. and Wigren, R. (1997) Byggkostnader i Norden. En analys av kostnaderna för att bygga flerfamiljshus i de nordiska länderna. *Tema Nord 1997: 508, Nordiska Ministerrådet, Köpenhamn*.

Eriksson, P-E. (1993a) *Flerbostadshus i USA – god standard till låg kostnad*. Utlandsrapport från Sveriges Tekniska Attachéer, U.S.A. 9304.

Eriksson, P-E. (1993b) *2-tim-4 Ryggraden i amerikanska flerfamiljshus*. Utlandsrapport från Sveriges Tekniska Attachéer, U.S.A. 9305.

Eriksson, P-E. (1995) Trästommar i flerfamiljshus: Erfarenheter från byggande och förvaltning. *Trätek rapport P9504018*.

Hansson, T., ed., (1997) *Flervånings trähus*. Nordisk Industrifond, Stockholm.

Miller, T., Stone, G., eds, (1995) *Multifamily Housing in the U.S.A. and Sweden: A Comparative Study*. The Swedish Federation for Rental Property Owners, Stockholm.

Nordstrand, U. (1993) *Byggnadsprocessen: projektering, uphandling, produktion, förvalting, ombyggnad*. Stockholm: Liber.

Norén, J. (1996) Brandklassade träkonstruktioner i U.S.A., Kanada och Sverige. Några direkta jämförelser. *Trätek Rapport P9609078*.

Östman, B. (1997a) Brandsäkra trähus – ett Nordic Wood projekt. Slutrapport – fas 1. *Trätek Rapport P9702014*.

Östman, B. (1997b) Fire Design of Timber Frame Buildings: present knowledge and research needs. Paper presented at the COST Action E5 Workshop Fire Safety of Medium-Rise Timber Frame Residential Buildings. VVT, Finland, June 1997. *Trätek Rapport L912103*.

Östman, B. (1998) Träteks FoU-projekt 1997. Resultatöversikt. FoU-område 7 Träbyggnadssystem och byggprodukter. *Trätek Rapport L9801004*.

Persson, S. (1998) *Wälludden trähus i fem våningar: Erfarenheter och lärdomar*. Rapport TVBK-3032. Lunds Institute of Technology: Department of Structural Engineering.

Rosenberg, N. (1994) *Exploring the Black Box: Technology, Economics, and History*. Cambridge University Press, Cambridge.

SCB (2002) *Bostads- och byggnadsstatistisk årsbok*. SCB-Tryck, Örebro.

# 4  Conscious use of others' interface knowledge

## How IKEA can keep the price of the Lack table constant over decades[1]

*Enrico Baraldi and Alexandra Waluszewski*

### Mobilizing a network

The two previous empirical chapters made us aware of all the specific knowledge that is activated when economically heavy resources are embedded into related user interfaces. We saw how specific knowledge changes each interface and the relationship between interfaces. We also saw how difficult it is for new knowledge and new solutions to find a demand in such settings, i.e. to become embedded into a structure of tightly related interfaces – especially when only a few actors representing them are actively involved. What the focal resources in the two previous chapters also have in common is that although they are of great importance in the supply of certain end products, they are also hidden from their users. In this empirical chapter we will consider the organising of interfaces with a somewhat different character. Here the focal resource is also a very visible end product, IKEA's Lack table (see Figure 4.1). Alone this table cannot be considered as an economically heavy or important resource. In fact, Lack is one of IKEA's cheapest furniture products. However, when we consider the organising

*Figure 4.1* Grey, white and black variants of the Lack table.

of the interfaces behind the supply of Lack, another picture emerges. We will see how a restricted network of firms are mobilised to contribute to the development and shaping of a vast array of different physical and organisational interfaces, with the common denominator that they all are related to the creation of Lack.

### Launching a new product and a constant need for development

When IKEA introduced the bedside and sofa Lack table in 1981, the aim was to launch it with a price so low that no competitor could even approach it. With a launch price of only SKr99, or US$9.90, Lack was indeed a huge sales success and soon became a symbol of IKEA's low-price philosophy. This induced IKEA to make a very bold decision: to keep Lack's retail price constant for as long as possible, while covering all of its production and distribution costs. What was less evident in 1981 is that this decision would make Lack the object of never ending development endeavours – a true development odyssey that is still ongoing. In fact, to keep both the price and the profitability stable, the construction and production technologies of Lack had to be constantly improved.

Even before Lack existed as a physical product, the idea of introducing a table at a price under the ten dollar barrier kept IKEA's product development unit, IKEA of Sweden (henceforth abbreviated to "IKEA" for the sake of simplicity) busy. The first challenge was to find a technical solution enabling the production and worldwide distribution of a table at a cost that no other producer had ever matched. For products like tables, materials and transport are major cost factors. Therefore, a solution that would allow saving materials and reducing the product's weight was explicitly on the agenda. As often happens to IKEA, such a technology was found among one of their suppliers. However, this solution was far from a ready-made one for table production – it was developed and used in the house-building material industry. It was when a product developer from IKEA visited a door manufacturer that he almost stumbled on a technical solution that perhaps would allow for the production of a resistant, but lightweight and inexpensive sofa table.

For several decades the production of inner doors relied on a technology known as "board-on-frame". A wooden frame was filled with honeycombed paper and covered by a resistant thin sheet of wood (usually high density fibreboard, HDF). This technology resembled the method for producing wooden airplane wings, for which low weight is pivotal. Similar to airplane wings, inner doors need to be light to reduce wear on the metal supports attached to walls. With the board-on-frame technology, IKEA saw the possibility of producing a visually attractive, but low-weight and material-saving table. However, this technology also had its shortcomings: it was applied to inner doors, which do not need to be as resistant as furniture pieces. The Lack table demanded a strength that allowed a person to stand on it without damaging the table.

Nonetheless, IKEA decided to test board-on-frame. The door supplier, in cooperation with its own suppliers and IKEA, began refining the technology to overcome the resistance problem. Among other things, a special type of honey-combed paper (with smaller hexagons and better glues) was introduced, along-side an exclusive use of the high resistant HDF to cover tabletops (see Figure 4.2). However, attaining a resistant structure turned out to be possible only with very thick surfaces, exactly like those of inner doors. For this reason the Lack table got its peculiar design: its tabletop had a very unusual thickness for sofa tables of five centimetres. And most importantly, the modified board-on-frame allowed IKEA to launch Lack in 1981 for a retail price of only SKr99. Exposed in the IKEA catalogue and in all retail stores (which grew to over 200 in 2006), this small table (55×55 cm) with its thick tabletop became a very visible item among more traditional tables and soon turned out to be an incredible sales success. Almost a quarter of a century after its birth, Lack is still a best seller, selling 2.5 million pieces per year worldwide, one of IKEA's largest sales suc-cesses ever. But most important is that 25 years after its launch, Lack is still available at the very same retail price of SKr99, or €9.90. Achieving this bold target – at least so it seemed in 1981 – was however not easy; it required IKEA and its suppliers to engage in almost 100 extensive technical development pro-jects, some of them involving up to ten cooperative partners, including both small firms and large multinationals.

To keep Lack's price and design constant, IKEA had to embark on a develop-ment adventure whose path was far from clear in the beginning. IKEA did not know much about the concrete steps to be taken, as they would become only clearer along the way while the technical development process was unfolding. This uncertain process was full of many surprises, unexpected routes and detours that IKEA and several other firms encountered when they began to forge, modify and handle a series of resource interfaces that progressively

*Figure 4.2* Inner structure of the Lack tabletop.

emerged as relevant along the way. To understand all the physical and organisational interfaces that were involved during these development efforts, the next sections are devoted to a thorough analysis of two components that were in focus during these changes: Lack's legs and tabletops. If any Lack customer ever decided to cut apart a table bought in the early 1980s and compare its inner construction with a table bought in the early 2000s, several striking differences would appear. Some substantial technical changes took place both in tabletops and legs. By dissecting the changes in these two central components, we will try to grasp the character of some of these consciously initiated development endeavours. Let us start with a closer look at the development of an "empty-inside" solution for Lack's legs.

### Changes beneath the surface of "unchangeable" Lack legs

The construction of Lack's legs soon turned out to be problematic in combination with IKEA's general goal of keeping Lack's price and profitability constant without changing its design. Lack's legs were still rather heavy and material consuming – especially when compared to the light and "empty" tabletops. However, applying the smart board-on-frame technology to the legs was not technically possible. The narrow surface and the sheer depth of a table's legs made it difficult to fill them with honeycombed paper, thus threatening its strength. IKEA began struggling with the problem of Lack's legs soon after the launch of Lack and engaged several suppliers in testing different materials and constructions. However, despite the many tests carried out throughout the 1980s, no fully satisfactory solution capable of combining low weight, low cost and aesthetically appealing features was found.

For several years, IKEA was stuck between two unsatisfactory technical solutions: plastic-based or massive wooden legs, each having some positive features but also entailing negative ones. For instance, plastic legs were inexpensive and light, and thus easy to transport. But coating them was a nightmare – at least if exactly the same colour as the wooden tabletop had to be obtained – and aesthetic results were usually very poor. As a consequence, only when cost pressures were strongest did IKEA produce Lack tables with plastic legs. On the other hand, technical reasons (ease of coating) and stylistic reasons (colour uniformity with tabletops) pushed IKEA towards using massive wooden legs, which were a heavier and expensive solution.

This was the situation in the late 1980s, when Swedwood Poland became the sole supplier of Lack tables. IKEA brought up the technical problems concerning the production of Lack's legs and, in close interaction with Swedwood, the search for a new solution began. As board-on-frame was out of the running, what other solution could provide "empty" but resistant legs while providing a visible image of being made of solid wood? To receive some technical help, Swedwood invited the equipment specialist Wicoma to take part in the development efforts. Wicoma was the small but skilled company that for many years had maintained, repaired and adapted Swedwood's machine park. Around a drawing board the technicians from Wicoma and Swedwood literally figured out how one could obtain stable and resistant legs starting from as few materials as possible.

The first solution for Lack legs was an inner construction based on a few square pieces of chipboard, placed horizontally above each other at 20 cm intervals. Second, a light and flexible HDF sheet was bent and glued around the chipboards to hold them together, thereby creating the leg's external, vertical surface. Chipboard was already used for tabletop frames and Swedwood knew that this material was both relatively light and inexpensive. HDF, also already in use to cover tabletop frames, was chosen for its resistance and flexibility, despite its high cost. Here, Wicoma's competence in mechanical engineering turned out to be essential to devise a particular, unique machine for combining the qualities of these two materials, HDF and chipboard, into "empty" legs.

The development of the machine to automate the insertion of pieces of chipboard into HDF sheets required investigating such issues as technical functions, output capacity, speed and precision level. The carving step is an illustrative example of the complexity of this task. To bend and have HDF sheets exactly stick to the chipboard's lateral surfaces, it was necessary to carve each HDF sheet along three lines. Thus, the new machine had to be able to precisely carve the right depth (not too much, as that would break the sheet, nor too little as that would make it impossible to bend the sheet) and with the right carving angles (to allow HDF to stick exactly to the corners of each piece of chipboard). Furthermore, the machine also had to perform the gluing and pressing operations to obtain a complete leg for Lack.

Being engaged in adapting Swedwood's production equipment over many years gave Wicoma experience with such technical issues as basic operations, architectural design and choice of key subsystems (e.g. engines). However, the detailed technical specifications of the new machine had to be developed in close interaction with Swedwood, the only firm that actually knew how the new machine should combine such process materials as chipboard, HDF and glues. To summarise, it was only through daily interaction, stretching over months, that technicians from Wicoma, Swedwood and, at least initially, from IKEA, could identify and concretise this technical solution.

### Changes in the surface of the "unchangeable" Lack tabletops

Creating the colours and the surface of tabletops, Lack's most visible aesthetic and quality-signalling features, is one of the most costly parts of its production. The surface treatment process, which includes both veneering and coating, accounts for about one third of Lack's production cost (see Figure 4.3). It is therefore not surprising that IKEA kept surface treatment under close scrutiny. The role of colours and the veneers is not only to create a visibly attractive tabletop, but also to make it resistant to scratching and wear (and to the accumulation of dust, which can happen if the coating texture is too rough).

One of the most costly parts of surface treatment was the veneer, which alone

*Figure 4.3* Veneered version of the Lack table.

represented 30 per cent of Lack's material costs. To this one must add a complex manufacturing process that required additional time and costs, compared to non-veneered tabletops. To tackle these issues, in 2000 IKEA invited some of its suppliers to engage in a cooperative effort to address Lack's veneers. Much like the "empty leg" project, this project had no strictly specified technical goal; the idea was simply finding solutions that would reduce the costs associated with the veneering operation. Swedwood's plants produced Lack's surfaces relying on two coating suppliers, Becker-Acroma and Akzo-Nobel, who were invited to take part in this technical project. Of these two, only Akzo-Nobel became immediately interested because it had a possible solution, which it had successfully tried with some of its customers, namely producers of parquet and of wooden benches for outdoor environments (e.g. parks). Akzo suggested literally substituting veneers with a printed veneer-like pattern.

Enticed by this possibility, IKEA and Swedwood, in cooperation with Akzo, launched the "printed veneer" development project. IKEA set the requirement that any alternative solution to veneers had to respect a quality constraint. Because veneers are essential for Lack's aesthetics and durability, the new solution should give the customer the same feeling as real veneers. Thus, this excluded the possibility of using easy-fix solutions, such as papers or plastics with veneer-like patterns. The goal of the project progressively concretised into a specific goal from which the name of the project was coined: to develop a technology that could allow printing a veneer pattern directly on a wooden surface, such as the HDF used for Lack's legs and tabletops.

In Akzo's early drafts this new technology resembled offset printing more than traditional industrial coating. This meant that it was a technology of which Akzo had only limited knowledge. Furthermore, it meant that the coating lines installed at Swedwood would not work for the new process. For this reason, Swedwood and Akzo had to involve the two coating line manufacturers Bürkle and Sorbini in the project. These two engineering firms already had a dozen of their lines installed at Swedwood, although they were used for applications other than printing veneer patterns. They had also been involved in development projects with Akzo to introduce coating lines that could print on wooden benches and parquet for customers other than IKEA's suppliers. However, Lack's "printed veneer" project entailed a new challenge: printing on finer furniture such as tables required much better quality, consistency and smoothness of the veneer-like patterns than those the coating lines and materials used for rougher benches and parquet could attain. Thus, to allow the printing of a veneer pattern directly on the HDF of the Lack table, IKEA, Swedwood, Akzo-Nobel, Bürkle and Sorbini had to change and fine-tune both the coating machines and the lacquers and inks.

Printing on wood turned out to require equipment quite different from that used in traditional wood coating: the core of the process required an entirely new station that resembled an offset printing press. Two such presses by Bürkle and by Sorbini were integrated into two of Swedwood's existing coating lines. These printers are equipped with three types of cylinders that, respectively, apply a ground lacquer layer, absorb excess coatings and apply the special inks provided by Akzo-Nobel. The latter type of cylinder is particularly important because it is engraved in steel and is responsible for reproducing the exact veneer pattern, with all the necessary colour nuances, on the ground lacquer. This not only required Akzo-Nobel to develop new types of lacquers and inks that would fit into the process at Swedwood, but also an Italian cylinder engraver had to be involved in the project. This firm was in charge of a crucial part of the process: digitally separating the colours in the photographs of veneer patterns provided by IKEA's designers and specifying the detailed colour nuances that Akzo-Nobel had to achieve with its special lacquers and inks.

Engraving and colour specification required extreme precision, but the most demanding and time-consuming phase in the "printed veneer" project was that performed on the shop floor at Swedwood's Polish factories. With engraved cylinders in the new printing presses, new special inks and detailed colour instructions were, in fact, just halfway from obtaining good quality veneer patterns printed on Lack. Achieving this result required hundreds of tests at Swedwood's plants, during which technicians from all the involved firms (except the Italian cylinder engraver) met and observed the concrete outcomes. While evaluating these tests the technicians discussed improvement alternatives. They gradually tuned the coating lines (in their speed, pressure and temperature) and identified the adequate combinations of lacquers and inks. In fact, even if Akzo-Nobel's laboratories had already refined and adapted the basic chemical properties of inks and lacquers to print on fine furniture, concrete tests were still necessary to understand how the materials actually behaved in interaction with the specific coating lines installed at Swedwood, considering even such very local environmental conditions as factory humidity.

Akzo-Nobel was the actor that alone had the most scientific and technical knowledge of coating processes. Therefore, this actor assumed a supervising role during these tests, despite the fact that they were held at Swedwood's premises. However, the final word for accepting or rejecting the quality of test outcomes was IKEA's. Only after more than a year of extensive test work was it possible to reach results that satisfied IKEA, who gave the approval to prepare the large-scale introduction of the print-on-wood technology for Lack. In this way, after hundreds of rounds of trials and error, the knowledge that emerged from the "printed veneer" project consolidated and was ready to be exploited to contain Lack's costs and maintain its price, without compromising its aesthetic appeal.

However, when Swedwood was about to start producing the new printed-on Lack tables an unexpected event changed the direction of the development around this product. In the meantime, IKEA's purchase offices around the world had never stopped looking for convenient sources of veneers. And it was in this search that IKEA stumbled on a very large supply of surprisingly high quality veneer, available for a very good price. IKEA was suddenly confronted with a new situation: the need to find a use for this precious process material, which could help lower the high cost of veneers on the Lack tables. It did not take long for IKEA of Sweden to decide that the Lack table was the candidate for making use of this highly convenient resource to reduce veneering costs.

This choice created a completely new scenario for the newly developed "print-on-wood" technology, in which a large investment had been made at Swedwood. This new technology could not simply be left unused after all efforts and development costs. And luckily, even if the extensive investment in "printed veneer" had been tuned to serve primarily such a large application as hundreds of thousands of Lack tables, Swedwood still produced many other products for IKEA that utilise veneers. Therefore, the first commercial application for the print-on-wood technology was found in such furniture as IKEA shelves: Swedwood started producing them with a printed veneer pattern in late 2001 and they were then launched in all IKEA stores. After all the efforts to substitute veneers in Lack tables, this solution may sound ironic, but what IKEA was indeed trying to get rid of was expensive veneers, and finding inexpensive ones corresponded to the original goal. Besides, whenever IKEA runs out of this convenient stock of veneers, the "printed veneer" technology will be there waiting to see if the time is ripe to be introduced on Lack tables as well.

## Physical and organisational interfaces behind Lack legs and tabletops

A striking aspect of the development endeavours addressing Lack's legs and tabletops is how these developments connect so many different physical and organisational interfaces, within and across the borders of the involved firms. These endeavours not only connect already existing technical and organisational solutions, but also imply changes of these solutions. But how did these "meetings" or "interfaces" between physical and/or organisational resources really occur? Clearly they were neither the result of a company's exclusive use of its internal resources or knowledge, nor of its relying on the known solutions that the market could supply. Instead, these resources and interfaces were consciously searched for by IKEA and its suppliers, then actively constructed by IKEA and each single firm, each one in interaction with external actors.

The previous sections showed how technical solutions originating from a wide variety of organisations were brought together, tested, discarded and developed. Different organisational units all played central roles due to their knowledge of and experience with these solutions. But, most importantly, regardless of how much knowledge about a resource was available in advance, any deeper understanding of how it will function in a novel combination must be created. Thus, the creation of the new solutions for Lack's legs and tabletops required handling physical and organisational interfaces stretching to the entire network around IKEA and Lack. Some of these physical and organisational interfaces are displayed in Figure 4.4. The diagram is a simplified version of the physical and organisational interfaces (indicated by the double-headed black arrows) that had to be created and handled to realise Lack's new legs and tabletops.

In this section, we take a closer look at some of the organisational and physical interfaces behind Lack's new legs and tabletops. IKEA has played a key role as initiator and supervisor of Lack's entire development history. In fact, the unit IKEA of Sweden is in charge of product development and range management for all IKEA products. However, the empirical illustration has revealed that Lack's development is far from being the result of IKEA managing its internal resources towards a given pre-defined direction. Instead, IKEA appears

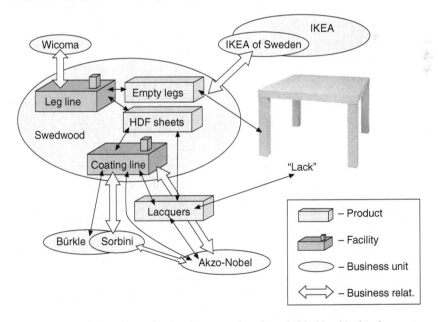

*Figure 4.4* Physical and organisational resource interfaces behind Lack's development.

as the very careful and skilled user of others' knowledge, consequently investigating what others can contribute, using their knowledge and their physical resources in new combinations. However, to be able to use others' knowledge, IKEA also needs to be something in itself.

The organisational unit in charge of Lack belongs to IKEA of Sweden, employing over 700 people with abilities ranging from purchasing to logistics and from marketing to technology. The unit in charge of Lack counts 56 specialists in the above fields. More precisely, for the last 25 years, a team composed of a couple of purchase strategists, four to five technical specialists and a product manager has been dedicated to promoting Lack's conceptual and technical development. From Lack's organisational unit, a key organisational interface was built with Swedwood Poland, with the three production facilities in charge of manufacturing Lack. In interaction with this producer the main technical solution for Lack, board-on-frame, was improved over the last 15 years. Moreover, this organisational interface was pivotal in handling a whole network of physical and other organisational interfaces concerning Lack's two main components. The double-headed arrows in Figure 4.4 point, for instance, to the following interfaces:

- *Physical interfaces*: between empty legs and their key component HDF, between empty legs and Wicoma's leg line, between lacquers and HDF, between lacquers and the new coating lines, and between HDF and the new coating lines (with engraved cylinders).
- *Organisational interfaces*: between IKEA and Swedwood, between Swedwood and Wicoma, between Swedwood and Akzo, between Swedwood and the two coating line suppliers, and between Akzo and the latter. Even if these organisational interfaces are essential for developing Lack, IKEA of Sweden is directly involved in only some of them: whereas this unit may try to affect these interfaces "at a distance", many indirect organisational interfaces develop and evolve under the initiative of external units.

The above physical and organisational interfaces together produce important effects on both physical and organisational resources. Let us see a few examples:

- *Effects on physical resources:* Lack's tabletops were the first to become "empty" inside, followed a few years later by its legs. But, to do this, new components had to be introduced: more resistant honeycombed paper and glues, HDF and, finally, chipboard inserts for legs. The same holds for the new lacquers and inks necessary to print veneer patterns on HDF: they had to be greatly modified to be used for Lack's special requirements. But for materials and components to interact and be put together into the new solutions for Lack, a parallel development of production facilities was also necessary; some equipment had to be engineered ad hoc (e.g. Wicoma's leg line), some core subsystems had to be specifically configured (e.g. engraved cylinders), some new methods had to be introduced (e.g. digital colour separation), and some additional lines had to be purchased and installed. To this must be added all the required field testing and tuning at Swedwood Poland, for all the above physical resources to properly function together.

- *Effects on organisational resources:* even if all the involved firms were somehow affected in some key dimensions (size, revenues, competence, etc.) by participating in the constant development of Lack, two units are clearly most strongly affected, Swedwood Poland and IKEA of Sweden. Thanks to Lack, Swedwood became an absolute expert on the board-on-frame technology and its employees grew to 1,300, mostly in the last ten years, following the success of Lack. Sales for the three plants reached SKr900 million, also thanks to the fact that board-on-frame was extended to be applied in several IKEA products. Today Swedwood is so experienced that suggestions for improving Lack's quality or reducing its costs often derive from this unit, which has dozens of technicians who both further develop the installed coating lines and leg lines and know which product changes in Lack would best fit Swedwood's installed machinery. The effects of Lack's developments on IKEA are also remarkable: board-on-frame is now a very strategic technology for all of IKEA in view of the cost advantages derived from its application to an increasing number of products. Today, the interaction with the Swedwood units is so intense that at least one technician, purchase strategist or Lack product manager is always on a visit to these Polish plants to learn, suggest or test new development avenues for Lack.

Handling the physical interfaces involving products and facilities requires specialised expertise – and the use of others' knowledge. Thus, the organisational interfaces between the units and relationships reflect how others' knowledge is acquired and used – and consequently developed in new directions. To cast light on the interplay between knowledge and resource interfaces, the two following sections delve more precisely into a few selected physical and organisational interfaces intervening in the "empty leg" and in the "printed veneer" projects, respectively.

### Knowledge and selected interfaces in the "empty legs" project

The main physical interfaces in this project, presented in the upper part of Figure 4.4, include:

1  *Interfaces involving empty legs*: obtaining light and material-saving legs for Lack had been a puzzle for a few years. In the early 1990s, the large and steadily increasing sales volumes justified a substantial investment to develop a new, tailor-made and long-term solution. The key technical vision was then to replicate the idea of "air-filled" furniture, that is, the construction of a structure that was empty inside, while relying on a resistant frame made out of some key material, possibly already in use for producing Lack.

2   *Interfaces involving HDF sheets*: HDF sheets turned out to be one of these materials already employed for Lack's tabletops. Next to Swedwood's experience with this material, utilising HDF entailed a series of technical advantages; HDF is a very resistant composite material. The other positive feature is that this resistance can be obtained with a very thin sheet. In this sense, the sort of HDF that Swedwood had always utilised for Lack is extreme, because it is only three millimetres thick. Finally, thin HDF is also easier to bend to create the external part of a table's leg. However, thin HDF must be carved with great precision (just a millimetre or so) to avoid cutting apart HDF sheets. This requirement had to be seriously taken into account when developing the machine that would automate leg production (see next point).

3   *Interfaces involving the leg line*: this machine, developed in cooperation with Wicoma, was conceived as a solution to automate as many operations as possible in leg manufacturing. The machine processes three input materials (HDF sheets, chipboard and glue) into a finished leg; larger HDF sheets are cut into smaller strips that are carved with great precision along three parallel lines. A square chipboard insert is simultaneously cut and glued on the HDF sheet. Finally the HDF sheet is literally bent, glued and pressed around the chipboard insert (and along the carved lines) as if it were a sheet of wrapping paper wrapped around a package. By combining mechanical elements such as engines and carving blades, a highly specialised and single-purpose machine was developed.

Considering the above physical interfaces, a broad range of expertise and knowledge had to be activated. Product calculations pointed at the techno-economic importance of developing less expensive empty legs out of the same materials already used for Lack; while marketing expertise suggested respecting stylistic needs by developing a solution compatible with tabletops; knowledge of the property of materials was necessary to understand the exact amount and structure of the specific materials that could be used to create empty legs; mechanical engineering helped in constructing the highly specialised leg line, but only in combination with a detailed knowledge of all the specific operations and precision requirements it would be able to cope with at Swedwood.

To have these competences interplay and be applied to the specific technical problems of empty legs, three business units directly intervened in this project. IKEA of Sweden contributed its competence in marketing and product costing and calculation; Swedwood had the most extensive experience with using HDF, chipboards and gluing them together into highly resistant structures; and Wicoma was the mechanical engineering workshop that had not only great general competence in machine construction, but also had direct experience with adapting and servicing all of Swedwood's machines and of their interfaces with the two key materials, HDF and chipboard. Wicoma was necessary (1) to translate the technical needs of Swedwood (and indirectly of IKEA) into a machine with specific functions and sub-functions, and (2) to devise all the technical details of such a machine.

Combining these competences became possible through the organisational interfaces among the above three firms. We now take a closer look at these interfaces. Starting from Wicoma, this unit was not randomly chosen for this project or through a market-like mechanism, but because of its highly specific knowledge of Swedwood's processes and materials. This experience had grown from over a decade of daily technical interactions. Thus, from an early stage, practically since IKEA and Swedwood decided together to move along the "empty inside" solution, Wicoma was chosen as the right partner with which to proceed. A couple of technicians from Wicoma met daily and cooperated with Swedwood production engineers, facilitated by the fact that Wicoma is located just 100 metres away from Swedwood's main plant in Zbaszyn (Poland). Thus, relying on an established relationship and on long-term experience with the reciprocal needs and technical capabilities, Wicoma and Swedwood could identify the concrete solutions to manufacturing empty legs, including, for instance, the need to carve the HDF sheets at appropriate angles.

What about IKEA and the organisational interfaces with Swedwood during the "empty leg" project? Even if IKEA of Sweden initiated this development effort and provided the initial inspiration, its personnel were not directly involved in devising or testing the empty leg machine. However, from a techno-economic point of view, IKEA, with its purchasing experience and knowledge of the needs of final markets, was indirectly on the map. In fact, increasing the utilisation of HDF could have created potential sourcing problems for Swedwood and IKEA, because the unusual thickness (3 mm) of the HDF used by Swedwood Poland made this unit one of the very few customers in Europe demanding this odd-sized HDF. However, a substantial and steady increase in the amount of HDF utilised, which the stable relationships to IKEA and its large market needs could secure, would hopefully induce KronoPol, the sole supplier of HDF, to dedicate more production capacity to Swedwood.

### Knowledge and selected interfaces in the "printed veneer" project

The key physical interfaces in this project, shown in the lower part of Figure 4.4, include:

1   *Interfaces involving design and retailing*: the printed-on Lack needs to be eventually sold by retail stores, hence the importance of its techno-economic interfaces with consumer tastes in terms of veneer patterns and quality, and especially of the *costs* that will affect the retail price. The engraved cylinders that trace the veneer pattern are essential for Lack's aesthetics and were based on design and photographs of the real veneers produced by IKEA's designers.
2   *Interfaces involving lacquers and inks*: the chemical properties of these materials affect many of Lack's features. It is from the interplay among lacquers, inks, HDF and coatings that quality (e.g. resistance to scratching) and costs are defined. Something new with "printed veneers" was that both

lacquers (the base layer) and industrial inks (that trace the actual veneer pattern and nuances) needed to be employed, making it more complex to treat a given HDF surface and requiring changes in the chemical compositions of both lacquers and inks, which needed to be more adapted to each other.

3   *Interfaces involving new coating lines*: a special type of line had to be engineered, with serially positioned cylinders with different functions, each one interacting with a different type of lacquer or ink (like in an offset printing press). The right speed, applied pressure and amount of coating applied on each square centimetre of HDF was carefully evaluated and tuned. Depending on such key dimensions as the porosity of the HDF surface, the above parameters needed to be changed (more porous surfaces requiring more coating). It was thus necessary to engineer a machine sensitive and flexible to these dimensions of processed materials. Curing stations are other important sessions of coating lines, where the chemical properties of materials are exposed to ultraviolet (UV) rays to have them stick to HDF surfaces. To obtain good results and the sought-after colour nuances (measured on light reflection scales), it is crucial to tune UV lamps and the speed of the transportation belt to expose the coated surface to UV rays for a sufficient time.

This wealth and complexity of physical interfaces required combining widely varied expertise and knowledge for the "printed veneer" project: design and marketing was necessary for the choice of appealing veneer patterns, of reasonable quality and of prices that could be applied to the new Lack by sales units. Industrial chemistry defined the chemical properties of lacquers and inks that should fit in the new coating process, mechanical engineering helped the construction of the new coating lines, and physics and optics were necessary to tune curing operations and for measuring the actual colours after coating.

This variety of competences was mirrored by the participation of several business units in the "printed veneer" project, each one contributing some specific competence to the project, thanks to the organisational interfaces created among the involved units. IKEA contributed marketing and design and imposed quality and cost constraints that mirrored the interface towards retailing. Akzo-Nobel stood for competence in industrial chemistry, optics and physics, derived from being a large chemical producer and one of the world's largest manufacturers of industrial coatings, with a unit specialised in coatings for wooden and furniture products selling for about SKr10 billion. This unit also has R and D labs employing hundreds of chemists that constantly develop new coatings and inks, such as those required in the "printed veneer" project. But these competences are also more concrete and relationally oriented. Akzo-Nobel had supplied Swedwood with coatings and technical support for over a decade, thereby having extensive direct experience with the coating lines and processes installed at the Polish plants. Sorbini and Bürkle contributed their mechanical engineering skills. Finally, Swedwood had extensive hands-on experience with both the coating processes for Lack and with IKEA's quality and cost requirements. This unit acted as the test facility where hundreds of production tests had to be performed – and indeed could afford sacrificing hundreds of Lack tables to achieve reliable coating solutions. In fact, Swedwood was the business unit that had to implement and concretely exploit the print-on-wood technology.

During the "printed veneer" project many organisational interfaces among the above units emerged or were consolidated. Moreover, such interfaces are quite complex. For instance, even if Swedwood was the actual test site and the user of the new process, it was the coating supplier, Akzo-Nobel, that assumed a supervising role during the most technically oriented phases of this project. This was due to its specialist competence, its overview of the whole coating process, its extensive experience in coating line installation (at over 100 sites) and in developing new types of coatings. We review below two of these organisational interfaces, with specific reference to the context of the "printed veneer" project.

- *Swedwood-Akzo:* This interface can be better understood by looking beyond it. In fact, Swedwood is not just an isolated customer for Akzo, but is part of IKEA's supplier network, a major source of sales for Akzo. Thus, Swedwood obtains the prices negotiated centrally between Akzo and IKEA and is treated as a key account. Moreover, the large exchanged volumes (tens of SKr millions per year) and the technically advanced requirements of Swedwood induced Akzo to let a dozen support technicians visit Swedwood's plants on a weekly basis, spending even a month there for large projects. These field technicians were very experienced in furniture coating and in the functioning of Swedwood's coating lines. Their work helped (1) to identify the requirements for coatings and special inks to be used for printing veneers and (2) to formulate and send these requirements to Akzo-Nobel's laboratories in Sweden. The organisational interface Swedwood-Akzo was further consolidated on the shop floor. In fact, after Akzo's chemists had devised the chemical composition for the new coatings and inks, Akzo's field technicians, together with Swedwood's production technicians, performed the repeated tests that were necessary for tuning the newly installed printing stations to the new coating materials.
- *Swedwood-Sorbini (and Bürkle):* the strength of this interface and the involvement in this project of these two suppliers is reduced by the fact that their coating lines are not fully adapted technically to Swedwood's specific needs. Moreover, Sorbini and Bürkle have only an "intermittent" relationship to Swedwood, concomitant with the cycle of sales and installation of machinery purchased every second or third year – and they have no relationship with IKEA. As these are much smaller units than Akzo, a permanent presence of their technicians at a customer like Swedwood can only be justified for a short time, that is, until a line is installed and ready for general-purpose operations, certainly not until all possible coating materials have been tested under the newly installed line.

What about IKEA's role in the "printed veneer" project? The variety and the depth of knowledge and competences necessary to handle so many complex interfaces implied that IKEA was not in a position to supervise the whole thing, let alone to master the details of each single technical step. Some physical interfaces and competences are quite far away from IKEA, being handled within "indirect" relationships (e.g. between Swedwood and Sorbini, or between Sorbini and Akzo, as shown in Figure 4.4). Even if IKEA could not handle these indirect relationships, it had personnel attending the project meetings and tests, which provided updated insight in the technical discussions ongoing between the various specialised units. But most importantly, IKEA had the final word on declaring the project concluded by accepting or refusing the quality of the printed veneer patterns. IKEA would not have had the competence to take a leading position in solving specific technical problems, and thus technical supervision was "delegated" to Akzo, a unit in a better position to supervise and connect the many and variegated skills required in this project.

In fact, "printed veneer" required the combination of knowledge from research (the chemical formulas at Akzo's laboratories) with the practical knowledge required for concrete industrial coating applications. The field of industrial chemistry is actually still wrapped in a quasi-alchemistic aura. There may be such codified principles as chemical formulas (and even patented compounds) or general rules to obtain curing reactions or on how to engineer coating lines. But there is also a lot of tacit knowledge and hidden experience that combine such different knowledge fields as chemistry, physics, optics and mechanical engineering, all brought together to solve specific problems for a customer through concrete testing. During the "printed veneer" project this variegated knowledge was contributed in different ways by several different specialised business units.

For instance, Sorbini and Bürkle contributed their tacit knowledge by embedding it in their printing stations. But these two units also contributed codified knowledge in the form of the installation manuals delivered with the coating lines to Swedwood. In turn, these manuals, which also included highly structured electronic databases, build on the installation experience that Sorbini and Bürkle accumulated with hundreds of customers around the world and contain suggestions on how to handle such technical dimensions as workable sizes, coating line speed, curing temperatures and electrical power. But the knowledge embedded in the physical artefacts and codified into installation databases was not sufficient to solve Swedwood's coating problems. To find a satisfying technical solution for printing veneers on wooden surfaces it was necessary to combine the above knowledge with the tacit knowledge of Akzo and Swedwood's technical personnel, by means of many trials and errors.

## The depth of resource interfaces and the knowledge around Lack

How are the above interfaces related to each other? Let us consider how these interfaces are related depending on the depth of each interface among the resources in Figure 4.4. We will evaluate the relative depth of three types of interfaces: physical (involving products and facilities), organisational (involving units and relationships) and mixed (connecting physical to organisational resources). We proceed according to the following steps: (a) we develop a map of the relative depth of the selected resource interfaces, (b) we break this map down into a matrix form, and finally, (c) we analyse the patterns that emerge when looking at all these interfaces together. But, before starting with the mapping, we need a scale to "measure" relative depth. The various levels on this scale need to be defined differently for the three different types of interfaces, given their different natures, but for all three types we use here a 4-level scale, from 0 (minimum depth) to 3 (maximum depth). Table 4.1 shows the meaning of the 0, 1, 2 and 3 markers for the three types of interfaces.

In the above definition of the scale levels, the basic dimensions along which we measure depth are (1) adaptation/coordination, (2) reciprocal importance/ dependence and (3) substitutability among the couple of resources involved in each interface. Depth increases when the first two dimensions increase and when the third decreases: we have maximum depth in the interface between two resources if they are well adapted to and dependent on each other and for each one of the two there are no substitutes. These three dimensions do not overlap, even if they partly affect each other. For instance, adaptation between two components can be low even if they are highly functionally dependent on each other. Substitutability is related, but different, from both adaptation and dependence: two very adapted and reciprocally important components can be substituted by others, depending on the availability and flexibility of substitutes

The depth of an interface indicates how specific the combination between the involved resources is in relation to alternative combinations. Thus, the deeper and more specific the interfaces behind a technical solution, the less useful general knowledge and commonly available standard solutions will be in developing this solution. As we shall soon see, the very deep and specific nature of several interfaces around Lack implied that the knowledge to solve the specific technical problems we saw in the previous section could not be "shopped around" on a market or picked from a scientific library. This knowledge needs to be specifically developed, combined and tested in relation to those deeper interfaces.

In Figure 4.5 we assign a depth to the interfaces among the resources presented in Figure 4.4. For simplicity, Figure 4.5 does not map mixed interfaces and just considers as organisational interfaces only those between pairs of business units, thereby excluding the interfaces between a unit and a relationship. Thus, business relationships are the same as organisational interfaces and are used to symbolise them (the thick empty arrows). To simplify our analysis we also exclude indirect interfaces (for instance that between Wicoma and IKEA: see notes 2 and 3).

Table 4.1 Measuring the depth of resource interfaces

| | Technical interface (e.g. component–product) | Organisational interface (e.g. two business units) | Mixed interface (e.g. facility–relationship) |
|---|---|---|---|
| 0 (no depth) | No adaptation. Totally standard resources with minimal functional or economic importance for each other. | No interaction and minimal financial, commercial, learning effects on each other. | No adaptation in function, structure, knowledge or behaviour. Low reciprocal importance in working, utilisation or goal achievement. |
| 1 (minor depth) | Minor adaptations (unilateral or reciprocal) and some functional/economic importance for each other. | Some interaction with minor adaptations. Basic reciprocal trust, but no real business relationship. | Some modification in above features to fit the other resource. Relatively important for each other. |
| 2 (moderate depth) | Strong adaptations (reciprocal). Strong functional/economic impact on each other. | Continuous interaction with strong behavioural/organisational adaptation. High trust and a real business relationship. | Resources modified to work better together. Substituting one damages the other due to high reciprocal importance. |
| 3 (maximum depth) | Perfect matching in functional needs due to being designed-engineered together. Hard to use the resources in any different combination. | Very intensive interaction with total adaptation and trust. A very strong business relationship, for which no substitutes could be found. | One resource cannot work without the other. No substitute exists + strong reciprocal effect: machine cannot be used by others, or building is suited to only one firm. |

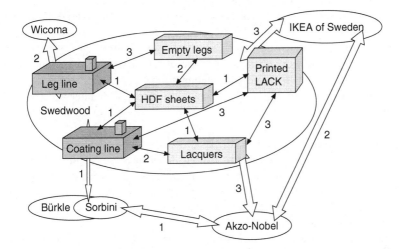

*Figure 4.5* Depth of physical and organisational interfaces behind Lack's development.

### The depth of physical interfaces around Lack

The physical resources (products and facilities) involved in the "empty legs" and "printed veneer" projects are listed along the rows and columns of Table 4.2, to point out the interfaces between each of them. Besides 1s, 2s and 3s, the matrix includes also some "–" symbols to indicate that two resources are not technically related with each other at all, that is, they do not have a physical interface at all.[2] Therefore, it would be improper to attribute to that pair a "0", that is, an interface with no depth due to a totally standard solution.

Starting from the first row and moving down through the matrix we have these interfaces:

- *Interfaces involving HDF:* HDF is relevant for both projects (no "–" signs appear here), but it has no very deep interface. The interface with the leg line is minor (1) because this machine was not conceived to exclusively handle HDF, which was not specifically adapted to the leg line. The interface with empty legs is instead a bit deeper, a moderate (2): the legs'

*Table 4.2* Matrix over the depth of selected technical interfaces around Lack

|  | HDF | Leg line | Empty legs | Lacquers | Coating lines | Printed Lack |
|---|---|---|---|---|---|---|
| HDF | 1 | 2 | 1 | 1 | 1 |
| Leg line |  | 3 | – | – | – | – |
| Empty legs |  |  | – | – | – |
| Lacquers |  |  |  |  | 2 | 3 |
| Coating line |  |  |  |  |  | 3 |

construction relies on having an external HDF structure of 3 mm thickness, but this material is not specifically adapted to Lack's legs. HDF has minor depth interfaces (1s) with the resources in the printed veneer project because it is the material on which coating lines apply lacquers, but here no specific adaptations were made: the use of this material was simply taken into account when developing the technique.

- *Interfaces involving leg lines:* this facility has a deep interface (3) with empty legs engineered specifically and exclusively for this purpose, to which it is totally adapted.
- *Interfaces involving lacquers:* the lacquers developed for the printed veneer project are rather adapted to the coating lines' process (depth 2), but they are not fully reciprocally adapted, as the printing presses existed already and were only retuned. Lacquers have instead a major interface (3) with the printed Lack, being pivotal for its existence: no other lacquers could allow printing on Lack.
- *Interfaces involving coating line:* the physical interface to the printed Lack is very deep (3), because this coating line was introduced and tuned specifically for printing on Lack and no other facility could do the same. But, as the coating line's printing stations previously existed and were simply retuned, this interface is not as strong as the one between empty legs and the leg line (see above).

### The depth of organisational interfaces around Lack

The key business units involved in the "empty legs" and "printed veneer" projects are listed along the rows and columns of Table 4.3 to point at the interfaces between each of them. Like Table 4.2, this matrix presents a few "–" symbols to indicate that two units are not directly related[3] because they intervened in just one of the two projects (e.g. Akzo and Wicoma) or because they have not yet interacted on specific issues (e.g. IKEA and Wicoma).

Let us now look at the detail of the six relevant organisational interfaces mapped in Table 4.3:

- *Interfaces around IKEA of Sweden:* this unit has a strong relationship (depth 3) with Swedwood and extensive contacts (depth 2) with Akzo for both economic and technical issues.
- *Interfaces around Swedwood:* this is the central unit in the resource network of Figure 4.5, with most organisational interfaces concerning the two projects. But there is a clear variation in the depth of these interfaces: deepest (a "3", although less deep than the one with IKEA) is the relationship with Akzo, a key supplier involved in pivotal technical development work and with technicians that reside at Swedwood's premises; moderately strong (2) is the relationship to Wicoma, an important technical partner, but with intermittent contacts; a minor strength (1) relationship is entertained with the coating line suppliers Sorbini and Bürkle, due to infrequent contacts.

*Table 4.3* Matrix over the depth of selected organisational interfaces around Lack

|  | IKEA of Sweden | Swedwood | Wicoma | Sorbini/Bürkle | Akzo-Nobel |
|---|---|---|---|---|---|
| IKEA of Sweden | 3 | – | – |  | 2 |
| Swedwood |  | 2 | 1 |  | 3 |
| Wicoma |  |  |  | – | – |
| Sorbini/Bürkle |  |  |  |  | 1 |

- *Interfaces around Sorbini/Bürkle:* there is a minor depth interface with Akzo. Even if Akzo does not purchase from the coating line producers, there is still intense interaction at the moment when a new line is installed and between installations some form of dialogue is kept open.

The matrices of Tables 4.2 and 4.3 show no "0s" in the depth of resource interfaces. This means that in the context of the "printed veneer" and "empty leg" projects no purely standard technical solution was introduced and that the market mechanism did not organise the interactions among the involved firms. This holds for the most techno-economically important resources and interfaces addressed in the two projects. Moreover, the depth of organisational interfaces is closely related to the strength of the physical interfaces to be handled and the knowledge necessary to do this, as we saw in a previous section. However, in regions of the network not traced and covered by our analysis there are many thin interfaces ("0" depth). For instance, only minimal interaction exists between Swedwood and the provider of honeycombed paper for Lack. As for physical interfaces, the cellophane foils around which Lack tables are wrapped before packaging are totally standard.

### The depth of mixed interfaces around Lack

The mixed interfaces shed light on the issue of handling physical interfaces through organisational ones. Moreover, mixed interfaces hint at the specific knowledge that intervenes and how it is combined at inter-organisational levels to handle the physical interfaces. Now we will take a deeper look at mixed interfaces formed by how specific physical resources interplay with organisational ones, such as a facility with a business unit or a product with a relationship. Because of the way we defined the strength of mixed interfaces (see Table 4.1), for the first time Table 4.4 will show thin interfaces (our "0s") among the resources on Figure 4.5. A difference from Table 4.3 (including only business units as organisational resources) is that we now also include business relationships, which are themselves organisational interfaces with a depth of at least 2. The reason for doing this is that many physical interfaces are handled not only within a single organisation, but also across two or more tightly interacting units. There are four such relationships: IKEA of Sweden–Swedwood, Wicoma–Swedwood, Swedwood–Akzo, and IKEA of Sweden–Akzo. The matrix of Table 4.4 lists in its columns nine elements of organisational resources and in its rows

Table 4.4 Matrix of the depth of physical-organisational interfaces around Lack

| | IOS | Swedwood | Wicoma | Sor/Bür | Akzo | IOS-Swedwood | Wicoma-Swedwood | Swedwood-Akzo | IOS-Akzo |
|---|---|---|---|---|---|---|---|---|---|
| HDF | 1 | 1 | 0 | 0 | 0 | 1 | 1 | 1 | 0 |
| Leg line | 1 | 3 | 2 | – | – | 1 | 3 | – | – |
| Empty legs | 2 | 3 | 1 | – | – | 2 | 2 | – | – |
| Lacquers | 2 | 3 | – | 1 | 2 | 2 | – | 3 | 2 |
| Coating line | 1 | 3 | – | 2 | 2 | 1 | – | 2 | 1 |
| Printed Lack | 2 | 2 | – | 1 | 2 | 2 | – | 2 | 1 |

six elements of physical resources. The vertical line separates the five business units from the four relationships, while the middle horizontal line separates the two projects (for simplicity HDF was attributed to the empty legs project).

As anticipated, Table 4.4 presents a few "0s", that is, mixed interfaces with some reciprocal techno-economic effect between a physical and an organisational resource but without any changes in behaviour and knowledge of the unit or the relationship to handle this effect. For instance, HDF impacts the functioning of Wicoma's leg lines, of Sorbini and Bürkle's coating lines and of Akzo's lacquers, but HDF does not affect the thoughts and actions of these units, nor does it enter discussions and actions in the relationship IOS–Akzo. At the opposite end of our strength scale we have several very deeply mixed interfaces ("3s"). Looking across the rows of Table 4.4 (starting from each physical resource), none of the deepest mixed interfaces involves either HDF or the finished printed Lack. Instead, the deepest mixed interfaces involve the leg line, empty legs, lacquers and coating lines. The leg line and lacquers each have two very deep interfaces. These "3s" for leg line reflect its very adapted nature, handled both by the unit Swedwood and within the relationship with Wicoma; the "3s" for lacquers reflect their adapted nature to the printing process, which needed to be handled both jointly within the relationship Akzo–Swedwood and on the factory floor of the latter unit.

Taking the perspective of organisational resources, we can go down each column of Table 4.4. The social resource with the least and the thinnest mixed interfaces are the units Sorbini and Bürkle, followed by Wicoma. However, Wicoma's relationship to Swedwood is involved in a larger number of mixed interfaces, including a very deep one with leg lines. Swedwood is the only unit with the deepest mixed interfaces (four in all), while the remaining two very deep interfaces involve two business relationships (Wicoma–Swedwood and Akzo–Swedwood). These many deepest interfaces involving Swedwood are not surprising, because this is the unit in charge of producing Lack and because both projects directly involve this unit.

The distribution of the depth of mixed interfaces across all the organisational resources in Table 4.4 helps to show how physical resources were handled through organisational ones. The question is, apart from Swedwood, where do we find other deep mixed interfaces? Table 4.4 shows that IKEA has many rather deep interfaces with all physical resources, even if none of its mixed interfaces reach the depth of those of Swedwood. This indicates that the major responsibility for the technical developments of Lack has been attributed to Swedwood. However, such developments are important for IKEA as well, as appears from the rather deep mixed interfaces between the relationship Swedwood–IKEA and all the involved physical resources. The only relationship with so many mixed interfaces is the one between Akzo and Swedwood, where some of these are even deeper than the ones involving IKEA. In relation to lacquers we have a maximum depth interface because this component is the reason why this relationship becomes so strong, with great effort jointly dedicated to improving this product. The mixed interfaces of the Akzo–Swedwood relationship are deeper than those involving Akzo individually: lacquers are more important and stimulate more joint work in the Akzo–Swedwood relationship ("3") than at Akzo's labs ("2"); HDF is handled much more in the Akzo–Swedwood relationship ("1") than at Akzo's lab ("0").

### Organizing deep physical interfaces

Organisational and mixed interfaces handle physical ones, so it is interesting to compare the depth of the former with that of the latter to see whether there is any match in the depth of the two types of interfaces. In other words, are deep physical interfaces matched by deep organisational/mixed ones? We can start from HDF: Figure 4.5 shows that it is the only physical resource that interfaces with all other physical resources. Therefore, HDF is a technically central resource, and was in fact placed at the centre of Figure 4.5. However, HDF remains a relatively standard component: only its thickness was partially adapted to the other resources. Thus the physical interfaces around this component are thin and shallow (only one "2"). What about the organisational interfaces that handle the physical interfaces around HDF? Are they also thin and shallow? The first row of Table 4.4 clearly shows that HDF is the technical resource with the largest number of mixed interfaces with organisational resources, but all these interfaces are very thin (at most "1s"). Therefore the nature of a central, but rather generic product is reflected in the mixed interfaces that involve HDF: this product is neglected by many units and by the relationships it affects (the "0s" in Table 4.4) or only superficially occupies their concerns (the few "1s").

Thus, HDF shows a clear match between thin (although many) technical interfaces and *thin* organisational and mixed interfaces. What about deep technical interfaces instead? Lacquer is a physical resource with very deep physical interfaces (see Table 4.2). A couple of deep organisational interfaces involving IOS, Swedwood and Akzo (see Table 4.3) correspond to these deep physical ones. Moreover, the mixed interfaces of Table 4.4 show a great number of moderate depth ("2s") and very deep ("3s") interfaces. Thus, there seems to be a match between deep physical interfaces and deep organisational and mixed ones.

However, this is not a linear and necessary match between the depth of physical interfaces and of organisational/mixed ones. Things are more complex; for instance, the "printed Lack", a physical resource with an even larger number of deepest physical interfaces than lacquers, has fewer deep mixed interfaces than lacquers. The fact is that there will always be physical interfaces that are "missed", maybe willingly, at organisational level; while deep organisational interfaces can be present even if the corresponding physical interfaces are thin. For instance, Swedwood–IOS is a very strong relationship that handles physical interfaces (between Lack and IKEA's own physical resources) that are rather thin.

Whatever the initial depth in physical interfaces, it is only when actors consciously attempt to organise and handle physical interfaces via organisational ones that we see a tendency to match deep physical interfaces with deep organisational ones. Moreover, there is the opposite tendency that existing deep organisational and mixed interfaces make certain physical ones deeper, as the strong relationship Swedwood–Wicoma made deeper the physical interfaces emerging around the leg line.

In both the "empty leg" and the "printed veneer" projects, no single actor envisaged all the reviewed complex and deep physical interfaces and forged them alone. Neither did IKEA actively seek the specific partners to instrumentally handle each of these interfaces. First came many relationships among established partners (e.g. Swedwood, Wicoma or Akzo). These relationships became springboards to start envisaging and forging deeper physical interfaces (e.g. around leg lines and coating lines). Further on, some partners pointed out that some physical interfaces were indeed relevant for a project, and eventually some of the emerging deep physical interfaces induced the already involved units to invite new partners and relationships, some of which were of minor strength (e.g. Sorbini and Bürkle).

This non-deterministic and non-linear interplay between physical and organisational/mixed interfaces holds not only for a single development project, but extends back to the time Lack was launched in 1981. Back then IKEA had no clue that the continuous technical changes would lead to the emergence and deepening of all the physical interfaces concerning Lack. IKEA did not even know then which organisational interfaces would be necessary to handle the new emerging and unexpected physical interfaces. But during the process of technical development, we can see a tendency of organisational and physical interfaces to match each other's depths. At the same time, as deep physical interfaces push to be handled through deep organisational and mixed interfaces that concentrate specific knowledge efforts on them, existing deep organisational interfaces (especially business relationships) allowed the depth of certain physical interfaces to increase to levels that do not exist in nature or in other contexts of use.

To summarise, physical interfaces, on the one hand, and organisational and mixed ones, on the other hand, affect each other's depth. Deep physical interfaces need to be handled organisationally, as much as deep organisational and mixed interfaces stimulate a deepening and better fit of physical resources with each other or with the using organisational context. The Lack case shows that this matching process can happen in three ways:

1   *Inside a single business unit:* a deep mixed interface emerges only inside the organisation that uses the resource with deep physical interfaces, through changes in the structure, knowledge and routines of this organisation. For instance, the interface HDF-empty legs is of moderate depth and mostly handled within Swedwood.

2   *Between two units:* the provider and the user of the resource with deep physical interfaces closely interact with each other. For instance, leg lines have a deep interface to empty legs and this interface is handled in a rather strong relationship ("2") between Swedwood and Wicoma.

3    *Through a third unit:* neither the user nor the provider of the resource with deep physical interfaces, but a third party intervenes. For instance, coating lines have physical interfaces of depth 3 and 2, but the relationships with their suppliers (Sorbini and Bürkle) are organisational interfaces only of depth 1. Therefore, someone else had to take care of this deep physical interface on the user's side. This someone was not the user Swedwood (despite its deep mixed interface to coating lines), but Akzo-Nobel, the supplier of a complementary product (lacquers).

These three ways of handling deep physical interfaces can complement each other, but they are also alternatives. A user receiving extensive external support to handle a deep physical interface can dedicate fewer internal social resources to adapt to and take care of that interface. What counts is that when deep physical interfaces appear someone takes care of them, intra- or inter-organisationally, and when there is someone capable of identifying and forging them, they will tend to become even deeper. The case of Lack also shows that it is possible to combine several external organisational interfaces alongside mixed ones to handle a cluster of related and deep physical interfaces. For instance, the cluster of interfaces around lacquers and coating lines is taken care of by two close relationships, Akzo–Swedwood and Akzo-IKEA, and within the unit Swedwood. But such combinations of organisational interfaces need to be somehow coordinated to avoid confusion, duplication of efforts or neglect of important physical interfaces. In fact, to coordinate and create responsibility for the outcomes of complex technical projects, such as the "printed veneer" project, Swedwood, backed by IKEA, assigns a leading role explicitly to selected partners such as Akzo-Nobel.

## Using others' knowledge to create balance between unique and general knowledge

What the empirical picture presented above illustrates is that the innovations around IKEA's Lack table are neither the outcome of general market forces nor of technological determinism. It was not through competition that IKEA managed to keep the price of Lack constant over 25 years, but through a systematic use of others' knowledge. And the technological solution behind Lack cannot be considered as following one specific technological path, but rather as a creation of new cross-roads between different technological paths. Thus, we have seen how innovations emerged from a mix of actors interacting to solve different types of problems that, in one way or another, were connected to the creation of Lack. Certainly, IKEA made conscious efforts to mobilise others' knowledge; several actors were directly engaged in the process of developing specific organisational interfaces. But we have also seen how IKEA's efforts to mobilise others would have been worth little if the mobilised actors could not have combined IKEA's ambitions with their own and their counterparts' need for problem-solving.

Thus, the use of others' knowledge is systematically related to the specific economic interests of the involved "others" (e.g. Akzo's interest in selling more to IKEA's suppliers or IKEA's interest in reducing Lack's costs). Such combinations, where actors' different interests and different possibilities are moulded into specific interface patterns, might be a key driver for technological development – and for economising on these efforts.

We have also seen that no actor was "selling" a previously known specific knowledge to IKEA, but was closely involved in development projects where specific technological and organisational problems defined what knowledge was useful. Thus, IKEA is very far away from shopping around for bits of knowledge, either from research or from business, as no such knowledge would solve the specific problems of need for interface development around Lack. Instead, the knowledge that was needed had to be developed or re-created through a very specific and directed trial and error. The physical setting where a lot of knowledge concerning the interfaces around Lack was tested, discarded, modified or accepted was in many cases Swedwood's premises. Thus, the process of combining others' knowledge was characterised by active participation of motivated actors, all representing specific knowledge fields related to Lack.

However, we have also seen how the creation of unique, deep physical interfaces includes a lot of standard solutions. The utilisation of standard solutions in combination with specific adaptations appears as absolutely vital from an economic point of view. It makes it possible to create specific combinations of the knowledge provided by some of the involved actors, (e.g. Wicoma's knowledge about Swedwood's processes) with much more general and non-specific knowledge and expertise (e.g. Sorbini's knowledge of coating processes).

Thus, how to create a balance between the use of general and highly contextualised knowledge appears as a delicate and important economic issue. The need for highly contextualised knowledge is illustrated by issues related to deep physical interfaces; for instance, how to automate the folding and gluing of 3 mm-thick HDF around chipboards to obtain a highly resistant structure. To solve, or even just to identify this type of problem means bringing together different types of knowledge that all are tacit and non tradable. This knowledge is not evenly distributed and available to everyone, either from science (i.e. as a "common good") or upon payment to patent-holders. The only way to acquire such knowledge is to interact with those representing the specific interfaces. However, along with the need for specific knowledge, the general aspect is also vital. The fact that a unique solution is always more expensive to deal with than a standardised one has at least two important implications. First, as soon as a unique solution is used in an interface it has to be embedded into a larger pattern of interfaces in a business context, for which it is better that most of them are standard. The distance in terms of the number of interfaces between the unique and the standard should be as small as possible. Second, the solution developed for a unique interface might also have a content that, to some extent, can be useful in other interfaces; i.e. the economic result will be improved if features from the unique solution are embedded into more standardised ones. What is "standard" is continually developing due to all of the "unique" solutions found for different problems. This need for the creation of a balance between unique and general knowledge points to the importance of interaction through business relationships. Not only can the unique knowledge necessary for deep physical interfaces be created through organizational interactions, but relationships can also be related to general knowledge used in standardised interfaces – with both efficiency and development effects. Let us have a closer look at these processes. Specific organisational and mixed interfaces are important signs of contextualised knowledge. They indicate that specific knowledge has been developed for certain problems at hand in a specific context. Thus, specific organisational and mixed interfaces are the result of considerations regarding physical resources that need to be tightly linked. In the same way specific organisational and mixed interfaces can be seen as the result of interactions where just these needs for deep linking were prioritised in terms of investments in knowledge development and organisational arrangements. A key issue is how this prioritising is done – how are such issues raised and tackled? In the empirical part of this chapter we have seen that not only are single actors important in such processes, but that they cannot act in splendid isolation. Instead, they are dependent on the knowledge of many related actors being brought together both to set the details of development agendas (e.g. IKEA did not know in advance that cylinder engraving would be a key issue) and to find solutions to the problems that progressively emerged (e.g. Swedwood and Wicoma developed together the leg line). Such processes, where others' knowledge is identified, modified and used, constitute a first, basic function for business relationships. Arenas for such considerations are created through business relationships, and prioritisations can be made jointly by the involved actors.

The empirical part of this chapter also illustrated that there is a tendency for deep physical and organisational (and mixed) interfaces to develop to match each other. A deep organisational interface, such as a strong business relationship, not only facilitates communication but also makes it possible for the parties to jointly tackle certain problems. Thus, a second basic function of business relationships is that they facilitate the fusion of separate knowledge bodies into combinations that can be used in the existing interface pattern. Such tight combinations of knowledge also occur in mixed interfaces; for instance, when an organisational unit changes to fit the functioning of a particular facility or vice-versa, when the facility is tailor-made to the needs of that certain organisational unit (as the leg line was for Swedwood). In such situations, knowledge becomes so contextualised that it is almost impossible to separate it from the daily behaviour of the organisation or from the technical functioning of the machine.

A third important function of business relationships that was illustrated in this empirical chapter is the ability to find combinations of deep unique interfaces with more standardised ones. In fact, the knowledge combinations concerning Lack were created both through deep and through more shallow interfaces. Both of these kinds of interfaces were present in particular organisational arrangements: specific inter-firm technical projects wherein responsibilities and roles were assigned, depending on the distributed knowledge and on the existing business relationships. Some of these arrangements had deeper physical interfaces (e.g. Akzo–Swedwood) than others (e.g. Swedwood–Sorbini). These organisational arrangements helped to create new problem-specific knowledge that was at least partly possible to integrate with other "standard" interfaces. But nobody knew from the beginning of a project what knowledge would need to be combined to solve the specific technical problems that would later emerge. This explains the flexibility that can exist in this network setting, the ample delegation of responsibilities to more competent partners and the variety in the type of projects conducted throughout these 25 years. In fact, the "empty leg" and the "printed veneer" projects differ from each other in terms of the organisational interfaces that intervened; different types of business relationships were involved and combined.

To summarise, through a mix of business relationships it is possible to create both a correspondence between deep physical and organisational interfaces accompanied by highly specific and adapted combinations of knowledge, and suitable "trading" zones to more generalised and standardised interfaces related to them. It is such combinations of deep and standardised interfaces that can create solutions that are both unique and cost effective.

However, we should not forget that any nice fitting knowledge combination that we can identify ex post (i.e. if we deconstruct a technical solution into the knowledge behind its deep physical interfaces) is the result of a complex and open-ended process. Ex ante (i.e. at the beginning and even during the development process), knowledge did not exist in such a form that it could be used in these combinations. Furthermore, not even the involved actors knew that they had relevant knowledge until the connections with others involved in the specific interfaces were created. In this empirical chapter there were some fuzzy ideas of potentially fruitful knowledge combinations that induced IKEA and Swedwood to involve other actors depending (1) on their special knowledge and (2) on existing organisational interfaces, like the close relationships to Wicoma or Akzo. Then, a great deal of joint learning began with the creation of new, very specific resource combinations. In this sense, the deepening of organisational and physical interfaces go hand-in-hand with and sustain the contextualisation of knowledge around these deeper interfaces.

Finally, just a brief look at the small "universe" of the Lack table illustrates that there is no single or optimal configuration of organisational interfaces that is capable of covering all possible technological development problems or all physical interfaces. Projects requiring a rather restricted knowledge span, such as the "empty leg" project, can be tackled within tighter and more direct links (starting from IKEA) to just a couple of business units (Wicoma and Swedwood). On the other hand, extensive projects that require combining very diversified and widespread knowledge, such as the "printed veneer" project, need several business units to be involved, through links that (taking IKEA's perspective) can be very indirect (e.g. to the cylinder engraver) and not all of which need to be tight (e.g. to coating line suppliers).

In conclusion, the development journey begun in 1981 with IKEA's ambition to keep Lack's price constant, is clearly a construction in hindsight. In real time this journey included a large number of smaller, unconnected "trips". These trips had rather different goals, and no coherent picture of whether the types of knowledge they would end up with already existed. At any point of time during this process relevant knowledge was dispersed but, in many respects, also incomplete. The picture emerging (that was only one among many alternatives) was created interactively by the involved actors along the way, when they combined their specific knowledge into new forms fitting the technological and organisational problems they faced together. Thus, the emergence of the knowledge embedded into specific deep physical interfaces is a process that cannot be planned in advance. When successful, it can create highly effective and innovative solutions.

## Notes

1   The empirical basis for this chapter is presented in a VTI doctorial thesis, Baraldi 2003. This thesis features an extensive case study concerning the utilization of IT in relation to IKEA's table Lack. The investigation started from this focal product and was extended to its interactions with a set of key physical and organisational resources involved in developing and daily producing Lack. The empirical material was collected primarily through 70 interviews conducted in 2001–2003 at over 20 firms operating in the network around Lack. These firms include, next to several of IKEA's business units, Lack's sole supplier, Swedwood, and its major sub-suppliers. The interviewees were, for instance, product managers, purchase strategists, order managers and technology specialists at IKEA, and production managers and technology experts working in the other firms. A dozen visits to IKEA's and these firms' facilities were also used to collect empirical material, together with first-hand written documents, such as technical product specifications, orders and production schedules. A comprehensive list of sources is presented in Baraldi (2003: 246–248).

2   An example is leg line-coating line: this pair has no physical interface within the context of the two projects. There is, however, an indirect interface between the two facilities simply because they are sequentially related in a production flow whereby empty legs from the leg line need to be coated by the coating line. Therefore, time and capacity interdependencies give rise to a physical interface among these two lines. However, since such interfaces are completely beyond the two reviewed technical projects, we do not analyse them here. On the other hand, it would be possible to trace indirect (or hidden) interfaces among ALL the resources in Figure 4.5.

3   However, the units marked with a "–" may well be indirectly related, through what they deliver (an extra-speed coating line by Sorbini/Bürkle may require Wicoma to deliver more leg lines or to improve the speed of existing coating lines), or because they affect each other sequentially (Wicoma's leg line meant a lot for the possibility of introducing empty legs, a major change in the Lack product that affects IKEA).

## Reference

Baraldi, E., 2003. *When Information Technology Faces Resource Interaction. Using IT Tools to Handle Products at IKEA and Edsbyn*. PhD Thesis, Department of Business Studies, Uppsala University.

# 5 Handling resource interfaces in a planned economy

## How Tipografiya solves interaction issues without direct interaction[1]

*Martin Johanson and Alexandra Waluszewski*

### Company life in the planned economy

The previous empirical pictures of how knowledge is embedded into resource interfaces can be characterised as "variations on a theme". Although we saw different patterns surrounding the embedding of knowledge, the processes described in the three previous chapters have at least two general themes in common. First, they took place in an economic system where business actors are allowed to interact directly with counterparts on the supplier–customer side. Second, they occurred in business contexts where the actors are so aware of the need to interact with counterparts concerning related resource interfaces that this skill is taken for granted. Third, they illustrated that conscious handling of resource interfaces over company borders can create economic effects that are impossible to reach through the economic theory's way of exchange, i.e. through competition among anonymous actors exchanging given resources.

But how is the embedding of knowledge into resource interfaces handled in economic systems that do not allow direct and deep interaction among companies? Such situations are common in planned economic systems. However, they can also be found in their "opposites", i.e. in economic systems organised according to the economic theory's view of a market. In the first case, direct and long-lasting interaction between customers and suppliers is regarded as a threat to the planning function and, in the latter, as a threat to the market mechanism.

In this empirical chapter we will meet a company working in a planned economy – the Soviet economic system. How could an individual company handle resource interfaces related to the supplier and customer side during this era? Moreover, what happened with the organising of interfaces after the transition, when this task was left to the market by the planning authorities? We will consider these issues through the "eyes" of Tipografiya, a medium-sized printing house located in Novgorod, 200 kilometres from St Petersburg. Before we take a deeper look at Tipografiya's struggles with resource interfaces related to its suppliers and customers, let us consider some of the main characteristics of the economic system in which this company functioned.

## *Organising resource interfaces in the Soviet economy*[2]

Organising resource interfaces in the Russian context during the Soviet economy was nothing that a company could develop from the perspective of its own and its counterparts' interest. Instead, an elaborate institutional framework regulated the relationships among companies, especially their relationship to the planning authorities. The Soviet institutional framework regulated almost the whole economy, and each company had to live with centrally planned production volumes, qualities and standards, as well as centrally fixed prices and costs. Furthermore, this economic system was organised according to a separation of change and development of technology on the one hand, and implementation and use of the new technology, on the other hand. The development of new technological solutions was an issue for the planning authorities, while embedding the outcome into resource interfaces was an issue for each company to carry out by themselves.

An important ingredient in how resource interfaces were handled in the planned Soviet economic system was price. During this era, prices were mainly used as control mechanisms. They were stable and fixed by the planning authority GOSKOMTSEN, and could not be affected by the companies themselves. This meant that the main function of price was for planning, control, accounting and measurement purposes.

The prices were set on a cost-plus basis and included profits, turnover taxes and handling charges. They were aimed to cover average costs in each branch of the economy, with the intention that each firm should be self-financed.

In practice, this meant that interaction was an affair between the planning authorities and the individual company. All issues concerning how an individual company should relate to their customers and suppliers were handled indirectly through the planning authorities. This meant that when companies were engaged in development processes, in product or process development, these issues were carried out in relation to the planning authorities and, consequently, coloured by this perspective. Thus, what technologies should be developed, and how this development would affect a producing company, its suppliers and customers, were questions interpreted and preceded by the planning authorities.

For an individual company, this meant that the quality of both its input and output were regulated through GOST, the governmental standards body. The individual company had no direct influence over choice of supplier, or the quality and price of the product. Increasing the quality of the output had no direct economic effects on its well-being. It could not increase the price of the output, it was not allowed to search for new customers that better fit its production and it could not increase the products delivered to existing customers. Thus, any change in the production process would only have internal effects. On the other hand, each firm had to fulfil the quality standards set by GOST, otherwise the buyer could reject the output. Rejections were deducted from the firm's production and could lead to failure by the buyer to fulfil its agreement. Despite GOST, the firms often had to give priority to the production of quantity at the expense of quality.

Running a company during the Soviet economy was not mainly an issue of how to relate to customers and suppliers, but how to relate to the plans delivered by the planning authorities. In parallel to companies there also existed a number of governmental organisations with the task of planning the development and use of economic resources. In total, over 20 state committees and other agencies with ministerial status answered for some specific aspect of the development and use of economic resources. For instance, GOSPLAN had the task of developing a general plan and the methods and means to implement it. GOSSNAB was responsible for the physical distribution of products and controlled the fulfilment of the plans. GOSPLAN did the planning all the way down to the production level, but it was the ministries that had the actual executive power and made the plans for each firm concrete. Thus, the ministries had extensive power over both the supply and use of resources, and the individual company had a limited ability to exert any influence.

Consequently, knowledge that should be used in a business setting was determined by authorities in a linear and hierarchical process. Planning for and developing new technologies was the authorities' task and using them was the companies' task. This meant that development of new technological solutions was usually isolated from actual practice, i.e. from the resource interfaces where the new were supposed to be embedded. Formal research and development was performed by the Academy of Science, the ministries or state committees and was remote from problems the companies and their counterparts experienced and, most important, from economic consequences of the new technology. Development of new technology was based on the assumption that central planners had more knowledge of society's needs and the innovation process on the assumption that perfect knowledge existed. Those who planned change also knew perfectly how the new technology should be used and the consequences of doing this. Thus, the main role of the company in development issues was to implement the innovations commanded by the authorities. However, in practice excluding both the focal user and its suppliers and customers from the development process meant that the outcome was difficult to embed into these actors' contexts. As a result, companies became reluctant to use new knowledge or new technological solutions. How could an individual company then handle resource interfaces it was dependent upon to its suppliers and to its users in such an economic system? In the following, we will consider these issues through the life of Tipografiya.

Tipografiya, located in the city of Novgorod, is an old firm; it was established before the Russian revolution. When we first meet Tipografiya in the mid-1980s, it was formally owned by the regional district administration, Oblispolkom. Tipografiya's activities were organised around the production of forms and local newspapers – a direction given by the planning authorities. Forms constituted the most important product Tipografiya produced and sold from the middle of the 1980s until 2000 (see Table 5.1). It is forms that are the focus of this chapters' analysis of use of knowledge. How was knowledge acquired and embedded into resource interfaces related to the supply and use of forms, when the main

*Table 5.1* Products sold 1993–1998. Share of total sales in %

| Products | 1993 | 1994 | 1995 | 1996 | 1997 | 1998 |
|---|---|---|---|---|---|---|
| Forms | 63.5 | 45.4 | 37.6 | 35.7 | 36.1 | 31.4 |
| Newspapers | 12.6 | 22.2 | 22.4 | 22.4 | 23.5 | 27.3 |
| Remaining products | 23.9 | 32.4 | 40.0 | 41.9 | 40.4 | 41.3 |

Source: Author's own calculations based upon internal data from Tipografiya.

Note
"Remaining products" stands for books, labels, booklets, folders and certificates, stamps and seals, plates, strips for cash registers, papers for printers, and writing papers.

interaction around them was directed one way, from the planning authorities to each company?

The chapter is organised in the following way. In the first section we will consider how Tipografiya was involved in handling resource interfaces during the planned economy. The focal product is presented and some critical resource interfaces are identified. Then we will make a brief overview of the changes in the economic system that occurred during the transition, which took place during the first half of the 1990s. The final part of the chapter concerns handling of resource interfaces in the transition economy.

## Tipografiya's activities during the planned economy

The vast majority of forms Tipografiya printed were for the regional branches of the Soviet Post Office Administration, and Tipografiya supplied them over the entire planned economy period.

Tipografiya had no influence on what products or what quality it should produce, or for which customers. Instead, its production of forms was standardised by the planning authorities in terms of quality of the paper, size and layout – and these standards did not change over the years. All regional branches of the Post Office Administration in the Soviet Union were governed by Lensvyazsnabkom-plektatsiya (LSSK), which also was responsible for all allocation of forms. The Soviet Post Office Administration used about 60 different types of forms, but Tipografiya only supplied ten of them, while other printing houses printed the remainder. It was LSSK's decision that Tipografiya should print these ten types of forms, and they were annually depicted in the Ministry of Transport and Communication's catalogue. The regional branches specified the volumes of each type of form for the coming year and sent them to LSSK. Then, at the beginning of the year, LSSK allocated production plans to Tipografiya. These plans specified what products and quantities should be produced. The plan also included decisions about salaries of Tipografiya's employees, as well as the prices of the input and output. However, although the planning authorities decided what quantity and quality Tipografiya had to produce, the company could decide how this production should be distributed over the year.

When LSSK sent the plan to Tipografiya, it was received by the planning and production department. The production of forms started when one of the three employees at the planning and production department gave the production specifications to the printing shops. Tipografiya's planning and production department was also responsible for the production timetable.

Before the forms were printed, the composition room prepared the matrices that were used in the process. The preparation of printing lead blocks was done manually. The composition room was a large and demanding part of Tipografiya, and it was also the company's most intense and lively department. It worked in two shifts. The composition also included preparation of the right quality and quantity of the paper that was going to be used in production. Paper was stored in a special stock room, where one employee worked. She reported to the accounting department and she made the calculation and estimation of the paper used in production. She also took the paper to the printing shop.

The forms were printed almost exclusively on the relief printing presses, as they were usually standardised and did not require any adaptations. By the end of the 1980s they were occasionally printed on the offset machines. The relief printing shop was situated partly on the first floor, but there was also a room with a few printing presses on the ground floor. Altogether, Tipografiya had eight relief printing presses that were supplied before 1986 (see Table 5.2). A critical resource both for composition and printing was the employees involved in the production. It was not unusual that there was a shortage of staff, which partly influenced the quality of the forms printed and partly meant that Tipografiya sometimes had difficulties in producing on time. In such cases Tipografiya used typesetters from other printing houses.

After the forms were printed, they were brought to the bookbindery, equipped with paper cutters (without computer programming) and equipment for bookbindery. The equipment was exclusively from a producer in the Ukraine. After the forms were cut, they were taken to the stock of finished products, which was located on the first floor. One employee managed the stock of finished products. (The parts of Tipografiya involved in the production of forms are summarised in Table 5.3.)

*Table 5.2* Relief printing machines bought before 1986

| Name | Year of acquisition | Size of paper (cm) | Revolutions per minute |
|---|---|---|---|
| Grafopress | 1982 | 21 × 30 | 40 |
| Grafopress | 1984 | 21 × 30 | 40 |
| PS 1M | 1968 | 42 × 60 | 26 |
| PS A3 | 1977 | 60 × 84 | 38 |
| PT 4 | 1970 | 21 × 30 | 28 |
| PT 4 | 1970 | 21 × 30 | 28 |
| PBG 84–2 | 1974 | 60 × 84 | 300 |
| PVG 84–2 | 1978 | 60 × 84 | 300 |

Table 5.3 Administrative units, products and facilities activated in the production of forms at Tipografiya

| Administrative units | Products used in the administrative units | Facilities used in the administrative units |
|---|---|---|
| In the *planning and production department* three people received the plan orders and prepared production notes, that were given to the stock room for paper and the composition room. | No products were used. | Two small rooms on the second floor, close to the printing shop. Telephones, fax machines and computers were also used. |
| In the *composition room* 12–15 typesetters were involved in setting the text in types that makes text out of different metal letters.<br>In the *stock room* one employee controlled the consumption of paper and took the paper from the stock room to the relief printing shop. | The products used in the composition were matrices made out of different metals, including lead to make type.<br>Writing paper, mainly from DAO Bumaga or Syktyvkarskiy TBK, was stored in the stock room. | For composition the typesetters used linotype machines that set type in metal strips as long as a line.<br>No machines or equipment were used. The stock room was located on the ground floor, but often the paper was stored in corridors and other free spaces at Tipografiya. |
| In the *relief printing shop* around ten printers were working. | The ink applied on the paper was supplied from Torzhorskiy Krasok. Ink was usually stored right in the printing shop. | The relief printing shop was located on the first floor, but there were also two presses on the ground floor. Tipografiya used big relief printing machines. |
| In the *bookbindery* two or three employees cut the forms and took them to the stock room for finished products. | No products were used in the bookbindery. | The bookbindery was situated on the first floor, besides the relief printing shop. The equipment used was paper cutters supplied from a producer in the Ukraine. |
| In the *stock room* for finished products one employee was responsible for the finished products. | In the stock room for finished products the forms were kept until it was time to deliver them to the customer. | No machines or equipment were used in the stock room for finished products. The stock room was located on the first floor close to the gates. |

### *Tipografiya's relationship to its suppliers during the planned economy*

The relationship between Tipografiya and its suppliers was almost exclusively handled by Lensvyazsnabkomplektatsiya (LSSK), the authority responsible for the planning of all branches of the Soviet Union Post Office Administration. Tipografiya's main input products were paper, ink and material needed for composition. LSSK sent orders to suppliers; the pulp and paper plants, and to ink and matrix producers, specifying the quality and quantity of products to be supplied to Tipografiya. When the paper was delivered to Tipografiya, it was LSSK – and not the paper producer – that received the payment.

The writing paper Tipografiya was supplied with was the standard used for production of forms, and it was mainly either DAO Bumaga Arkhangelsk or Syktyvkarskiy TBK, which supplied the paper. The most traditional supplier of ink was Torzhorskiy Zavod Krasok, located in the neighbouring district of Kalinin (which in the 1990s changed its name back to Tver). Poligrafresursy had supplied matrices and Leningradskiy Shriftoliteyny Zavod provided lead over a long period.

One of the most important materials in Tipografiya's production, paper, was also one of the products that caused most troubles in the production. It fell on the paper and pulp plants to secure the transport of the paper. The paper was usually transported by train, and Tipografiya received the deliveries a couple of days after Tipografiya was informed that the paper was on its way. When the paper was delivered, Tipografiya did not even know what paper mill was behind the actual delivery. However, over time Tipografiya's employees had learned to identify the differences in the paper quality from the various suppliers, and how to use it in production.

The fact that Tipografiya could not influence the supplier, the quality, the quantity, or the transportation of the paper caused problems for both Tipografiya and its customers. Tipografiya had to live with a constant shortage of paper, and the company had to be satisfied if they had a sufficient quantity of paper in its stock. This meant that Tipografiya preferred to receive the largest quantities possible and to keep them in stock for long periods. The paper supplier delivered paper adapted to the quality standards set by the planning authorities – and both Tipografiya and its customers, the Soviet Union Post Offices, were excluded from this process. The pulp and paper plants supplied the paper according to the plan orders they got from LSSK, and neither LSSK, the pulp and paper plants nor the post offices had any knowledge of how much paper was left in Tipografiya's stock room.

Altogether, this often resulted in situations where there was either too much or too little paper in stock at Tipografiya. Having too little paper meant that Tipografiya could not start production when it was time. Having too much paper, which from Tipografiya's production point of view was considered a strength, however also meant that the paper was piled in a room where the temperature and humidity could not be regulated. When taken to the relief printing shop for production the paper was therefore usually yellow, instead of white, and wavy, which affected the interface with ink, stereotypes and printing press and the finished forms and its interfaces with the users', the Post Office's resources.

The supply of resources related to composition was handled in much the same way as the paper supply. When Tipografiya needed material for composition, it had to turn to KPI (Komitet po pechati i informatsii), which was a committee at Oblispolkom (the District Administration), with the responsibility of dealing with issues related to the printing industry and mass media. KPI made centralised inquiries and was completely responsible for the supply of consumables such as ink and stereotypes, but the goods were delivered directly from the producers. Tipografiya often had to wait, usually for a long time even though they had already sent the money. KPI actually had a small stock of various consumables, for instance, it received ink and Tipografiya received its ink from this stock. It was common for KPI's inquiries to be sent to Moscow, turned into production orders, and distributed to the producers. Although there was a shortage of these consumables as well, they were not as vulnerable as paper. They could easily be kept in stock for a long time without losing quality. The consumables used in the composition were kept in stock right in the composition room.

If Tipografiya wanted to make any investments, it had to turn to its formal owner, Oblispolkom (the District Administration), which handled this issue. The allocating of investment resources was also the only role Oblispolkom had in relation to Tipografia. These decisions were tied to political priorities or centralised decisions made in Moscow. However, it was KPI, the committee at Oblispolkom, the District Administration, that financed the investment in new equipment such as printing machines. Tipografiya had no opportunity to save any money for future investment since all profit was transferred to the government as taxes.

### Tipografiya's relationship to its customers during the planned economy

No one at Tipografiya knew what happened to the forms after they left the stock room for finished products. The company generally had no direct contact with its customers. Despite the fact that Tipografiya had delivered forms to regional branches of the Soviet Post Administration for decades, none of them was ever paid a visit.

Form delivery from Tipografiya to the Post Office Administration was handled by the railway company. At the beginning of each month, Tipografiya gave the railway information about volumes and destinations. The railway company required that Tipografiya fulfil the delivery according to this timetable.

However, the Post Office Administration did not pay when the products were delivered, but when products were produced, and no credit was given. The price the Post Office Administration had to pay only included expenses in terms of physical work carried out by Tipografiya. Expenses for insert material, such as paper and ink, were covered by LSSK. Despite the lack of direct interaction between Tipografiya and the Post Office Administration, the latter did not have any complaints about Tipografiya.

## Tipografiya faces severe changes in its business landscape

When the dismantling of the Soviet planning system, the "transition", began around 1990, Tipografiya was facing a dramatic change in its economic landscape. Along with the major transition from planned economy to market governance, Tipografiya's life was also affected by the abolition of entry barriers, liberalisation of foreign trade and of the change of corporate governance.

By 1991 Tipografiya was already transformed into a leasing company, one year before the large-scale privatisation of Russian enterprises started in 1992. In 1993 Tipografiya became a joint stock company and the employees acquired the stock from the state. Thus, from being controlled by its owner, the regional district administration, Oblispolkom, and its committee, KPI, Tipografiya was to be managed in the same way as any traditional private company. However, in practice it was the same people that managed Tipografiya before and after the transition, and it was also this management that became responsible for the privatisation of Tipografiya.

The relationship to the main customer group, the regional branches of the Post Office Administration, was still handled through LSSK. However, now LSSK worked as an intermediary for whose services Tipografiya had to pay. Some years after the transition, in 1994, Tipografiya perceived that LSSK's importance for its relationship with the regional Post Office branches was negligible. The contacts with LSSK were terminated and Tipografiya started to do business directly with this customer group. In practice this meant that Tipografiya negotiated an agreement with each regional branch once a year.

The transition also had effects on Tipografiya's exchange patterns other than the ability to deal directly with the customers. When it was allowed to reassess exchange partners, a widespread dissolution of relationships occurred in the Russian economic landscape. This development was strengthened by the liberalisation of foreign trade and the abolition of entry barriers. More firms – reconstructed and new Russian firms as well as foreign companies – entered and a more complex structure of both competing and cooperating companies evolved. New printing shops emerged; at least one in Novgorod where Tipografiya was situated, and in other regions. Furthermore, the new business landscape was also affected by the actors' ability to determine prices. For example, Tipografiya lost a number of its old customers to Polex from Nizhny Novgorod, a trading company that engaged in printing activities in the middle of the 1990s. Along with offering lower prices to Tipografiya's old customers, this company also transported the forms.

In the mid-1990s, Tipografiya lost 45 of 75 regional branches to other suppliers. One of the 30 regional branches that continued to conclude agreements was the Leningrad (St Petersburg) district, one of Tipografiya's most important

*Table 5.4* Tipografiya's biggest customers within the Post Office Administration. Share of the total sales in %

| Customers | 1993 | 1994 | 1995 | 1996 | 1997 | 1998 |
|---|---|---|---|---|---|---|
| Leningrad district | 2.6 | 1.2 | 2.5 | 3.9 | 2.4 | 1.9 |
| Yekaterinburg district | 2.4 | 1.2 | 1.6 | 0.9 | 0.5 | 1.0 |
| Komi Republic | 1.3 | 0.7 | 1.5 | 0.5 | – | – |
| Arkhangelsk district | 0.3 | 1.8 | 1.2 | 0.4 | – | 1.9 |
| Lipetsk district | 0.7 | 1.0 | 0.8 | 2.1 | 2.9 | 2.1 |
| Primorskiy Krai Vladivostok | 3.0 | 0.7 | 0.7 | 1.1 | 0.4 | – |
| Kemorovo district | 0.6 | 0.6 | 0.4 | 1.6 | 0.1 | – |

Source: Author's own calculations based upon internal data from Tipografiya.

customers during the planned economy. Another important customer during that time, the Yekaterinburg district, gradually decreased its purchased volumes. The opposite was true for the Kemorovo district and the Lipetsk district. They first increased their volumes over the previous five years, but in 1998 the Kemorovo district chose not to buy from Tipografiya. The same thing happened with Vladivostok (Elektrosvyaz Primorskiy Krayi), UPFS in the Arkhangelsk district and UFPS in the Komi Republic. On the whole, the 1990s meant that Tipografiya lost the majority of its customers among the Post Office's regional branches. Three of Tipografiya's seven biggest customers preferred to buy forms from other suppliers, and production decreased significantly (see Table 5.4).

### A slowly emerging interaction between Tipografiya and its customers

Even though Tipografiya began to interact directly with its customers, and many customers left because they thought they were getting better service from other suppliers, the printing house did not significantly change the way it related to the users. Although the forms were still Tipografiya's most profitable product, the printing house regarded the production as simple and standardised from a technical point of view, and saw no need to adapt in the area of customer relationships. The design of the forms was still standardised and depicted annually in the Ministry of Transport and Communication's catalogue. The layout of the forms had not changed since 1992, but during 1997–1998 there were some small changes in the design; the logotype and the organisation names were replaced.

Although Tipografiya began interacting directly with the regional branches of the Post Office Administration, the way they related to customers was similar to the planned economy tradition. Yearly negotiations with the regional branches of the Post Office Administration were close to LSSK's tradition. Tipografiya distributed a standardised contract to the regional branches with prices stipulated. If the customers intended to use Tipografiya as a supplier for the following year, they specified, signed and returned the contract. When the customers had signed the contract, it was still Tipografiya's planning and production department, now called the production and finance department, that was in charge of receiving orders, preparing price lists, controlling production times, invoicing and following-up on price calculation.

However, in 1997 Tipografiya re-organised the activities concerning forms to the regional branches of the Post Office Administration. The responsibility for all the regional branches was moved to the newly founded business centre. The main idea behind the business centre was to create a better match between Tipografiya's production planning and its suppliers' and customers' activities. The business centre co-ordinated supply with working out orders to the composition room and the print shops. It also monitored production and registered incoming and outgoing orders, prepared invoices and received the payments. The business centre was located on the ground floor and had its entrance on the street.

The transition also meant that Tipografiya took over the responsibility for transporting the forms to customers. The deliveries were made in the same way as during the planned economy – in containers sent by train, and occasionally some deliveries were made by mail. One customer, the Leningrad district, regularly sent a driver to pick up the forms. After 1992, the deliveries began to take place once a month, but in 1996 Tipografiya took over the responsibility for transportation to this customer and used its newly purchased van.

### A slowly emerging interaction between Tipografiya and its suppliers

The transition not only affected Tipografiya's interaction with its counterparts on the user side, but also on the supply side. New suppliers appeared. However, the most significant change was that Tipografiya was allowed to interact directly with its suppliers. Although Tipografiya was owned by all its employees, decisions of what to buy became a top management issue. The managing director took over the responsibility of purchasing paper. The emerging purchasing strategy was strongly coloured by Russia's financial crises. When Tipografiya began to purchase insert materials by itself, it was the ability to reduce the price without affecting the quality that initially attracted its interest.

From a cost point of view, paper remained the most important product purchased; the cost of paper was approximately 75 per cent of its current assets. However, from a quality point of view paper was also one of the most important products, with a strong influence on the shape of the finished forms. Due to the managing director's strong attention to keeping the costs low, the production staff could not influence the choice of paper or suppliers. Although of less financial importance, the chief engineer was in charge of purchasing consumables, and his decisions had no influence on the setters or printers who had experience with the effects of quality on the consumables.

Thus, during the transition Tipografiya's purchasing strategy was to search for the cheapest paper available, and to buy in large volumes. The supply of paper was also characterised by an increasing variety, since both fixed prices and most governmental standards for paper qualities were abandoned. In the mid-1990s Tipografiya developed its low cost strategy a bit further, and switched to a printing paper that was of lower quality and lower in price. This measure was intended to allow Tipografiya to decrease the price of the forms, which also was welcomed by the customers.

Paradoxically, Tipografiya's low cost strategy resulted in the same quality situation as during the planned economy: a large constant stock, which meant that much of the forms were printed on wavy yellow paper. However, Tipografiya's management regarded a large stock as a strength, though for different reasons; the ability to purchase large amounts of paper at a low price. The paper was still stored in the stock room for paper and kept there until it was taken to the printing shop.

Despite decreasing production volumes, Tipografiya still bought wagonloads of paper that were delivered by rail. In the beginning of the period, Tipografiya continued to buy from the same plants as during the planned economy, but in the mid-1990s it changed suppliers when several intermediaries entered the business landscape. The intermediaries offered lower prices than the producers of writing papers and Tipografiya began buying from them instead of buying directly from the producers. By 1996, Tipografia's paper purchasing was done mostly by intermediaries. One of the new suppliers was the intermediary Nevskaya Bumaga, which managed to cut its costs and, consequently, the price of the paper. An additional big advantage was that Nevskaya Bumaga did not require prepayment.

Along with paper, ink continued to be the biggest product in terms of volume. Ink was stored right in the printing shops. Tipografiya bought all the ink for the relief printing from Torzhorskiy Zavod Krasok, one of its traditional suppliers. A few times a year, ink was collected by Tipografiya in its own van. However, due to Tipografiya's decreased production, and because more of the production was done on offset machines, the quantities of ink purchased from this supplier gradually decreased by 1998. Ink for offset printing was purchased from Heidelberg or Ipris in St. Petersburg. Tipografiya continued to buy matrices from Poligrafresursy and sometimes from Shadrinskiy Zavod Poligraficheskikh Mashin in Kurgan. The increased use of offset printing also meant an increased use of offset plates. Until the mid-1990s offset plates were bought from Poligrafresursy, but then Tipografiya began purchasing them from Ipris.

The ability to attain a higher quality form and the decreasing production volumes led to Tipografiya's movement of the main production of forms from the relief printing shop to the offset equipment. Small batches made it more beneficial to print the forms on the offset presses than the relief presses. Printing on the offset presses also meant that the composition could be done by computer. The first offset machine was delivered in 1977, but it had been used solely for producing other products. When the changes in the economic system began, Tipografiya had eight offset machines. The first computers appeared at the end of the planned economy. Tipografiya bought three new computers in 1991, and in the mid-1990s Tipografiya bought seven new computers. After the forms were produced they were still cut in the bookbindery by the same equipment and taken to the room for finished products.

## Company life affected by planned economy thinking – effects on resource interfaces

Tipografiya's company life is an expressive illustration of how much an overall economic system affects an individual company and its interaction pattern. Tipografiya's way of handling resource interfaces also stands out in distinct contrast to what we have seen in the three previous empirical chapters. Although these empirical studies concerned different types of industries, technologies and products, the way resource interfaces were handled must still be considered as a variation on a theme; interfaces were developed in direct interaction with those representing related resources, almost regardless of whether they were located within or beyond company borders. For example, the development of resource interfaces around the Lack sofa table resulted in a hundred development projects stretching over two decades, with important technological and economic consequences for all the involved actors. Almost nothing of this direct interaction took place in relation to Tipografiya's production of forms. Instead, all technological and organisational interfaces related to the supplier and user sides were handled through a "middle-man" – the planning authorities (see Figure 5.1).

Also, what Tipografiya actually could communicate to this "middle-man" was affected by the overall economic system. Although Tipografiya had a certain interaction with the planning authorities and could bring up issues like the need for new equipment or input materials, the lack of experience with the counterparts' total resource structures meant that Tipografiya only had general knowledge of what could be achieved in relation to others. Tipografiya was treated as if it was an island by the planning authorities as well as by its customers, suppliers and by itself. If there was any dialogue around the features of input and output, it was between Tipografiya and the planning system, not between those producing and using them. For Tipografiya this meant that although, for example, the setters had certain knowledge of how the interfaces between the resources like paper, ink and printing machines could be developed

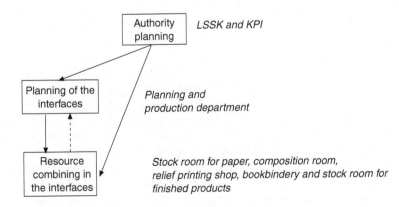

*Figure 5.1* Planning and resource combining in the interfaces during the planned economy.

to increase both efficiency and output quality, this was never used in direct inter-action with those representing these resources. Instead, development of the resources Tipografiya exchanged became an issue for the planning authorities. Changes in both the input and the output, in terms of qualities, quantities and prices, were designed by the planning authorities. What Tipografiya actually could do, besides communicating their experiences to the planning authorities and waiting for effects, was to engage in an internal interface development process, as long as the result did not interfere with what was stipulated by the planning authorities. Thus, Tipografiya's activities were directed to internal pro-duction management and to protect the internal functioning through, for example, a large stock.

What the planning authorities got through the interaction was Tipografiya's and other companies' internally developed knowledge about how the resource combinations functioned from their own production perspective. This meant that the interfaces between Tipografiya's and its counterparts' resources were organ-ised from a particular perspective – the planning authorities' perspective of how the resources could be combined. Through combining and bridging each company's "island" perspective of resource interfaces, the planning authorities designed what was assumed to be the "right" interface pattern.

Thus, the interaction pattern created during the planned economy affected Tipografiya in terms of who it did interact with and, furthermore, in terms of what problems and what opportunities were framed in this interaction. The planned economic system gave each single episode, where Tipografiya was involved, a specific content by determining who was interacting and with what perspective and knowledge.

### Tipografiya's way of handling resource interfaces after the transition

The problems that Tipografiya experienced, suffering from static activities and lack of development, were also what international economic expertise saw as the main drawbacks with the planned economic system. Furthermore, the main solu-tion to this problem was also rather clearly articulated. What Russia needed was a market economy, i.e. an economic exchange system that allowed flexibility and where resources were allocated through the price mechanism.

For Tipografiya the transition to a market economy began when LSSK and KPI lost influence over Tipografiya's *and* its counterparts' company life. Tipografiya, which became employee owned, got a management dedicated to utilising the flexibility of the new economic system. However, the management used this new feature of the economic system in a specific way; the focus was on how to utilise the freedom to exchange resources, not on how to develop resources. Thus, management's behaviour became very close to what is depicted in economic theory's characterising of the interplay between the "market" and the "economic man". The managing director and the chief engineer responsible for Tipografiya's businesses developed a strategy in line with the assumption that all necessary information about the exchanged resources is in the price. The purchasing strategy was characterised by buying from the supplier who offered the lowest price, and trying to play out competitors against each other. This meant that purchasing became an issue between management and the suppliers. In the same way as during the planned economy, none of the personnel responsible for the production and use of the purchased resources became involved in these discussions. Thus, during the transition Tipografiya had a management that focused on short term efficiency issues, i.e. that acted as if the exchanged resources were homogeneous and as if there were no need to consider either internal or external resource interface development.

An interesting observation is that when Tipografiya became managed from a market perspective, the effects on development issues were almost the same as those caused by the planned economy. Neglecting the resource interfaces in favour of short-term efficiency issues again resulted in a large stock, with quality consequences such as paper that was yellow and wavy when it arrived at the production facility. When LSSK and KPI withdrew as planning authorities Tipografiya and its suppliers and customers also lost some forces that actually did demand a certain quality standard of the exchanged resources. And, since no new interaction pattern that could replace these quality demands emerged, for example a direct interaction between customers and suppliers, the new flexibility initially had negative effects on the quality. Thus, the transition from a planned to a market system left no immediate imprint in terms of quality development. Instead of having a planned system that actually handled certain development issues, the price mechanism assumed to breed resource development did not automatically deliver any such effects. On the contrary, the initial effect was a decreased degree of focus on quality and interface development.

The new flexibility of the economic system, however, gradually made Tipografiya aware of the need for development of both cost and quality dimensions. Tipografiya lost most of its Post Office customers, and the competitors not only offered lower prices but also better solutions in terms of more precise and adapted deliveries. Tipografiya's development of a new organisational unit can be regarded as a sign of an increasing awareness of the need for resource interface development. The aim of the new business centre was to create a closer coordination between the customers' requirements and Tipografiya's supply and production. However, at least as long as we are following Tipografiya, the role of the business centre in interface development was rather immature. The supply of paper and consumables was still managed by the managing director and the chief engineer, and although they did not have any background in the printing industry they preferred to make all the decisions. The experience of the personnel involved in handling the interfaces where these resources were activated, like during the planned economy, was not considered by the management (see Figure 5.2.)

What the life of Tipografiya before and after the transition illustrates is that knowledge about how to develop resource interfaces is nothing that a change in the overall economic system can rapidly supply. Instead, this appears as the result of conscious interaction between directly related exchange partners over

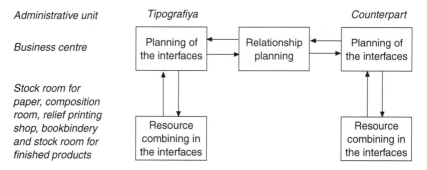

*Figure 5.2* Emergence of relationship planning.

time, in a context that rewards not only utilisation but also resource development.

Thus, the fact that it takes such a long time for Tipografiya to begin interacting with its counterparts probably has both internal and external explanations. First, before Tipografiya can begin to interact with its external counterparts it must create an internal organisation that is aware of and can handle such an exchange pattern. It must develop an internal organisation that can handle an extended interaction – and that can utilise the experiences made through these processes. As long as Tipografiya has no internal organisation for utilising others' knowledge, then it does not matter how much it starts to interact externally – it will still not have any major effects. However, with an increased awareness of what can be achieved through interaction with external counterparts, the external interaction pattern will affect the way the company is organised internally. Thus, a company's way of using its external interaction pattern has to be mirrored through its internal organisational design. This mutuality in external and internal organisational design can only be developed over time.

Second, it is not just our focal company Tipografiya that needs time to develop an internal organisation adapted to direct interaction with external counterparts, but also the counterparts must go through the same process (since they stem from the same business landscape). However, even if the counterparts are grounded in another business landscape, i.e. in a Western economy, they will still need time to develop knowledge about how to interact with this changing partner. If we compare Tipografiya's situation with the companies appearing in the three previous chapters, which all are grounded in a business landscape where companies have decades or even centuries of traditions of interaction with counterparts embedded as organisational knowledge, then it appears unfair to expect that Tipografiya should be able to achieve the same with such short experience.

## Conclusions

Tipografiya's life before and after the transition illustrates how it, like any company, is coloured by the interaction pattern into which it is embedded. This interaction pattern is formed by an overall economic system in combination with the companies' own experiences of how to organise internal and external resource interfaces. This interaction pattern influences both how the company identifies problems as well as the opportunities to solve them. Thus, each company is embedded into a "normality" of interaction patterns, determining the common way to function, the way to frame the economic environment, i.e. what the relevant problems are and what opportunities can be created. To challenge and break such interaction patterns is never easy, whether it is an individual company, like IKEA, that is developing a new way to relate to its counterparts, or if it is many companies, as in Tipografiya's economic landscape, which are forced to adapt to a new overall economic system. Still, any such change will affect each company's and its counterparts' development and economic outcome.

When the overall economic system is so clearly articulated, as it was in the Russia before and after the transition, it is easy to recognise the effects it has on each company's interaction patterns and dynamic. However, these experiences can be seen as arguments for also considering what effects more minor variations in the business landscape have for resource development. If the overall business landscape is dominated by some few owners (whether families, multinationals or governments) with a short-term profit goal, and/or by a "top-bottom" management style, there are reasons to believe that this will negatively effect resource development. On the contrary, if a business landscape has a more interactive nature, i.e. if it is dominated by a heterogeneous owner structure, by decentralised management style and technologically skilled workers and middle management, this will probably have positive effects on resource development.

## Notes

1 This chapter is based on a VTI thesis *"Searching the Known, Discovering the Unknown. The Russian Transition from Plan to Market as Network Change Processes"* (Johanson, 2001). The focus of the thesis is how resources are used and exchanged in a network of relationships during the Russian transition from a planned economy to a market economy. The case selected for the study illustrates how a formerly state-owned firm, Tipografiya, met these requirements. Tipografiya is the biggest printing house in the Novgorod district, 200 kilometres from St Petersburg. The study concerned Tipografiya's relationships with its most important customers and suppliers and analyse how they had developed during the transition from a planned economy to a market economy. The data collection combines two temporal approaches. While the period 1987–1995 was studied in retrospect the data collection for the period 1996–1998 was conducted in real time. Altogether 33 interviews were made. The question guides were translated and checked by the author and a Russian researcher. The question guides consisted of open-ended questions. The interviews were made by the author in Russian and tape-recorded, but transcribed by two other Russians. The interviews were made between September 1996 and June 2000. Besides the interviews, the author followed the work at the printing house and spent altogether five weeks at the firm. He also studied the building and the equipment, and had short conversations with the employees. Moreover, documentary sources were used for the period.

2 The following section is based on Berliner (1976), Ericson (1991) and Nove (1984).

## References

Berliner, J.S. (1976) *The Innovation Decision in Soviet Industry*. Cambridge, Massachusetts, and London, England: The MIT Press.

Ericson, R. (1991) The Classical Soviet-Type Economy: Nature of the System and Implications for Reform. *Journal of Economic Perspective* 5, 4, 11–27.

Johanson, M. (2001) *Searching the Known, Discovering the Unknown. The Russian Transition from Plan to Market as Network Change Processes*. Doctoral dissertation, Uppsala: Department of Business Studies, Uppsala University.

Nove, A. (1984) *The Soviet Economic System*. 2nd edn. London: George Allen & Unwin.

# 6 Use of knowledge in the model world

## Lessons to learn from economic literature

*Benjamin Ståhl and Alexandra Waluszewski*

### Use of specific knowledge and models about generation of knowledge

Although the empirical chapters above concern different types of industries and different economic contexts, they have at least one thing in common. All business actors are engaged in the development of specific knowledge, i.e. knowledge of how to combine and utilise certain resources. We have seen how, in order to contribute to economic results, any kind of knowledge has to be created or re-created in relation to how some specific resources are activated in combinations that stretch beyond company borders. Furthermore, we have also seen that when the economic landscape allows such production and use of knowledge to occur in relation to activated resource interfaces, it has important effects on both efficiency and development issues.

What insights in these processes, i.e. the use of knowledge in a business setting, can the economic literature then contribute? Awareness of the importance of knowledge is high. In both the academic world as well as in society, the contemporary business world is often labelled the "knowledge economy". Or, as Castells (1996, p. 218) puts it, when he tries to grasp the soul of this new business landscape, "The source of productivity and growth lies in the generation of knowledge."

However, the empirical accounts presented in the previous chapters brought forward some specific questions concerning this "source of productivity and growth". A main question concerns the "generation" of knowledge; what features characterise the generation of knowledge that can be used in a business setting, and what are the effects of this use? A related question concerns the novelty that knowledge in a business setting is ascribed. There is nothing in our empirical accounts indicating that the need for development and use of knowledge of how to utilise resources beyond company borders is a completely new phenomenon. Has not specific knowledge about related resource interfaces always been an important ingredient in businesses' ability to turn material and immaterial things into economic resources? Is there anything new with the role of knowledge in the knowledge society? Let us start with considering the last question.

## The increasing importance of others' knowledge

Yes, says some spokesperson for the knowledge economy, the role of knowledge in a business setting has changed over time. However, the main difference is perhaps not that contemporary businesses are increasingly dependent on human resources' ability to cope with advanced and changing solutions. It is that these changes, to an increasing extent, are occurring outside the company, on both the supplier and user sides. As was discussed in Chapter 1, although the activities undertaken by a company's customers and suppliers always have been important, the amount of related activities that are taking place outside a focal firm have increased over recent decades. Or, as economic anthropologist Steven Gudeman illustrates this change:

> In the early part of this (the 20th) century, textile, shoe and other manufacturers had on-site machine shops to produce and maintain their capital equipment: today these workshops are museums, because specialist maintenance workers are hired by contract and brought by helicopter when needed. Accountants, tax advisors, lawyers, public relations experts, long-range planners, management consultants, and financial advisors are hired to complete special tasks, but later they may work for competitors.
>
> (Gudeman, 2001, p. 145)

Thus, in comparison to the traditional firm, where knowledge about how to develop insert material, production processes and products could largely be handled in-house, the amount and variety of knowledge-related resource combinations the contemporary business is involved in has greatly increased.

Typical for the new knowledge economy is, says Stiglitz (1999), that there is a "systematization of change itself". A main characteristic of this systematization is, as among others Piore and Sable (1984), Powell *et al.* (1996) and Castells (1996) have made us aware, that any change has to be related to the processes occurring among related counterparts, i.e. any change has to be related to the development of the business network of which each company is a part. In this ever changing business landscape the ability to develop innovations is, underlines Stiglitz (1999), critical for the survival and prosperity of firms. Or, as it is phrased by Gibbons *et al.* (1994, p. 111), "the competitive advantage on which advanced industrialised economies rely depends increasingly upon their ability to reconfigure knowledge". This ability to develop and reconfigure knowledge is also considered as critical for the survival of the individual firm. "Survival among organizations depends less than previously on access to material resources or markets and more on access to knowledge", underlines March (1999, p. 181). In a knowledge economy, companies are urged to think less of products or business units and instead focus on their underlying "core competencies" (Prahalad and Doz, 1987; Prahalad and Hamel, 1990).

The late 1990s and early years of this century have also seen a tremendous effort to unravel, explain and efficiently manage knowledge issues. However, although the interpreters of the new knowledge economy underline both the importance of knowledge and its systemic features, the main attention is still directed to how to create and how to transfer knowledge, while issues of how knowledge becomes useful in connections between businesses is rarely touched upon. Furthermore, the creation of knowledge is mainly treated as an internal business activity, i.e. it is something that companies are assumed to carry out in fierce competition against each other, and not in relation to each other.

Why then do so many scholars, after acknowledging knowledge as *the* economic resource, neglect to discuss how to make it useful in a business landscape populated by interdependent companies, in favour of a discussion of how to breed and transfer it? Do we, as Stiglitz (1999) suggests, simply have difficulties embedding the concept of knowledge in an economic model world that, in its main building blocks, is highly coloured by the assumptions made in economic theory?

If the resources that traditionally have been dealt with in economic theory allowed economists to consider them as homogeneous, it is far more difficult to translate knowledge to a homogeneity assumption. This problem has been solved with the assumption that the generation of knowledge is something that takes place outside the economic world, to be automatically absorbed by the economic actors when manifested in new economic resources (Wilk, 1996). However, as soon as we want to treat development and use of knowledge as an integral part of the business world, we need to reconsider the homogeneity assumption. Or, as Stiglitz (1999) puts it, if knowledge cannot be treated as a homogeneous resource, the handling of this issue "necessitates a rethinking of economic fundamentals".

Yet, the use of knowledge in a business setting was a central issue in economics during its conception as a field of inquiry. Since then, however, it has also been forgotten, neglected and marginalised by many, "assumed away" by mainstream neoclassical economics. Let us make a brief overview of this development, including earlier, somewhat forgotten insights. However, it must be underlined that the following overview is far from a complete review of how knowledge has been treated in economic theory. Rather it is a highly selective rendition of the dominant strands of thought that can be related to the subject matter of this book – knowledge from a user perspective. Thus, it is intended to be an examination of others' ideas, and how they relate to issues that have been brought forward in the previous chapters.

As mentioned above, emphasising the importance of knowledge is nothing new; it has always been regarded as central to economic theory. However, when it comes to our main theme, how knowledge is used in a business setting, it is more of an exception than a rule that this issue has been highlighted in economic theory. This implies that the ideas we start out with cannot be considered as "mainstream" economics, but rather some "dissident" thoughts in this field. We then turn to how the role of knowledge has been treated in a field where it has received far more attention, and where it also has been extensively investigated – management literature. However, here the discussion also pertains mostly to the acquisition of knowledge or its production – rarely to how it is used and how it is connected to others. The last section argues that we can nevertheless gain some valuable insight from research and theory regarding knowledge acquisition – learning – for our purposes.

## A brief history of how knowledge has been approached in economic theory

In any overview of how knowledge has been treated by economists, it is useful to begin with Adam Smith, who built a theory of welfare growth on the assumption of increasing knowledge through specialisation. He offered a useful definition of knowledge in his analysis of "the principles which guide and direct philosophical inquiries, illustrated by the history of astronomy" (discussed in Loasby, 1991). Smith saw a psychological need in humans to explain and link together in their minds a sensory phenomenon, to invent for themselves *connecting principles*; "one of those arts which address themselves to the imagination" (quoted in Loasby, 1991, p. 7). The more extensive the connecting principles, the more attractive. For Smith, Newtonian physics was a great achievement, not because of how "true" it was, but as a useful, persuasive, systematic invention of Newton's imagination, that might well be (as it has been) displaced by other connecting principles. As Loasby argues, the notion of connecting principles, or networks of knowledge, is "particularly useful in coping with phenomena which threaten to escape far beyond the bounds of human rationality – which [...] is characteristic of economics" (Loasby, 1991, p. 6).

The great contribution of Adam Smith was to make the division of labour central to economics. Smith argues that the wealth of a society depends on productivity, which increases with specialisation. People tend to specialise due to the difficulty of self-sufficiency, in other words to individually produce all that which is desirable to consume or own. By becoming skilled at a particular activity, however, one can produce more of that than others can, and induce them to trade the fruits of their expertise with one's own. That is what Smith means when arguing that blind self-interest leads to communal benefits, not because people are unrelenting egotists but only because it promotes the division of labour, which raises productivity through specialisation. In other words, using knowledge is to become skilled at a task. The value attached to goods differs between a buyer and a seller due to their special skills. This is what enables trade, what motivates people to act on their beliefs, to "bet" on the future course of events on the basis not only of information, but on the belief in their own skills, on how they use their knowledge. In other words, the entire discipline of economics is founded on the insight that using others' knowledge leads to greater welfare, via specialisation and resulting trade based on absolute advantage.

According to Smith, specialisation (the division of labour) increases productivity ("the skill, dexterity and judgment" with which labour is directed or applied) by three things. The first two are readily understood – the increase in dexterity of every worker when repeating a particular task and "the savings of time which is commonly lost in passing from one species of work to another". The third reason is innovation – "the invention of all those machines by which labour is so much facilitated and abridged" – which is the result of special-isation. In other words, resources are connected by (among other things) how they facilitate their respective usage.

Smith argues that such inventions are the result of the workers themselves, who have time to direct their attention to particular tasks, and much to gain from automating them; from businesses that have become specialised in the making of machines; and from "philosophers or men of speculation, whose trade it is to not do anything, but to observe everything; and who, upon that account, are often capable of combining together the powers of the most distant and dissimi-lar objects" (Smith 1776; I.1.9). This quotation could serve as an interpretation of the processes that have been caught in the previous empirical chapters; the combining and confronting of ideas and/or technologies in novel ways beyond company borders.

Although Smith's underlying argument of what enables trade, business devel-opment and increased productivity is businesses' ability to combine and integ-rate knowledge, specialisation and innovations, it is not this message that has been most elaborated by those following in his footsteps. Instead, Adam Smith is commonly credited with the notion of the invisible hand – how demand and supply can adjust and balance through the mere actions of individuals (rather than by intervention). This part of Smith's work also fits the central question of economics much better; the coordination of economic activities.

Another classical economist who also emphasised the role of knowledge in economy is Carl Menger, one of the instigators of "the marginalist revolution" and the founder of the Austrian School of economics (which we shall return to). Menger's work, together with that of Walras and Jevons, can be seen as termi-nating the period of classical economics. But unlike Walras and Jevons (who we also return to), Menger did not resort to mathematics or assume an omniscient "auctioneer" position. Instead, for his creation of a system of value and price theory, he was greatly concerned with the division of labour and with the use of knowledge. Like the classical economists, he was concerned with theory being founded on the empirical observation of how people actually behave. Know-ledge, he argued, was primary to goods, and not to be presumed – it could be lacking, incomplete, or even false. In this sense, using knowledge is what enables economic activity, and is at its heart. Menger essentially turned Smith's view of the relationship between increasing knowledge and economic progress on its head by viewing the division of labour as an outcome of more knowledge – indeed, division of labour for production is a more complex stage of know-ledge than is direct consumption – the growth of which was not confined to eco-nomic activities.

A related contribution is made by Alfred Marshall, who argued that know-ledge is not only the most important source of economic growth, but also creates interconnectedness among businesses. Marshall, too, straddled the shift from classical to modern economic thought. As an economist his heritage has been acknowledged by the neoclassical economists of the twentieth century. But they also criticised him for failing to develop a theory of perfect competition (which he, in his defence, did not set out to do, cf. Loasby, 1991). Marshall's analysis was wide in scope, and for our purposes, we need to highlight but a few ideas: the evolutionary principles of economies, the importance of knowledge and organisation, and the notion of external organisation.

Marshall was quite impressed by Darwinian evolution, and made frequent analogies to the biological realm, even though he cautioned against too eagerly accepting a firm as an organism. Although his attempt to reconcile evolution and equilibrium failed (Loasby, 1991), his biological analogy has two important implications. The first is that economies can be seen as open systems. This became a difficult concern for economists, just as Darwin's ideas were problematic for many of his contemporaries to accept. That is because if we accept the concept of evolution, and the processes that fuel it, then we also accept that there is no "goal", or destination, and that man is not the ultimate and final result of a great design. In other words, an economy can never be said to be "optimally efficient" in a meaningful sense, since it is the evolution of economies – through innovations – that provides the greatest benefits. The use of knowledge is not static, but constantly evolving.

A second implication of the biological analogy concerns the general rule of the connection between differentiation and integration. That is, economic evolution tends to increase specialisation on the one hand and increase the connections between specialised functions on the other. This means that as the use of knowledge becomes more sophisticated (specialised) it simultaneously becomes more interdependent (less self-sufficient), so that "any disorder in any part of a highly-developed organism will also affect other parts" (Marshall, 1920, IV.VIII.2).

In his *Principles*, Marshall spends much (indeed, most) of his discussion on the "Agents of Production. Land. Labour. Capital" on the importance of organisation:

> Capital consists in a great part of knowledge and organisation: and of this, some part is private property and other part is not. *Knowledge is our most powerful engine of production*; it enables us to subdue Nature and force her to satisfy our wants. Organization aids knowledge; it has many forms, e.g., that of a single business, that of various businesses in the same trade, that of various trades relatively to one another, and that of the State providing security for all and help for many.
>
> (Marshall, 1920, IV.I.2; emphasis added)

Two implications of direct interest to the experiences described in the previous empirical chapters are readily apparent from this quote. A first concerns the primacy of use of knowledge for business behaviour. A second concerns the interconnectedness of knowledge and the role of organisation in enabling the use of many kinds of knowledge for a common purpose. Note that Marshall considers organisation to extend beyond the firm itself; he envisions an external organisation, where a firm is linked to customers, suppliers and competitors. Such external organisation is, according to Marshall, very important in terms of not only limiting and enabling exchange, but also because it facilitates innovation. As such, the external organisation is viewed as part of a firm's capital, which can be of greater significance than its tangible assets and instrumental in its ability to create benefits.

To summarise, the era of classical economics was one where the connection to the real world of markets and business behaviour was central. The field was driven by induction, relevance to real life, and by a concern about how to foster prosperity. Political economy, as it was called then, was concerned with how economies developed, how the wealth of nations could increase, and why economic development differed among regions. The use of knowledge and innovation was at the core of theory and debate. These themes were all but abandoned in the era that followed.

## Role of knowledge in modern economic theory

In the late nineteenth century, economic thought became focused on equilibrium theory with a strong preference for mathematical modelling. This preference remains to this day. The economics of Walras, Jevons, Pareto and others defined economics as the analysis of equilibrium, especially under conditions of perfect competition. This required a closed system and rigid assumption concerning knowledge and information – basically getting rid of the idea of innovation as an endogenous variable. The attraction of this approach was, of course, its focus on logical completeness and predictability.

At the pinnacle of general equilibrium theory stands the so-called Pareto optimum. This describes a state at which point no actor can change his actions without worsening a situation for himself or someone else. By being able to define Pareto optimum, economic theory has implications for overall societal welfare and can be used ideologically. The prevalent ideology has mainly been to allow markets to work without intervention, as the ideal model of perfect competition at equilibrium is the most efficient in terms of resource allocation.

General equilibrium theory, however, requires rigid assumptions regarding what people know, how they use knowledge and how they act. Within these rigid assumptions both individual consumers and productive decision-makers (that is, companies) act with given preferences and given technologies, and with complete information. In other words, firms do not wield any discretion – not even being able to avoid maximising profits (Schumpeter, 1939). We find little, if any, help here concerning how adoption of knowledge and technology occurs from a user perspective.

This shift in attention to equilibrium modelling has had far-flung consequences. Economic thought has been, and remains, very much influenced by this perspective. Perhaps the most important effect (and, arguably, shortcoming) of general equilibrium theory has been the emphasis on Pareto optimality, the analysis of optimal resource allocation under perfect competition. For Jevons, for example, the "great problem of Economy" was formulated thus: "Given, a certain population, with various needs and powers of production, in possession of certain lands and other sources of required material, the mode of employing their labour to maximise the utility of the product" (quoted in Loasby, 1991: 29–30). That is, scarce resources and unlimited desire – what we are taught in basic economics textbooks.

This model world, however, requires that we assume that the use of knowledge is completely unproblematic. Knowledge – and other resources – must be considered as homogeneous, and accessible to anyone. Economic actors are not "allowed" to alter or adapt resources. Knowledge use is identical among all individuals. Instead, knowledge and resource development are treated as exogenous – that is, they are not developed inside the model (among actors in the economy) but somehow appear and are made readily available to all.

This model world also includes the assumption that economies represent evolutionary end states. The issue at hand is to utilise what exists in an optimal way, rather than devising new ways of doing things. However, this concentration on resource allocation efficiency, in terms of Pareto improvements, means that the whole issue of the role and impact of combining knowledge and innovations in economy on both a general and business level, is left out. Or, as Schumpeter illustrated, what is neglected with such a perspective, "add as many mail coaches as you please, you will never get a railroad by so doing."[1] Thus the stylised economic model world rests on assumptions quite far removed from the empirically based one that states that the evolution of economies is primarily one of new methods of production and exchange, rather than their optimisation. But, to this day much policy, e.g. competition policy and ideologies devoted to minimising market intervention, rests on the notion of allocation efficiency and given demand, rather than on empirical accounts concerning effects of combining of knowledge and innovations beyond company borders.

Although the ambition to track the development pattern that gave this line of thought such prominence goes far beyond the ambition of this book, some interpretations deserve to be mentioned. First, a theoretical model that can deliver high predictability is perfect from a user perspective. Another reason is that the mathematical form enables a scrutiny for logical errors (Debreu, 1991).[2] Moreover, the construction of the competitive equilibrium model provided a landmark intellectual achievement.

Another hypothesis is that economists chose the physical analogy rather than the biological analogy for their models. The great achievements within the field of physics made it, at the time, the envy of all scientific fields. It has been argued (Ormerod, 1997) that the relevant analogy to physics here concerns its mechanistic side (rather than complex and chaotic), envisaging the economy as a harmonious and smooth clockwork – certainly not the transitions envisaged by, e.g. Marshall or Marx.

It is of course not the case that economists in this era were unaware or ignorant about the importance of knowledge. On the contrary, the fact that there was so little theory surrounding it was lamented upon by the most respected of economists (Hayek, Machlup, Boulding and Arrow, for example). Rather, it was the difficulty of integrating the knowledge issue into the conventional equilibrium models. Much of this, of course, has to do with the properties of knowledge that distinguish it from the other variables in the model (for example land, labour and capital). First, it was notoriously difficult to find a measure of knowledge (Boulding (1966) noted this, and suggested that it would be convenient if one could find the measure of a "wit", a play on "bit" in relation to data). This problem is, of course, the source of the habit of equating knowledge production with the R&D function – data on this was more readily available.

Another problem is the non-exclusiveness of knowledge as compared to other kinds of property (if one possesses a piece of land, no one else can – if one posses knowledge, this may be shared with others yet still available to oneself). Yet another was the reluctance to distinguish between information and knowledge (indeed, Hayek used these terms interchangeably).

It should be noted, however, that special branches in economic theory were formulated around the particular properties of knowledge. For example, its non-rivalry nature means that a seller does not lose anything when knowledge is sold – it is acquired definitely, even if it is shared or sold. Likewise, a buyer need not buy the same knowledge even if it is to be used several times. Moreover, a buyer cannot accurately value the knowledge without acquiring it. This has important pricing, transaction and user implications, which have been considered at length. These and other concerns have inspired research on "knowledge industries"; "learning by doing", formulated as productivity gain due to the producer's past production experience; pricing with incomplete knowledge; and transaction costs arising out of (among other things) asset specificity brought about by local learning and knowledge development. Yet the role of knowledge was (and still is) marginalised and neglected in mainstream economics – but not by all. The next section considers some of the "dissidents" in this area, and how their ideas can relate to the use of knowledge.

### Some "dissident" thoughts on the role of knowledge

Although the role of knowledge in an economic setting received grudging treatment during the "neoclassical" era, there were some unrelenting voices that kept insisting on the centrality of this issue, and on the necessity to consider more than adjustments of price and quantity in response to given, exogenous events. A persistent line of thought that can help to shed some light on our focal issue, a user perspective on knowledge in a business setting, is the Austrian school of economics. The founder of the Austrian school was Carl Menger, whose ideas were discussed previously, and his adherents Ludwig von Mises, Friedrich Hayek and Israel Kirzner (among others) kept insisting on the role of knowledge in economic life.

A central thought among the Austrian scholars was that the market is a process of discovery and learning, about which Mises and Kirzner were adamant. Knowledge was approached as dispersed and subjective, which implies that the interaction between individuals over time was regarded as critical for the use of knowledge. Interaction serves both to alleviate uncertainty and to aid the discovery (and exploitation) of opportunities. This implies a focus on how knowledge is used. For Kirzner especially, the use of knowledge was synonymous with alertness, a fundamental condition of entrepreneurship. In other words, an entrepreneur is the driving force in the market process where economic actors are alert to how resources (including knowledge) may be combined and connected.

Another implication of the assumption of dispersed knowledge, pursued at length by Hayek, is the impossibility of extensive planning. In his essay "The use of Knowledge in Society" (1945), Hayek argued that dispersed knowledge not only necessitated local judgement and decision making, but is what actually creates a semblance of macro-coordination. Furthermore, he insisted that "a little reflection will show that, beyond question, there is a body of very important but unorganised knowledge that cannot possibly be called scientific in the sense of knowledge of general rules: the knowledge of the particular circumstances of time and place" (Hayek, 1945, H9). He goes on to argue that:

> Is it true that once a plant has been built the rest is all more or less mechanical, determined by the character of the plant, and leaving little to be changed in adapting to the ever-changing circumstances of the moment? . . . The fairly widespread belief in the affirmative is not, as far as I can ascertain, borne out by the practical experience of the businessman. . . . One reason why economists are increasingly apt to forget about the constant small changes which make up the whole economic picture is probably their growing preoccupation with statistical aggregates, which show a very much greater stability than the movements of the detail. . . . The continuous flow of goods and services is maintained by constant deliberate adjustments, by new dispositions made every day in the light of circumstances not known the day before, by *B* stepping in at once when *A* fails to deliver.
>
> (Hayek, 1945, H13–H15)

Hayek's picture of the role of knowledge in a business setting, all the "constant small changes that make up the whole economic picture", all the "deliberate adjustments" and "new dispositions made in the light of circumstances not known the day before", is an almost perfect characterisation of the knowledge using processes described in the previous empirical chapters. Thus, the message of Hayek is that we need to understand business practice, and thus economics, as a constantly evolving market process rather than the movement towards an optimal equilibrium. The price mechanism, he argues, serves as a grease to that process, where planning would undoubtedly fail. The argument is not that the price mechanism is all that which is required for coordination and interaction –

it is rather that the constant use of knowledge, as it changes, requires decisions to be made close to the problem. The fundamental difference between the Austrian and the neoclassical view, then, is that in the former ignorance is the starting point, rather than fully informed, rationally behaving economic agents.

The role of knowledge in general, and experience in particular, was also brought forward by Edith Penrose, who made these issues the heart of her theory of micro-level firm growth. She emphasised managerial experiences with resources – how they can be combined in many different ways to render productive services for exchange. This meant that she also underlined the need for a heterogeneity assumption concerning resources. Thus, firms evolve distinctly according to how they combine their resources – they are pools of resources under a particular administrative framework. Through planning, and through the execution of these plans, managers gain (experiential) knowledge, influencing their "imagination". Their imagination concerning how resources can be used provides the firm with its "productive opportunity", which serves as input to future plans. The growth of firms is thus fuelled, and directed, by increasing knowledge. Growth is limited only by the imagination of managers and by the time it takes for learning to occur and be incorporated into the firm. Unfortunately, Penrose's work was not influential in economic theory, but has lately been recognised in management and technology development studies.

These and other dissidents' insistence on the issues and difficulties associated with the use of knowledge are important to emphasise for two reasons. First, it means that the use of knowledge is a challenge – a constant challenge – for businesses, requiring sensitivity to surrounding resources, actors and processes in which they are involved. The message from the dissident is that the knowledge of local circumstances is indeed knowledge about others – including about their knowledge. Hayek posited that the price system is an extremely adept communicating medium, but this does not rule out the importance of other media, such as experience with counterparts and their business. Price, for the Austrians, is not given but a communication device through which negotiation, adaptation and discoveries are made explicit. Second, these insights imply that use of knowledge is also a challenge for scholars engaged in studying economic activities; what theoretical tools do we need to develop in order to grasp these issues? This leads us to that area where perhaps most research and thought concerning the use of others' knowledge has occurred – dealing with changing knowledge in general and innovation in particular.

Many theoretical interpretations of knowledge and innovations have been influenced by Joseph Schumpeter, who puts knowledge and the creation of "novelty" at the core of economic development, "The fundamental impulse that sets and keeps the capitalist engine in motion comes from the new consumers, the new goods, the new methods of production or transportation, the new markets, the new forms of industrial organisation that capitalist enterprise creates" (1975, p. 83, originally published in 1942). Thus, Schumpeter saw innovation as the fundamental driving force of capitalism, much like Marx, and saw competition as a process of "creative destruction" whereby new solutions replace incumbents. This idea has many implications, but of special concern to us is the large number of empirical studies that have shown, like our empirical experiences, that an innovation indeed can be a threat to existing solutions and to the businesses engaged in them. These insights indicate that using others' knowledge is not a straightforward process of adopting or sourcing a technology, but that this process can be problematic and painful for parties that both support and oppose it.

We are also provided with rich industry illustrations of how incumbent firms fail to foresee, adapt to, and sometimes even survive, new technology, as seen in the studies made by Tushman and Andersson (1986), Henderson and Clark (1990) and Christensen (1997). The problems related to new knowledge and innovations are explained as a consequence of several factors. Some main reasons are the difficulty of integrating the new with existing resources and activities, the dilemma associated with investing in unproven and uncertain knowledge as compared to existing knowledge, and the reluctance of actors such as customers, investors and employees to change. That is because knowledge exists in structures of other's knowledge, investments and business relationships. In sum, it points to the salience of the theme of the empirical studies presented in this book – to explore the issues associated with using others' knowledge.

The same contention concerning the painful side of using new knowledge is found in "evolutionary economics", the last strand of economic theory we shall look at here. The origin of evolutionary economics is Nelson and Winter's book *An Evolutionary Theory of Economic Change* (1982). The idea draws on the behavioural theory of the firm (Cyert and March, 1963) and the concept of bounded rationality, an emerging idea in the management sciences (see below). It also draws heavily on Schumpeter's ideas and posited that firms' behaviour is very much influenced by their past through routines. Routines are seen as the "genes" of the organisation and a consequence of repeated action, that is, knowledge in use. An important consequence say the evolutionary economists, is that firms have a tendency towards "inertia", an inability to change, because what they have learnt, they do well; what investments are made, influence available choices. However, evolutionary economics is concerned with dynamic firm behaviour on a macro (industrial) level, and uses quite a stylised model of routines and knowledge use. The ideas have been very influential for the development of concepts important in management studies, to which we turn in the next section.

To summarise, many influential – classical as well as contemporary – scholars have underlined that knowledge can charge and re-charges economic resources with the kind of novelty that acts as "fundamental impulses" for keeping the "engine in motion". Far less attention has been devoted to the actual processes where knowledge is brought into use. For example, this is evident in the voluminous research devoted to innovation adoption, which has primarily been concerned with macro-level adoption rates, using epidemic models and threshold models of innovation diffusion. The processes that make knowledge both available and useful in the development of the resource combinations that are behind such things as goods, production methods and production facilities, transport methods and transport facilities, organisational methods, rules and organisational units are still poorly understood. Thus, when considering how the use of knowledge has been treated in economic research, it is easy to understand the remark Edith Penrose made a half century ago: "Economists have, of course, always recognised the dominant role that increasing knowledge plays in economic processes, but have, for the most part, found the whole subject of knowledge too slippery to handle" (Penrose, 1959, p. 77). In the management sciences, the subject of the next section, more attempts have been made.

### The role of knowledge in the management sciences

Research in organisations, management sciences, poses profound challenges to the assumptions used in much economic theory. An important concept in this regard is bounded rationality. In fact, the idea of bounded rationality constitutes a rejection of the fundamental assumption in equilibrium models of what "rational" action is. The idea derives from how knowledge is actually used – that it is impossible to possess all the relevant information, to consider all possible alternatives, and to calculate all possible consequences given limited mental capacity, incomplete information and time constraints. Instead, purposeful decision-making is boundedly rational. People engage in limited searches that provide but a few alternatives, and adopt subjective levels of aspiration that permit satisfying (rather than optimising) (Simon, 1955; March and Simon, 1958). Simon's comprehensive research is aimed at building an understanding of decision-making (and administration) that rests on the human mind's actual capacities and processes, or "procedural" rationality, rather than "substantive" rationality, and on the information structures within which the mind operates. Regarding the former, bounded rationality is concerned with "limitations" of the human mind and the methods used to handle various tasks. These include recognition processes that specify information search, heuristics that guide such a search and specify termination points, and simple decision rules concerning how the information should be used (Gigerenzer and Todd, 1999). In addition, the workings of the mind must be related to the specific information structures in which actors find themselves: to understand the rationality of behaviour one must look at the context. This includes other actors, connected knowledge and resources.

In effect this switches the decision-making focus from optimality to aspiration levels, levels that are subjective and context-dependent. The standards that define what is satisfactory are objects of analysis themselves, and these standards, it seems, have little to do with optimal solutions and more to do with negotiated and acceptable solutions. In other words, satisfying is a short cut by setting a stopping rule that ends the search for alternatives at the point where standards are met, e.g. the payoff period of an investment.

With the concept of bounded rationality, organisations are vehicles for both overcoming bounded rationality – by coordinating effort and knowledge – and for capitalising on it. That is, organisational mechanisms and properties, both formal and emergent, shape how effort is limited and in effect focused. Job descriptions, for example, specify areas of responsibility; organisational structures specify authority and information flows; processes define how recurring tasks are performed. Other factors, like culture, can also have a profound influence, and formal patterns of interaction may be less influential than informal ones. Bounded rationality has become the foundation for a theory of business administration that looks upon organisation as a means to overcome the limitations of the human mind primarily through restriction of what employees should do, who has authority and so forth. It forces us to accept that knowledge is dispersed but connected, and to understand how it is used we must understand those connections to other knowledge and to other resources.

One prominent school of thought in management today, that builds upon the idea of bounded rationality, is the resource-based view. It emerged in the mid-1980s and 1990s, in the strategy subfield of management. It has been adamant in bringing both knowledge and innovation back on the research agenda. Largely in reaction to industrial organisation (e.g. Porter, 1990), knowledge is in the resource-based view emphasised as an endogenous variable. Firm behaviour is motivated more by the development of "capabilities" (bundles of resources) than strategic positioning vis-à-vis other actors. Firms differ, even in the same industry, and these differences are both persistent and matter for the performance attainable by the firm (Nelson, 1991; Foss, 1997). A main tenet of this approach is that heterogeneity is something that should be included in the analysis, rather than assumed away. The resource-based view builds on diverse strands of thoughts, including those of economists interested in firm growth (Penrose, 1959), evolutionary economics (Nelson and Winter, 1982) and the boundaries of the firm (Richardson, 1972), as well as sociologists (Selznick, 1957) and organisational theorists (March and Simon, 1958; Cyert and March, 1963).

The resource-based view is concerned with how resources are combined into "capabilities". Capabilities refer to the skills, activities and resources pertaining to value creation through exchange. They were invoked by Richardson (1972) to denote the knowledge, experience and skills needed to carry out certain activities. "Resources", or rather control over them, are commonly invoked as underpinning performance. But unless resources are defined so broadly that it is nonsensical ("anything that provides value to a firm") the actual source of an advantage must lie in how resources are combined and used. In this sense, Penrose discusses "bundles of resources" and Grant (1991) "teams of resources". As knowledge is embedded in the minds of individuals, in artefacts and processes, these "teams" or "bundles" are activated through knowledge integration (Grant, 1996). So, it is knowledge of resources that constitute capabilities, or more exactly the knowledge about the services, applications, that resources render when combined.

Capabilities are thus heterogeneous not only because the innate properties of resources differ – limiting how they can be activated – but primarily because the knowledge about how to use and combine resources differs, making their potential usages infinite but limiting the use to which they are put at any one time. Therefore, the use of resources can never be "optimal" since there are unknown, unexplored applications and combinations. They can only be judged in terms of relative efficiency in meeting the ends that, in turn, depend on value judgments that they are the means to achieve. Moreover, heterogeneity implies path-dependency, i.e. that decisions and commitments made in the present strongly affect that which is possible in the near future. So, capabilities are also constraints, and may be "core rigidities" (Leonard-Barton, 1992) as well as "core competencies" (Prahalad and Hamel, 1990). As firms specialise, their ability to adapt and learn outside the field of specialisation diminishes (March and Simon, 1958; Levitt and March, 1988) – firms are, to an extent, locked in a technological trajectory (Dosi, 1982).

The resource-based view, however, is not a unitary theory. The differences in assumptions, logic, modelling and implications between scholars are in some cases large. In particular, one may distinguish between the "equilibrium" and the "evolution" strands of thought (Foss, 2000). The former draws heavily from equilibrium theory and models accordingly, formally and frequently mathematically (Eisenhardt and Martin, 2000). Essentially the objective is to specify what the conditions are that are conducive to rent yielding, particularly emphasising heterogeneous resources that are difficult for competitors to imitate. This, however, decreases the applicability of the resource-based view for research into the use of knowledge, and particularly the use of others' knowledge.

That is because the theoretical development primarily has been concerned with how to acquire and/or develop knowledge and then to protect it. The big issue is to gain access to knowledge before others, to "store it" and use it as a "competitive advantage". Thus, if there are many recipes on how to gain access to knowledge, there are few on how to make knowledge so useful for others, i.e. how a certain kind of knowledge can render specific benefits for related companies on both the supplier and user sides. A limitation of this approach is thus that in its concern for endogenous sources of competitive advantage, it is limited in how it views interaction and exchanges between firms. The "black box" of the firm has been pried open and stepped into, so to speak, only to be closed again, so that the outside is not considered. The problem with this is that it neglects the very important issue of value (Kogut and Kulatilaka, 2001) and that business exists for the purpose of exchange (Snehota, 1990). The few observations about the external environment that enter into this perspective are often direct derivations of general equilibrium theory, particularly that advantages that are imitable will instantly attract entrants and dissolve any excess profits. For our present purposes the lessons from the resource-based view are somewhat limited.

Nevertheless, management literature deals more intricately with the concept of knowledge and its meaning for economic activity. Largely, this has come about through a more open dialogue with other fields – such as sociology and psychology. This may be due to the field being phenomenon-driven rather than theory-driven. To conclude this chapter, we shall look at recent advances in another field that deals quite explicitly with our current concern, the use of knowledge: the field of learning.

### The concept of knowledge and situated learning

In management sciences today it is commonplace to differentiate between explicit and tacit knowledge based on Polanyi's conceptualisation (although he wrote of a process, knowing, rather than a property), with corollary implications for knowledge acquisition. Explicit knowledge can be codified and explained (similar to Ryle's "know-what") and is thus transmittable. Tacit knowledge (akin to "know-how"), on the other hand, is "ineffable", i.e. partly inexplicable. It is therefore also inherently difficult to teach, and is rather acquired through experience and imitation. In other words, to use knowledge is also to produce it: to learn. For business, this has been formulated in terms of "learning by doing" (Arrow, 1962), "learning by using" (Rosenberg, 1982) and "learning by interacting" (Lundvall, 1988).

Other research has been even more rigorous in studying learning and the use of knowledge. Often, insights come from ethnographic studies of workers in action. An example of this is Lave and Wenger's theory of situated learning (Lave and Wenger, 1990; Lave, 1988; Wenger, 1998). Based on field studies, the theory stipulates that individuals attune themselves to each other and the enterprises they are engaged in through a process of interaction where practice is central. Learning is a function of the activity, context and culture in which it occurs – it is situated. "Constructing identities" is a process of "legitimate peripheral participation", whereby the individual engages in the practices of the community. In other words, learning is not merely a matter of content – such as formal and explicit descriptions of assignment – but a social process that "subsumes the learning of knowledgeable skills" (Lave and Wenger, 1990: 29). Knowledge, that is, cannot be divorced from the context within which it is used – including resources, actors and the particular activities taking place. Situated learning and communities of practice direct attention to the actual enterprise – or practice – that individuals engage in and thus may cross or delimit formally defined organisational structures and technologies.

This means that knowledge use should be considered in the context of other actors and resources. Thus, knowledge is unique to its context. For example, in the extensive ethnographic study conducted by Orr (1996) of Xerox service technicians, it is clear that they consisted of a specific community of practice that interacted with customers who had very different knowledge of copy machines, although they used them daily. That is, when we consider the actual use of knowledge, we may well learn that the knowledge that is used differs considerably in form and content from the "canonical" knowledge. Thus, different communities may not only hold different knowledge, but also know differently (e.g. Douglas, 1986; Dougherty, 1992; Carlile, 2002). Some groups may not be interested in a particular innovation (Dougherty, 1992) or be unable to actually identify it in the first place. In this sense, the idea of knowledge tacitness as a primary determinant is somewhat misleading. It is the idea of the existence of "pieces of knowledge" – in a finite sense – about a particular object or situation, that may or may not be written down. The point of distinction is not about the knowledge, but about the bearer of knowledge. This is a pragmatic view of knowledge – acting intelligently is about getting things done (see Carlile, 2002; Hohenthal, 2001). Moreover, the skill – or knowledge – depends on the context within which it is done. Mathematical proficiency, for example, varies whether performed by a vendor in her market, or by the same person in an examination situation with hypothetical problems irrelevant to her life (Lave, 1988).

But what constitutes the "relevance" of context? There has been a considerable amount of study devoted to communities of practice,[3] although there are certain discrepancies between foci. Most research has focused on communities in isolation (Lave, 1988), with few exceptions (e.g. Carlile, 2002; Bechky, 2003), even though in its original conceptualisation frequent references are made to interacting communities. While some studies on movement between communities exist (Østerlund, 1996), the scarce studies of inter-community interaction usually considers members of different communities that interact with each other (e.g. Tyre and von Hippel, 1997; Carlile, 2002; Bechky, 2003). For the purpose of examining the use of knowledge, then, we can be inspired by these theories of how knowledge is used and how learning occurs in certain communities, but we need to expand the focus and also consider resources and relationships with others. In short, context and relationships must be taken into account, as must resources themselves.

## More work is needed

The purpose of this overview has been to outline what we can learn from how the use of knowledge has been treated in economic theory by the "classical" scholars and by some of their followers. Thus, it has not been a complete review of existing ideas concerning knowledge, but rather a highlighting of arguments, thoughts and concepts that are useful when we discuss the empirical experiences made in the previous chapters, as well as when we consider the theoretical tools at hand. Although we owe a lot to some of the "classical" political economists, and what, in the perspective of the dominating contemporary economic thinking, appear as "dissident" thoughts, a main lesson is that much more work is needed. Knowledge figures extensively in economic thought, but most of the latter does not address how it is actually used, and how it relates to an economic world full of already existing and related resources. There must, as Hayek (1945, p. 519) argues, be something "fundamentally wrong" with theoretical constructions that "disregards an essential part of the phenomena with which we have to deal: the unavoidable imperfection of man's knowledge and the consequent need for a process by which knowledge is constantly communicated and acquired" (1945, p. 530).

The economic problem of society is thus not merely a problem of how to allocate "given" resources – if "given" is taken to mean given to a single mind which deliberately solves the problem set by these "data". It is rather a problem of how to secure the best use of resources known to any of the members of society, for ends whose relative importance only these individuals know. Or, to put it briefly, it is a problem of the utilization of knowledge which is not given to anyone in its totality.

(Hayek 1945, p. 519)

## Notes

1  Schumpeter, 1932, *Development: Festschrift offered to Emil Lederer,* published online: www.schumpeter.info/Edition-Evolution.htm
2  "Being denied a sufficiently secure experimental base, economic theory has to adhere to the rules of logical discourse and must renounce the facility of internal inconsistency. A deductive structure that tolerates a contradiction does so under the penalty of being useless since any statement can be derived flawlessly and immediately from that contradiction. In its mathematical form, economic theory is open to an efficient scrutiny for logical errors." Debreu, 1991.
3  See Teigland, 2003, for a review.

## References

Arrow, K.J., 1962. The Economic Implications of Learning by Doing. *Review of Economic Studies*, 39: 155.

Bechky. B., 2003. Sharing Meaning across Occupational Communities: The Transformation of Knowledge on a Production Floor. *Organization Science*, 14: 312–330.

Boulding, K.E., 1966. The Economics of Knowledge and the Knowledge of Economics. *American Economic Review*, 56(1/2): 1–13.

Castells, M., 1996. *The Information Age: Economy, Society and Culture. Volume 1. The Rise of the Network Society.* Oxford: Blackwell.

Carlile, P., 2002. A Pragmatic View of Knowledge and Boundaries: Boundary Objects in New Product Development. *Organization Science*, 13(4): 442–455.

Christensen, C.M., 1997. *The Innovator's Dilemma: When New Technologies Cause Great Firms to Fail.* Boston: Harvard Business School Press.

Cyert, R.M. and March, J.G., 1963. *A Behavioral Theory of the Firm.* Englewood Cliffs, NJ: Prentice-Hall.

Debreu, G., 1991. The Mathematization of Economic Theory. *American Economic Review*, March, 81(1): 1–7.

Dosi, G., 1982. Technological Paradigms and Technological Trajectories. *Research Policy*, 11: 147–162.

Dougherty, D., 1992. Interpretive Barriers to Successful Product Innovation in Large Firms. *Organization Science*, 3(2): 179–202.

Douglas, M., 1986. *How Institutions Think.* Syracuse, NY: Syracuse University Press.

Eisenhardt, K.M. and Martin, J.A., 2000. Dynamic Capabilities: What are They? *Strategic Management Journal*, 21(10–11): 1105–1122.

Foss, N.J., 1997. *Resources, Firms and Strategies.* Oxford: Oxford University Press.

Foss, N.J., 2000. Equilibrium and Evolution: The Conflicting Legacies of Demsetz and

Penrose, in N.J. Foss and P.L. Robertson, eds, *Resources, Technology, and Strategy*. London: Routledge.

Gibbons, M., Limoges, C., Nowotny, H., Schwartzman, S., Scott, P. and Trow, M., 1994. *The New Production of Knowledge: the Dynamics of Science and Research in Contemporary Societies*. London: Sage.

Gigerenzer, G., Todd, P. M. and the ABC Research Group, 1999. *Simple Heuristics that Make us Smart*. New York: Oxford University Press.

Grant, R.M., 1991. The Resource-Based Theory of Competitive Advantage: Implications for Strategy Formulation. *California Management Review*, 33(3).

Grant, R.M., 1996. Prospering in Dynamically-Competitive Environments: Organizational Capability as Knowledge Integration. *Organization Science*, 7(4), 375–387.

Gudeman, S., 2001. *The Anthropology of Economy: Community, Market and Culture*. Oxford: Malden.

Hayek, F.A., 1945. The Use of Knowledge in Society. *American Economic Review*, XXXV(4), September: 519–530.

Henderson, R.M. and Clark, K.B., 1990. Architectural Innovation: The Reconfiguration of Existing Product Technologies, and the Failure of Established Firms. *Administrative Science Quarterly*, 35: 9–30.

Hohenthal, J., 2001. *The Creation of International Business Relationships: Experience and Performance in the Internationalization Process of SMEs*. Uppsala: Department of Business Studies, Uppsala University.

Kogut, B. and Kulatilaka, N., 2001. Capabilities as Real Options. *Organization Science*, 12(6): 744–758.

Lave, J., 1988. *Cognition in Practice: Mind, Mathematics, and Culture in Everyday Life*. Cambridge: Cambridge University Press.

Lave, J. and Wenger, E., 1990. *Situated Learning: Legitimate Peripheral Participation*. Cambridge: Cambridge University Press.

Leonard-Barton, D., 1992. Management of Technology and Moose on Tables. *Organization Science*, 3(4): 556–558.

Levitt, B. and March, J.G., 1988. Organizational Learning. *Annual Review of Sociology*, 14: 319–340.

Loasby, B., 1991. *Equilibrium and Evolution*. Manchester: Manchester University Press.

Lundvall, B-Å, 1988. Innovation as an Interactive Process: From User-Producer Interaction to National Systems of Innovation, in Dosi, G., Freeman, C., Nelson, R., Silverberg, G., Soete, L., eds, *Technical Change and Economic Theory*. London: Pinter.

March, J.G., 1999. *The Pursuit of Organizational Intelligence*. Oxford: Blackwell Publishing.

March, J.G. and Simon, H.A., 1958. *Organizations*. New York, NY: John Wiley.

Marshall, A., 1920 (1982), 8th edn. *Principles of Economics*, London: Macmillan.

Nelson, R., 1991. Why do Firms Differ, and How does it Matter? *Strategic Management Journal*, Winter: 61–74.

Nelson, R. and Winter S., 1982. *An Evolutionary Theory of Economic Change*. Harvard University Press: Cambridge, MA.

Ormerod, P., 1997. *The Death of Economics*. New York: John Wiley.

Orr, J.E., 1996. *Talking about Machines: An Ethnography of Modern Job*. Ithaca, NY: Cornell University Press.

Østerlund, C.S., 1996. Learning across Contexts: A Field Study of Salespeople's Learning at Work. *Psykologisk skriftserie*, 21(1). Aarhus: Aarhus universitet.

Penrose, E., 1959. *A Theory of the Growth of the Firm*. New York: Wiley.

Piore, M.J. and Sable, C.F., 1984. *The Second Industrial Divide: Possibilities for Prosperity.* New York: Basic Books.

Porter, M.E., 1990. *The Competitive Advantage of Nations.* New York: Free Press.

Powell, W.W., Koput, K.W. and Smith–Doerr, L., 1996. Inter-Organizational Collaboration and the Locus of Innovation: Networks of Learning in Biotechnology. *Administrative Science Quarterly*, 41:116–145.

Prahalad, C.K. and Doz, Y.L., 1987. *The Multinational Mission: Balancing Local Demands and Global Vision.* New York: Free Press.

Prahalad, C.K. and Hamel, G., 1990. The Core Competence of the Corporation. *Harvard Business Review*, 68(3): 79–93.

Richardson, G.B., 1972. The Organization of Industry. *Economic Journal*, 82: 883–896.

Rosenberg, N., 1982. *Inside the Black Box.* Cambridge: Cambridge University Press.

Schumpeter, J.A., 1939. *Business Cycles: A Theoretical, Historical and Statistical Analysis of the Capitalist Process.* 2 Volumes. New York, London: McGraw-Hill.

Schumpeter, J.A., 1942 (1975). *Capitalism, Socialism, and Democracy.* London: George Allen and Unwin.

Selznick, P., 1957. *Leadership in Administration.* Evanston, IL: Row, Peterson.

Simon, H.A., 1955. A Behavioral Model of Rational Choice. *Quarterly Journal of Economics*, 69: 99–118.

Smith, A., 1776. *An Inquiry into the Nature and Causes of the Wealth of Nations.* Reprinted R.H. Campbell and A.S. Skinner (eds) Oxford: Clarendon Press.

Snehota I., 1990. Notes on a Theory of Business Enterprise. Doctoral thesis, Uppsala University, Department of Business Studies.

Stiglitz, J., 1999. Public Policy for a Knowledge Economy. Speech, World Bank Group, London, UK, 27 January 1999 (available from web.worldbank.org).

Teigland, R., 2003. Knowledge Networking, PhD dissertation, Stockholm School of Economics.

Tushman, M.L. and Anderson, P., 1986. Technological Discontinuities and Organizational Environments. *Administrative Science Quarterly*, 31: 439–465.

Tyre, E. and von Hippel, E., 1997. The Situated Nature of Adaptive Learning in Organizations. *Organization Science*, 8(1): 71–83.

Wenger, E., 1998. *Communities of Practice: Learning, Meaning and Identity.* Cambridge: Cambridge University Press.

Wilk, R.R., 1996. *Economics and Cultures: Foundation of Economic Anthropology.* Oxford: Westview Press.

# 7 Interaction

## The only means to create use

*Håkan Håkansson and Alexandra Waluszewski*

### Using resources and knowledge

Hayek's formulation concluding Chapter 6 is also an elegant formulation of how the problems related to the use of knowledge appeared in the empirical chapters. We have met companies that regardless of what business landscape they live in struggle with their resources due to the "the utilization of knowledge which is not given to anyone in its totality" (Hayek, 1945, p. 430). Thus, the use of knowledge is not an issue that can be solved within each company but, to an increasing degree, stretches across company boundaries. Furthermore, the same resource is most often activated in different resource interfaces, which means that it can never be totally adapted to perfectly fit one individual interface. This explains why trials to learn more about how different resources are already combined, and how this combining can be changed to use resources more efficiently, characterises both everyday activities and larger changes in each company.

Understanding how resources are combined and how this combination contributes to the bottom line is a main issue for any company. These considerations affect both physical and organisational resources. Any knowledge that sheds new light on resource combination methods, i.e. on the existing, related resource interfaces, whether produced internally or mediated through other companies or organizations, is greatly appreciated and can be used directly.

However, to begin using knowledge about new resources, or established but not yet combined resources, is another issue. Embedding such new knowledge into an ongoing process requires much more. The combining of resources into related resource interfaces starts from the beginning again, since the introduction of the new will have effects on all related interfaces. These complications draw attention to four specific features of the resource combining process:

- The importance of the "heavy" processes; i.e. the established supplier-user interfaces to which all use of knowledge in a business setting must be related.
- The impossibility of making individual decisions regarding resource combinations due to interdependencies between interfaces.

- The impossibility of separating out single knowledge processes due to the combination of different kinds of knowledge in the resource interfaces.
- The use of knowledge demands a simultaneous production (creation) of knowledge because any new knowledge has to be embedded into the "heavy processes".

The first point, the importance of the "heavy" processes, is related to the way companies work in principle. As illustrated in Chapter 1, there are some main processes dominating each company's life. These processes are related to key counterparts on the supply and user sides. There are few counterparts, suppliers of input and users of output that account for the largest volumes of resources going through the company, and thereby dominating its activities. For these reasons these counterparts are the most important contributors of knowledge that can be embedded into the existing resource combinations. Although knowledge – direct or indirect – can be mediated through other than these counterparts, it still has to be related and adapted to these heavy processes.

The second point, the impossibility for the individual company to alone decide whether any new knowledge will be used, is also related to these heavy processes. Whenever a resource combination is changed someone else is always affected. Thus, in a business world full of previously made investment in systematically related physical and organisational resources that are across company boundaries, and where people struggle with how to handle all these related resources, decision-making appears to be far from an individual process. Because of all resource interfaces that stretch over organisational borders, decisions are always part of collective processes. An interesting aspect is that those involved in this collective process not only represent affected social resources, they also represent a heavy structure of already made investments in physical resources.

The third point, the impossibility of separating out single knowledge processes, is related to the combining process. As soon as a company identifies any new knowledge as useful, the process of making it specific includes consideration of how to combine it with different resource items or artefacts representing different technologies. This means that it is always impossible to separate knowledge processes related to a specific technology, a specific scientific knowledge field or a specific industrial branch, i.e. processes with some clear core of knowledge. Although the embedding of new knowledge into use in a business is a specific process, it includes mixed knowledge fields.

The fourth point, the use of knowledge in a business setting, always demands a certain knowledge production because anything new must be related to the existing resource combinations. And this relating implies that new knowledge must be created to use any new knowledge. The fact that knowledge must be made specific to be embedded into resource combinations means that using new knowledge is interwoven with the creation of new knowledge. These processes where, with further production of specific knowledge, new knowledge is combined and used, are frequently much heavier and more costly than the development of the initial new knowledge. Within industry it is also an established truth that to go from positive laboratory trials of new knowledge to the first large-scale plant is a costly adventure demanding good problem-solving ability. Still, this is nothing compared to the need for knowledge development that appears when the customer begins using the output.

These four issues have all characterised the accounts of the empirical chapters. What they have in common is that they draw attention to the need to relate the knowledge issue to what is going on in the "heavy processes", i.e. in all the established supplier-user interfaces where the main part of companies' development processes take place. It is the economic consequences of these issues that we will discuss in this last chapter.

### Using resources is not "consuming" them

Resources and their utilisation have always been central to economic models. Typical issues include how to optimise the allocation of resources, the importance of scarce resources and how to substitute one resource for another. Resources are clearly at the heart of economics. It is interesting to note as we did in the last chapter that very little has been said about the use of resources, including how and why they are given a certain value. One reason could be that the use has been regarded as equal to consumption, as something that consumes the resource, or transforms it to "post-consumer-waste". This perspective includes the view that the consumption side is regarded as separate from the production side, traditionally the demand has been regarded as given, and a basic job for the producer is to identify a target market, develop a product and launch it.

Another closely related reason that the use of resources has been neglected is that this has simply not been defined as a problematic issue. If demand is given, then use cannot be dependent on any specific knowledge development process. Thus, traditionally the use of a resource has not been seen as an issue related to knowledge about its interfaces on both the supply and user sides. The empirical studies presented in this book started out from another perspective: the user side, resting on the assumption that neither the resources nor the demand are given but rather are created in interaction. Besides highlighting the issue of how to use resources as one of the main business considerations, this perspective also has put the issue of "production of knowledge" into a somewhat different light. As the empirical chapters above illustrated, any use of a resource in a business setting implies some production of specific knowledge related to this use. This observation implies that we have to treat "using" on the same level as "producing" knowledge. In this final chapter we would like to reflect on how knowledge affects the use of resources in a broader economic way.

We will use the four cases presented earlier as a basis for our discussion. In the first part of the chapter we will discuss the use of these resources from a physical point of view. The aim is to identify some important factors affecting the use of the resources – to find how knowledge related to physical factors affects the economic use of one specific resource. Thus, we are limiting the analysis to the physical use. In the second part we will bring the issue of use into an organisational context, and will discuss how and in what way organisational characteristics influence the economic use of a physical resource. Finally, we will summarise what effects these findings have on approaching and analysing the economic world.

## Physical factors affecting economic use

The development of technological systems has been at the core of research within the history of technology. The most general and obvious conclusion is, as discussed in Chapter 1 with the help of insights developed in several different research schools, that technological artefacts are always parts of larger systems. This is interesting from an economic point of view, since it indicates that physical resources are not free and independent in relation to each other. This general conclusion from the history of technology forces any analysis of economic effects of resources to start out from an assumption regarding how single physical resources are related. What can we assume regarding the interfaces between them? How simple and standardised are these interfaces? The more unique and complex the user interfaces are, the greater the need for knowledge. This is a key issue that we must consider when analysing the economic effects of using resources. Let us have a look at how this issue appears in our four cases.

*Case 1: Electricity for disc refiners*   Electricity can be regarded as a very homogeneous resource; so as long as it has the right voltage any electricity will work. However, as soon as we consider the volume aspect the use of electricity appears as somewhat more intricate. More than 2,200 KWH is used per ton of pulp for newsprint produced. This despite that 1,500 KWH per ton is enough to create a pulp than can be used for production of such a paper. Why then did the company go for more electricity? It was not due to any old and inefficient machine, but a conscious choice. By increasing the volume of electricity in the production, the input, wood chips, is transformed to a pulp with some features that create benefits in the processes where the finished paper is used. Thus, the volume of electricity used in the interface electricity-disc refiner is dependent on how some related interfaces are constructed such as wood-disc refiner, pulp-paper, paper-paper machine, paper-printing machine, and paper-ink. In the latter cases the speed of the printing machine and the ability to make colour print is directly dependent on the features in the pulp. The identified interfaces are, in turn, related to other interfaces, resulting in the focal interface being systematically related to a large number of more or less related interfaces.

*Case 2: Wood frames for tall houses*   After some big city fires in Sweden in the late nineteenth century wood frames were forbidden in houses higher than two stories. In the USA, however, the use of wood frames for tall houses continued. One hundred years later the Swedish law was changed and wood was again allowed to be used as a framing material. The difficulties of introducing the "new" (or old) frame materials in Swedish construction revealed all the interfaces the established frame material had with other resources. A large number of interfaces had been developed both when concrete (the most used frame material) was used in the production process and in the use of the final product – the building.

*Case 3: Wood components of a table*   IKEA launched the low priced Lack table in 1982, a low table consisting of a table top and four legs. To keep the same low price, IKEA carried out more than 100 development projects over 22 years. All components of Lack have been developed, and they are now produced in some specially designed facilities in Poland. Thus, in order to keep the low price all physical interfaces leading up to the finished table were changed. The product, on the other hand, still looks the same and 2.5 million of them are sold annually.

*Case 4: Printing forms in Russia*   In the first three cases we followed how companies struggled with combining resources in both internal and external interfaces. The fourth case reveals how a company struggling with handling resource interfaces in a planned economy faces a much more difficult situation. We saw how the forms printed for the post offices have some obvious physical interfaces both with the production of the paper as well as in the printing process. However, only a very restricted number of interfaces related to the supply and use of printed forms is within reach for our focal company. One of these was paper storage; storing it in the wrong type of room affected the quality of the finished forms.

Whether or not our case companies are working in a context where they are allowed and used to struggling with internal and external resource interfaces, the four cases highlight a common message: each identified physical resource is closely related to a number of other physical resources. All are combined with different products and equipment, and the interfaces are neither simple nor highly standardised. In all cases it is possible to identify what can be depicted as a physical using system. This using system is specific for the individual resource. In each case this consists of a set of products and facilities. But the cases also demonstrate that we can identify a producing system for each of the resources, which also have the same type of interrelatedness. The producing system of electricity has an interrelatedness that is of the same type as the using system of electricity when producing pulp. However, although the two systems have some common interfaces, they also have many different interfaces, and consequently different "borders". Thus, a main conclusion is that all physical resources, both when they are produced and when they are used, have very intricate interfaces with other physical resources. Consequently, knowledge of these interfaces is an important ingredient when making decisions regarding any resource as it will influence the economic outcome. Let us now look more closely at some economic decisions concerning a specific physical resource.

## Economic decisions regarding development, production and use of a specific resource

For a physical resource to be used it must be produced. Before it can be pro-duced it must be developed. If the economic world were characterized by independence, the decisions regarding development, production and use could be analysed as three related but "independent", and thereby isolated, decisions. For example, the use could be analysed as being dependent on the consumer/user and his/her utility function. The production could be analysed based on the producer's production function in relation to the market's total supply and demand, where the single user only has a marginal effect. Finally, the development could be seen as some kind of investment decision mainly based on a forecast of how the new resource differs from competing ones.

In fact, this is also the way decisions are analysed given a market environ-ment where independence is a crucial assumption, i.e. in most traditional eco-nomic models. However, as soon as we accept that interdependencies are a major feature of business life, there are problems in separating the three decision situations described above. The system aspect identified in the previous section must be considered, since it affects all three decisions, i.e. the decision maker needs knowledge from the others. We will try to make a first analysis by assum-ing that economic aspects are the only relevant dimensions (we could alterna-tively assume that all other aspects can be translated into economic terms). In all the three situations we will use ROI (return on investment) as the relevant outcome as this is the most used measurement in industry. ROI is a rather simple tool consisting of three components. It is the revenue minus costs divided by the needed investment. Let us now look at how ROI is influenced by the interdepen-dencies for each of the three decisions.

### The user

Any user wanting to increase ROI when using a specific resource can receive it by increasing revenues or decreasing costs or by decreasing the needed invest-ment. If we apply this to the using system, it is obvious that minor changes of a resource, which follow the established user logic, can increase revenues in a marginally positive way, without demanding a large investment or other costs. If the change is marginal it will generally only affect some few interfaces, and not the main dimensions of the using system. Such change is relatively easy to cal-culate; there are usually very few "others" who must be involved and their reac-tions are probably easy to predict. One interesting aspect is that the total revenue in this situation is very much volume dependent. The larger the volume, the larger the total revenue effect.

However, as soon as there are larger changes to a resource, the effects on the user system become much more problematic. Such changes will usually affect a large number of interfaces in a substantial way. These interfaces are often also related to each other in complex and multifaceted ways. Furthermore, these interfaces are not only found within an individual company, but between or within several companies. Thus, the knowledge about these interfaces is dispersed among a number of essentially related companies. As we have seen, sometimes those handling such related interfaces have close relationships, but sometimes they have no direct interaction at all. Regardless of the situation, seldom does any business actor have a good overview of all affected interfaces. The only chance an individual user has is to involve others who are affected, i.e. to mobilise them for a change. This does not mean that these others are going to make simple estimations but instead investigate what they could get out of the change if they could embed it into their use of resources. In this situation volume also has an interesting effect – a double one. It increases both the costs and the potential revenues. A volume user can benefit greatly from a large change, but it will also be extremely costly to make the change.

All this need for investigation of what and how resource interfaces will be affected by a change, implies that large changes will be both costly and highly uncertain for the user. Although it is often rather easy to identify some positive effects in some focal interfaces – where a new resource can appear as much better than the existing solution – they must be judged in relation to what this change requires of all other affected interfaces. Even if a new resource can mean substantial increased revenue in one or a couple of interfaces, these positive effects can easily be counteracted by smaller losses in several other, related interfaces. Furthermore, investment is often needed to be able to use a new resource. The introduction of a new resource might also affect existing investments in a negative way. In summary, the more marginal the change, the easier it will be to make an estimate of the ROI for the single user. The larger the change, the more difficult the ROI estimation will be in terms of effects of all involved elements (costs, revenues and investments), and the more dependent the individual user will be on mobilising others to determine the economic outcome.

### The producer

For a producer wanting an increase in ROI, the same three factors must be considered. The revenue comes from the users and is related to how large a ROI the latter will receive. The only way to determine this estimate is to involve the users, which in turn initiates the process described above. The costs as well as investment are closely related to the existing producing system. How does the production of the new resource fit into the existing production system? Can earlier investments be utilised? Will the production be based on input already used so there are some positive scale effects? Again a whole system is affected, several parts of which certainly lie outside the focal producer. Thus, others have to be involved to try out what the consequences will be. The more the producer can reduce the costs as well as the investment, the more the new production can be related to the existing structure. The closer the new production is to existing production methods, the easier it will be to make an estimate. The better the knowledge the producer has from the beginning, the easier it will be for the others to make their estimates. The more different the production is, the more difficult it will be to make any estimate at all.

### The developer

What are the consequences for the development decision? One problem is that in the development situation there might be very vague ideas about both the use as well as the production. This is very often the case for radical innovations. In such a case it might be impossible to make any forecasts about both the using and the producing systems. The only thing that might be known is that there will be big changes that will incur large costs and that it generally will take a long time. But, for less radical changes there are certainly possibilities for relating the development decision to the existing interdependencies. One solution could be to try to design the development so that it builds as much as possible on the existing structures both in production and in use. Another can be to focus on developments that solve problems in the existing structures. Both these ways are examples of how to use the existing structure as a base for development. Another way, but based on the same principle, is to try to design the development so it connects two earlier unrelated production structures.

Whether the introduction of new knowledge is considered from the user, the producer or the developer perspective, a common key issue is how the introduction of new knowledge systematically will be related to the existing structure. This issue will be crucial for whatever economic benefits the new knowledge creates. Let us once again return to our four cases to discuss how the revenues, costs and investment look in relation to a specific resource.

*Case 1: Electricity*   The use of electricity in the disc refiners developed over a number of years, in relation to several other interfaces on both the production and user side. The development was stepwise and it took time to relate the different interfaces to each other. The speed of the paper machine was gradually increased and the thickness of the paper gradually decreased due to changes in the pulp, which in turn is related to the total volume of electricity used. There were thousands of small and stepwise changes through the whole chain starting in the pulping process. Also, related interfaces branching out from each part of the chain were successively adapted. The total investment is considerable – but also impossible to calculate as it is so interwoven with other aspects. All these combinatory endeavours were carried out to reduce cost and to increase revenue in the use process. The developed use of electricity has created effects on several other interfaces in the user process. Newsprint, for example, has been improved in terms of the paper's ability to withstand colour printing, making it more attractive for advertisers. The paper's physical weight was decreased, resulting in a positive effect on the distribution cost. All these combinatory changes were made to reduce costs as well to increase revenue. However, hand in hand with the development of related user interfaces goes an increased interdependency, which means that any larger change in this user process would be very costly. In this way, the economic value of the use of electricity in the pulping process is highly interrelated to the use of paper, newspapers and several types of equipment and was created over time through an intensive interaction among a large number of actors who all tried to find a way to benefit from its use.

*Case 2: Wood frames*   The trials to introduce wood frames in the construction industry illustrate the difficulties of bringing in a new resource where resource interfaces have been chiselled out in relation to each other over time. An interesting aspect is that when the Swedish trials of using wood frames in tall buildings began, the production structure for timber products was well developed and as advanced as the one in the USA. However, on the using side, the construction and use of houses had, in a very distinct way, adapted to the use of concrete as the basic frame material (in combination with steel). When designing, constructing and using a building, there are two main "physical" processes that are strongly influenced by the use of a certain frame material. The first is the construction process, which in the Swedish context had been totally adapted to the use of concrete. The other is the use of the building, where stability and the way sound travels within the house are examples of important features. Both these processes, including the combining of thousands of resources, had been developed in relation to concrete as frame material. As soon as the construction company tried to introduce wood as frame material it removed some of the advantages that appeared in relation to concrete, they got into trouble in terms of consequences with related interfaces. Again we can see that the value of using concrete is based on a large number of adapted interfaces where different involved actors have tried to benefit from the use of concrete. It will take time and demand a substantial investment to create the same economic value for wood as a frame material.

*Case 3: Table components*   The introduction of new knowledge has, in this case, continued for over 22 years. However, compared to the processes discussed above this process has been very conscious and driven by one business actor. During this process several innovations in terms of new production designs were made. Although these processes were initiated to improve the resource interfaces behind Lack, they also became used for other similar products. More than 100 development projects were identified around Lack, where a number of resources were developed and related to each other. From the final users' perspective the end product, the Lack table, has always been the "same", even if the price in relative terms has decreased (been constant in absolute terms). Thus, the development endeavours have not been visible for any outsiders, although a substantial investment was needed to decrease the production costs. The economic value was increased through a systematic interaction between involved actors and where they have all tried to find a way to benefit from the process.

*Case 4: Printed forms*   Despite large changes in the economic system, we have seen only smaller changes in terms of bringing in new knowledge in the physical interfaces between the resources used in this case. The development steps that actually are undertaken are also independent from the changes in the economic system. However, the ability to develop direct interaction between those producing and using related resources indicates that in the long run, the interfaces will be handled in another way.

Together the four cases give us complementary pictures of the problem of using new knowledge in an existing structure of physical resources. Two main conclusions can be made:

- A physical resource usually has important interfaces to other physical resources, combined inside and outside of the company.
- These interfaces have distinct effects on the economic consequences that must be considered when making decisions about development, production and use of a new resource.

From an economic point of view, this means that in order for a new or changed resource to be put to use, it has to be given a place within an already existing structure. We have seen that this can be done in a number of ways, and that the existing structure provides both possibilities and restrictions. The last case is an interesting illustration of what happens when a larger economic structure goes through a major change in some, but not in all dimensions. The clue is how to establish an economic logic between the existing and the emerging structure. Every resource decision – development, production or use – must account for how interfaces to other resources look and how the decision will affect them. To get such pictures, knowledge from others, sometimes very detailed, is necessary. This implies that learning and teaching about resources and how they are combined in established interfaces is a key issue when making economic decisions. This in turn, draws attention to the importance of organisational resources.

## Organisational factors affecting resources

The empirical chapters not only painted us a picture of how physical resources influence the development, production and use of new knowledge, but also how organisational resources interfere in this process. This is also in line with experiences of scholars engaged in the social dimension of resources, which was discussed in Chapter 1. The first conclusion above underlined that one specific physical resource usually has close connections to some other physical resources. In our four cases we also saw many examples of such interfaces between products, between equipment and between products and equipment. However, none of these interfaces are given, but are created in interaction. This implies that the creation is due to how the resources are organised.

There are two main dimensions to this organising process. One concern is how resources are brought together within individual organisations. These resources are brought together due to a certain knowledge and capability within that organisation. Thus, the organisation in itself is a resource as it is able to combine and relate other resources to each other. Second, these organisations are related to each other in a more or less systematic way, through interaction and the development of business relationships. The interaction implies that a "new" organisation is created – a business relationship – with a certain capability in combining resources across company boundaries. Thus, both organisational units and organisational relationships are important resources from an economic point of view, since they both bring important "knowledge connections" to physical resources. So, organisational resources have the multi-faceted role of "mobilising", "developing" and "cementing" physical resources into related interfaces. Although the organisational resources in many ways are not as distinct and easily identifiable as the physical resources, they will still function in much the same way. Our cases, especially the fourth, give us insight into the features of organisational resources in a planned economy. The knowledge and experience of how to combine physical and organisational resources is an ability of the individuals representing them – but it is also a collective knowledge, influenced by a larger economic system.

Consequently, a company will consist of a set of physical resources combined with a set of organisational resources, divided into departments, groups or individuals. These resources are combined with each other according to a certain economic logic (which can be more or less clear, more or less formal). However, the internal resource structure is combined with single as well as sets of resources located in other companies and organisations. A physical resource in a company, for example, may be closely related to another physical resource, as well as to another organisational resource within the company and to a third physical resource and a second organisational resource in a customer company. The latter resources might, of course, then be related to some other resources. The number of potential combinations is usually extremely large and of the entire group of combinations, just a few are actually used and developed. Furthermore, every interface is always arbitrarily defined – it is never completely fixed or given by nature. Interfaces are and will always be constructed. New interfaces are continuously created by dividing the resources that were earlier seen as one unit, and through merging of pieces that were earlier seen as separate units. However, these two examples are just two points on a larger scale of how interfaces can be related. Each interface can be developed in terms of how the two surfaces are adapted to each other. This can be illustrated by how two organisations can develop a business relationship in a number of different ways to utilise each other's resources in a better way.

The description above gives reason to point out that the resources have more than one interface and are always used in between. Thus, every resource connects two or more interfaces to each other. As all resources do this, we get interrelated chains of connected interfaces where certain interfaces are focused.

Let us now look at the four cases from this point of view.

*Case 1: Electricity*   There were important organisational resources involved in the development in the electricity case. Several of the involved companies have substantial resources – both physical and organisational – and they expended great effort in developing the combinations internally. Consequently they have important knowledge regarding technical interfaces that is more than useful to their counterparts. Some of the organisations worked together for several decades within very established business relationships, which facilitated the development of relating some interfaces to each other. But the opposite can also be seen. For a long time the organisation owning the disc refiner had problems working with one of the most competent suppliers of such equipment, because the owner was seen as a 'competitor'. Much time and effort were invested in the interaction between the involved companies and where technical and organisational interfaces are developed and systematically related to each other.

Furthermore, the existence of long chains of interfaces is quite obvious in this case. One good example is the wood-disc refiner-electricity-pulp-paper machine-paper-newspaper-advertisement chain-consumer. However, a number of other chains involving different equipment producers or complementary products (such as ink) are also found.

*Case 2: Wood frame*   The importance of the organisational resources and how they are related clearly influenced the development of the use of the wood frame. One of the problems with the changing of frame material surrounds the decentralised structure of the construction companies. Knowledge of the combination of technical interfaces was distributed over many vaguely connected units of the organization. To change all of them each of the organisational units had to learn about the new possibilities. Thus, the internal way a company is organised greatly affects how it relates to important counterparts in technical dimensions. Another important factor was that the work was organised in separate projects, where the main economic control was directed towards these projects. Thus, the cooperation within projects is enhanced but there are problems with coordinating between projects. This makes it difficult for the construction companies to develop more long-term business relationships with both customers and suppliers. This way of organising the work makes it difficult to find smooth development processes. Instead, all changes must be made in more distinct steps where all involved (the whole structure of companies) have to change at the same time. This affects technical developments in a negative way.

*Case 3: Table components*   Here we saw one actor drive the development in a very strategic way in its specific direction. IKEA is the main initiator of the changes and they are all directed toward reducing the cost of the final table. The case is a good example of how the combining of several interfaces – both organisational and technical – is done to find new and innovative solutions through mobilising a whole set of suppliers. But, and this is important, the changes are done cooperatively, where the goal is to find solutions that are also useful in other applications. If IKEA just requested adaptations, the economic process would not be beneficial in the long run. The key is to find those developments that can be combined to make it beneficial in several different ways.

*Case 4: Printed forms*   The organisations in the Russian planning economy were isolated from each other; instead planning authorities gave them instructions for how to act. The interaction between suppliers and customers was very restricted, and mainly indirect. However, the freedom to organise economic activities in other ways, which appeared due to the change in the economic system, was, in the first phase, not used to increase interaction with others. To develop knowledge about what could be gained through supplier–customer interaction, and about how to develop and organise this process, appeared to be a very time consuming process.

There are several important conclusions to be made concerning how organisational resources affect interface development. A first observation is how much the existence of business actors with very strong ambitions to drive development can influence the interface development in a certain direction. IKEA is without doubt the reason for the specific development that took place in the production of the table. A second observation is that so much of the development occurs between the different actors. It is the interaction between the actors that seems to be the main development force. This becomes especially clear in the fourth case from Russia where almost nothing happens because this force is missing. A third observation is how the lack of consciousness can "freeze" a poorly developed relatedness between interfaces over a very long time. Although the organisational actors related to Tipografiya's production and use of printed forms after the transition are allowed to interact directly with each other, and also make internal changes without asking for permission from a central planning authority, the lack of organisational resources for handling such issues hindered interface development. While engagement in endeavours to develop resource interfaces outside their own company constitutes "normality" in the first three cases, concerning how to use electricity, wood frames and table components, external business partners' involvement in such issues represents something strange and unfamiliar for the organisation carrying imprints from a planned economy. A fourth observation is how organisational resources are mobilised in processes that are contradictory to each other. One of the more obvious examples is the electricity case, where the involved business actors are very aware of the energy issue, which amounts to a reduction in electricity consumption while also being aware of the fact that the users can still benefit from a high volume of electricity in both the paper production and printing process.

## Conclusions

### The importance of others

The pictures outlined in the empirical chapters, as well in the analysis of economic decisions above, have in one sense a very clear and distinct message. Others are not just important, they are a determinant for the result of any attempt to use new knowledge. Let us exemplify by the development of a new or existing product. In such a case, one very influential group of others is, as we have seen in all empirical chapters, the customer – a reflection that probably does not surprise anyone. However, what is challenging is that the customer side not only includes the customers themselves, but also those with whom the customers interact. It can be other suppliers, customers of the customers or complementary producers. It is possible to identify a whole set of important actors around most customers who are affected by the use of new knowledge. Furthermore, these actors might have rather different views on the change of a product, as compared to the initiating supplier and customer.

The outcome of a new product or a new feature for the customer is, as we saw in the earlier economic analysis, directly dependent on how it affects the others. The economic outcome can be seen as constructed by the involved actors. They might be able to construct a world where the new features of the product can be well used by all affected actors. However, it might also be that only a few of the affected others can take advantage of the new product features due to the investments they have already made in existing resource combinations. Thus, it is the "using system" that determines the value of the new product. All the cases give ample examples. Perhaps one of the most illustrative is the problems for the construction company when taking advantage of the opportunity presented by the change in regulations for using wood frames. Despite the fact that the material is both well known and cheaper and the customer highly motivated, it is very difficult and will probably take some time before the potential positive effects materialise.

Another important group are those involved or related to the production of the new product. Direct suppliers and their sub-suppliers can be important in several ways. Both the technical design of the production system as well as important input materials or components can play a significant technical and/or economic role. Again, examples can be found in all the cases. The electricity case illustrates the wide ranging effects the use of a certain product may have for different companies. Electricity is utilised in a process in a specific machine but the feature created by the output is used by a number of companies active both in supplying the process and using the output in several subsequent steps. This example gives a hint about how intricate the use of a specific product might be. The constant combining makes the specific features of a product embedded and utilised in many different ways. This has obvious positive economic effects; the same feature is commercialised a number of times. Consequently, to use new knowledge in such an intricate supplier-user system is not only highly problematic but also potentially rewarding. If, for example, one product activated in such a system is changed, and if the new product can utilise the already existing set of interfaces or even create positive volume or quality, it can receive very positive support from the others. Thus, as soon as the existing structure can be utilised, the introduction of something new will be facilitated. Again, there are several important others. To benefit from the existing structure, any initiative for change has to include a dialogue about potential positive and negative effects with others that are affected.

A third group of important others are found around the development of a new product. Above we mainly identified a number of negative or conservative forces in relation to the use of new knowledge, but this is not the whole picture. As our cases demonstrated, companies do not always react positively to all changes, but they are all engaged in a constant search for new and better ways to solve needs and problems. All the involved companies are more or less constantly and consciously looking for new ways to utilise existing resources. These processes can be characterised as constant trials to combine resources in new ways. They also represent a great interest in finding new, complementary resources that can improve use, i.e. solve mismatches or simplify complicated activities. One consequence is that there is a large interest in new knowledge, and it is generally easy to create some interest in development endeavours. However, there is often a discrepancy about the benefits of new solutions between those who are involved in the development work and those who are thought to be able to create the production and use of the new product. Here any company has opportunities to be consciously selective by trying to involve others related to production and use at an early stage in the development process.

In this book we also had the opportunity to get a glimpse of how important the organising of the economic system is for these processes. Our Russian case gives a small but very illustrative example of how "badly" the interaction processes might work if there are limitations due to the overall economic system. It is not enough for the companies to suddenly be given the freedom to relate to others, they must also have some experience in doing so, especially with the problems and difficulties that are generally included in such interaction processes. It takes time to develop economic structures where interaction with others over company and organisational borders is regarded as natural and necessary. In all of the cases where these processes work they are the result of interaction over a very long time period. There are even companies that have more or less specialised in working with others, such as IKEA. The Lack table is a wonderful example of how much can be done through a systematic search for new knowledge for a rather uncomplicated and mature product. And if so much can be reached through systematic combining endeavours for such a simple product, there must be a great potential left in the existing structure for any product!

### The already engaged others

The conclusion in the preceding section is that others are decisive in the chance to use any new knowledge. However, these others are not necessarily aware of their important role, and even if they are, they may not even care about it. Most companies are already engaged in short-term and long-term problem solving endeavours. Interacting with customers and suppliers means to always be exposed to suggestions for change and, consequently, to problems with priorities. A general problem is that those who will be negatively affected by a change normally become quickly involved so as to hinder it, while those who might have some positive effect may not realise this in the same way. The negative aspects of a change will often be realised much quicker than the posit-ive ones. Due to all of the investment in the existing structure and all conservat-ive factors, the positive effects often come much later, when the new solution has become thoroughly embedded into a structure that also has changed. For example, in the construction case and the introduction of a new framing mater-ial, we saw many difficulties quickly appear, while the positive economic effects are (maybe) waiting in the future. This implies that among those who react spon-taneously to a change, there is generally an over-representation of those who are negatively affected. This effect can be found both in the total numbers and within every single one. Thus, when new knowledge is brought into use, there are differences in how others are affected and consequently in how they will be expected to react. This is an important variation that must always be considered.

However, along with the fact that the introduction of new knowledge affects actors differently there is another dimension that might be of even greater importance. This regards how others interpret their own role in the change processes. How important is "change" in these others' business models, and how "given" is change processes assumed to be? To what degree are these others trying to develop solutions on either the buying or selling side, and to what degree do these others assume that change processes can influence and create something positive? For example, a company that is actively searching for new solutions and assumes that it can possibly influence others will be much more interested when IKEA approaches them to take part in a new, uncertain develop-ment project than those who do not share this understanding. Those who engage in a change process do not necessarily have to agree on all aspects of the change, but rather express a firm belief that it is possible to change in such a way that it provides them with a more positive outcome. By reacting in a specific way the involved companies might direct the change in such a way that it becomes posit-ive for them.

Thus, the effects of change depend as much on the reaction to them as on the initial suggestion. This also implies that a "change" is never finally defined. It will be altered due to how it is interpreted and reacted upon. Furthermore, this means that the more the counterparts are used to combine resources in inter-action with others, the more likely the change processes will be realised. Com-panies that are commonly involved in problem-solving processes with others generally know that these processes include re-formulation of main issues and consideration of how to transform unexpected negative consequences into posit-ive effects. A more "open" change process facilitates this; a change suggestion that can be reacted upon in many different ways is much easier to engage in than one that only allows a yes or no.

### The multifaceted others

The ability to use new knowledge does not only lie in the hands of others already involved in resource combining processes, it is also complicated by the fact that these others seldom are involved as "whole" organisations or businesses, but rather as parts of others. In the electricity case we find many products and facilities involved. Issues that concern larger changes or investment in major physical resources, such as the paper machine, usually involve the whole business unit, but most issues are handled by just a few people in each concerned unit. There might be one functional department, a production or product group or another small group of individuals that are concerned. Thus, many processes concerning how to use new knowledge, including how to change and adapt existing resources, are handled on a local middle management level.

This sometimes facilitates and sometimes complicates attempts to use new knowledge. If those who are affected by such change are others' local middle management, and if they are positive, then the process might run smoothly as long as it does not need any support from top management. If it does, the process can be hindered by lack of support. On the other hand, support from top management is not necessarily the same as a guarantee for a process to work. If top management cannot get support from middle management, this can create disturbances or hinder the use of new knowledge. Thus, others' internal "political" processes will appear both as disturbances and support in trials to use the new knowledge. For example, in the electricity case we saw how middle management could not work with a competent counterpart since it was owned by a company defined by the top management as a competitor.

There are several important consequences of these multifaceted or fragmented others. One is that personal networks are important for the ability to use new knowledge. It is critical for any organisation or company suggesting a change to interact not only with the top management of affected counterparts, but also to have broad contacts representing the whole organization. There must be interactions with all affected levels and with all kinds of related groups or even individuals. An interesting example from one of the cases is when all those working at one production unit, from management to production staff, visit corresponding representatives at an important customer. Through such interactions a vast amount of important knowledge from both parties can be brought forward, knowledge that is in the hands and minds of single individuals, without which it is hard to put any new knowledge to use.

A second consequence of the multifaceted others is that the embedding capability of the companies or organisations that want to use new knowledge is crucial. It is not enough to establish contacts and gain knowledge from others, it also has to be actively reacted upon internally. This implies that to use new knowledge, the internal knowledge handling process must include a solid interest for others' views and reactions – an understanding of the complex patterns that can be behind "strange" reactions. Thus, use of new knowledge puts a high requirement on the internal embedding capability, which, among other things, is affected by how internal political processes are handled; the abilities of the affected internal and external others to get involved in the process.

### The need for mobilising others

A commonality in all the above conclusions is that they draw attention to another important aspect of using new knowledge – that this is far from a neutral process. What all the empirical chapters have shown is that use of new knowledge is an active and more or less conscious process, where the usability of the new depends on the ability to combine it with the old. Thus, use of new knowledge depends on business actors who are willing to experiment with established combinations to find new possibilities for utilising old and new resources. This implies that mobilising others is crucial, not in terms of developing a certain strategy that others can join, but more in terms of creating endurance in the combining endeavours. For example, in IKEA's search for new knowledge to be used in the production of Lack, none of the involved counterparts knows exactly what kind of solutions they are searching for, only that they have to find solutions that allow IKEA to keep the price and the visible impression of Lack, which also requires that the solution must be possible to use also for other applications.

Thus, in such economic processes there is no given usable knowledge. Instead, the economic usability is created through a process where knowledge certainly is an "input", but where it is also an important "throughput" as well as "output". Knowledge is embedded by the use of others' knowledge into economic resources that create a useful outcome. In this way, knowledge is never given; it is both a raw material and a process material that are continuously confronted to create economic outcomes. It seems to be reasonable to assume that it is just this continuity or endurance that creates positive economic outcomes. As soon as this endurance is broken, there are reasons to expect declining economic outcomes.

Economic reasons are thus one of the major motives for mobilising others. However, it is not the only one. The empirical chapters also gave examples of other motives. One of those that are just as frequent is the technical/functional motive. There are many technicians involved in the combining processes and they are often interested in finding new technical or functional solutions without being driven by economic results (and sometimes even without considering the economic consequences). A third, which was described earlier, is strategic reason, which can make some actors very keen both in taking part and mobilising others for a certain change. Whether the motives to mobilise others stems from economic, technical or strategic sources, close relationships are often used as a means to convince others to take part in a specific process. And, as we have seen in the cases, behind many efforts to mobilise others there is often a mix of these motives.

### Consequences of using new knowledge in an economic setting

The discussion above about the importance of others in the economic use of new knowledge has some major implications for how to approach the role of knowledge in a business setting in general, including the role of science. If use of new knowledge is about determining what effects this knowledge creates when combined with established resource combinations, any such attempt means considering its positive and negative effects. Thus, to use new knowledge means being confronted with the issue of how this affects the revenue and costs created in the interplay between different but related economic actors. As the empirical chapters and the discussion above revealed, as soon as we start out from a user perspective, this issue presents itself rather differently as compared to how it is treated in traditional revenue and cost models, which are restricted to the single producer perspective. The user perspective brings forward at least three important messages about the role of knowledge in a business setting.

- *A first message outlined from a user perspective is that no knowledge has any economic value in itself – whether it stems from science or workmanship.* The fact that certain knowledge can be extremely important in one setting, science in an academic setting and traditional workmanship in a cultural setting, does not say anything about its usefulness in a business setting. Embedding new knowledge into physical or organisational business resources is a way to make it useful in an economic setting. However, for such a process to occur, we have seen that any new solution must be capable of being embedded into a number of related physical and organisational resource interfaces where it must have positive effects. The more the new knowledge breaks with the existing combinations, the more difficult it will be to embed it into economic resources. Thus, when new knowledge is activated in a business setting it is the effects on other resources that are important, not the sources of or the qualities of the knowledge itself. This means that science, or any other knowledge regarded as being of a specific quality in a certain context, loses this as soon as it is activated in a business setting.
- *A second message outlined from a user perspective is that the knowledge user does not need to know everything about it to embed it into a business resource.* The users who embed a certain new knowledge into a business setting do not need to have any deeper understanding about its internal constitution. For example, the designer of a table does not need to know all about the internal composition of a new material to use it. On the other hand, although a user does not need to know all details of how a new solution is constituted, it must understand the effects of using it in combination with other solutions. For example, what effects will a new table material have on the material it is coated with, on the coating machines, on its ability to resist wear, on the final table's weight, on its distribution costs, etc? Thus, to embed new knowledge, the user needs to create an understanding of the using effects that are rather different as compared to how the knowledge appears from the producers' perspective. This implies that the user must try to map how the embedding of new knowledge will affect directly and indirectly related established solutions. Furthermore, as soon as any

new knowledge is put to use it is combined with a certain amount of production of knowledge and thus transformed, making it difficult to be separated from the physical and organisational resources where it is embedded. Knowledge of use becomes a part of these resources, integrated in terms of different features.

- *A third message outlined from a user perspective is that when knowledge is used in a business setting it is always used in unique combinations.* Although the users of a new solution might be active in the same kind of industry, producing somewhat equal products, each supplier-user system still consists of unique combinations. This means that each user has to create its own understanding of the effects of using the new knowledge. Furthermore, this implies that different users (although they might belong to the same company) will have different views on the revenues and costs related to the use of a new solution. And they will bring forward different demands on how the new solution can be adapted to fit into their contexts. If the user systems consist of somewhat varied or similar combinations, each user can choose to use a new solution in a unique way. The differences in how to use a new solution will have effects on how different users consider the revenues and costs. Also this will point out different demands for how the new solution can be adapted to fit into their contexts. This implies that knowledge about combinations of resources is of a larger economic interest than knowledge about specific resources. The revenues and costs related to the use of new knowledge can be perceived rather differently by the users due to the variation among *users, using systems* and *use*. A final message from the empirical chapters is that the economic value of new knowledge lies in the hands of the users, struggling with combining it with existing physical and organisational resources. Or, to use Feyerabend's (1987, p. 7) wording: "Customs, beliefs, cosmologies are not simply holy, or right, or true; they are useful, valid, true for some societies, useless, even dangerous, not valid, untrue for *others*."

## *The importance of a constructed economic world*

We would like to end this book with a final remark concerning what consequences a user perspective on knowledge has for how to view and analyse the economic world. The empirical pictures presented above have a common message: the economic world is full of earlier investments – in physical and organisational resources – that are also related to each other in intricate patterns. No new venture, whether the new knowledge is presented in terms of products, processes, or services, will ever be met by an open and inviting economic world. Thus, no new knowledge will ever be met by a claimless demand. Instead, any new solution has to face a heavy and thoroughly elaborate economic construction made of physical materials such as steel, wood and bio-molecules, and organisational resources such as experiences, expectations and relationships, mixed together by human beings. This construction is under constant development but based on existing physical and organisational resources. For anything new to become a part of this construction it has to be embedded into the ongoing processes and have direct interfaces with at least some existing resources. From these meetings between new features and new solutions will emerge things that are more or less impossible to foresee, and consequently, whose effects are impossible to outline in advance. This implies that there only exists one general means in the economic world – interaction – getting involved and through interaction with others becoming part of the process of using and being used. This understanding is also close to the heritage from the "classical" political economists presented in the previous chapter. Or, as it was expressed by Carl von Linné, in his *Oeconomia naturae*, in 1749: "Everything gets its special task through a mutual serving" (our translation).

## References

Feyerabend, P., 1987. *Farewell to Reason*, London: Verso.

Hayek, F.A., 1945. The Use of Knowledge in Society. *American Economic Review*, XXXV, No. 4; September: 519–530.

von Linne, C., 1749. *Oeconomia Naturae (Naturens hushållning)* Available at www. linneanus.uu.se.

# Index